POLICE PATROL OPERATIONS

POLICE PATROL OPERATIONS

Editor
Elmar Pabst

DPH
DISCOVERY
PUBLISHING HOUSE

Published by:

DISCOVERY PUBLISHING HOUSE
4383/4B, Ansari Road, Darya Ganj
New Delhi-110 002 (India)
Phone : +91-11-23279245; 23253475; 43596065
Mobile : +91 9811179893 / +91 9871656464
E-mail : discoverybooksindia@gmail.com
orderdphbooks@gmail.com
namitwasan9@gmail.com
web : www.discoverypublishinggroup.com

Police Patrol Operations
Edited by: **Elmar Pabst**

International Standard Book Number: **978-93-6224-709-4** (Hardback)

Printed at:
Infinity Imaging Systems
Delhi (INDIA)

PREFACE

Whenever a heinous crime such as rape occurs within a country, the police department is invariably the first to face the intense scrutiny and pressure from the public, media, and political figures. The effectiveness of police patrols in crime prevention and enhancing public confidence in urban security cannot be overstated. The strategic design of patrol routes, the allocation of resources, and the planning of jurisdictional boundaries present many interesting and complex decision-making problems.

Many cities around the world have adopted structured and intelligent methods for police patrols, taking into account various operational and resource constraints. It is a widely held belief that a highly visible police presence acts as a strong deterrent to criminals and violent mobs, keeping them off the streets for fear of detection and arrest.

When planning patrols aimed at deterring criminal activity, it is essential to ensure that the patrol times and routes are varied and unpredictable. This unpredictability helps in effectively preventing crimes and maintaining public order. Police patrols play a crucial role in public service, as they respond to incidents, deter and prevent crimes, and provide a sense of security to those who need protection. They also serve to discourage potential criminals who might otherwise exploit the absence of law enforcement.

Patrolling is an indispensable function of police departments, integral to their overall operations. The goals and objectives of police patrols include crime prevention, criminal apprehension, and law enforcement, maintaining public order, providing public services, and enforcing traffic regulations. Through their multifaceted roles, police patrols contribute significantly to the safety and well-being of urban communities.

This book explores the various methods of police patrolling, analyses their outcomes and tries to measure their efficiency. The book looks at prominent patrolling experiments of the past and policing methods around the world. "*Police Patrol Operations*" is designed to provide a comprehensive overview of the principles, strategies, and practical aspects of police patrolling. Aimed at both aspiring and current law enforcement professionals, as well as criminal justice students, this book offers in-depth coverage of the essential functions and responsibilities associated with police patrol duties.

The book deals with various topics crucial to effective patrolling, including crime prevention techniques, methods of criminal apprehension, and the enforcement of laws. It explores the importance of maintaining public order, delivering community services, and managing traffic enforcement. Readers will gain insights into the development and implementation of patrol strategies, focusing on optimizing resource allocation to ensure maximum safety and efficiency.

It also addresses contemporary challenges faced by police officers, such as dealing with limited resources and evolving community expectations. It highlights best practices for building community trust and fostering positive relationships between law enforcement and the public. Through case studies and real-world examples, the book illustrates successful patrol operations and offers practical advice for navigating complex and dynamic environments. Intended for a readership that includes police officers, law enforcement trainees, criminal justice educators, and students, this book serves as a vital resource for understanding and enhancing the effectiveness of police patrol operations in today's society.

I would like to express my sincere gratitude to the numerous individuals and organizations whose contributions have enriched the content of this book. This work would not have been possible without the valuable information sourced from widely regarded references.

I extend my heartfelt thanks to the editors, researchers, and experts whose pioneering work has laid the foundation for the topics covered in this book. Their dedication to advancing knowledge in their respective fields has been instrumental in shaping the content presented here.

Editor

CONTENTS

1 THE PSYCHOLOGY OF POLICE

INTRODUCTION

Police is body of officers representing the civil authority of government. Police typically are responsible for maintaining public order and safety, enforcing the law, and preventing, detecting, and investigating criminal activities. These functions are known as policing. Police are often also entrusted with various licensing and regulatory activities.

However, police scholars have criticized this popular understanding of the word police—that it refers to members of a public organization having the legal competence to maintain order and enforce the law—for two reasons. First, it defines police by their ends rather than by the specific means that they use to achieve their goals. Second, the variety of situations in which police are asked to intervene is much greater than law enforcement and order maintenance. There is now a consensus among researchers, based on a definition first proposed by American sociologist Egon Bittner, that the common feature among all the different agencies engaged in policing is the legal competence to enforce coercive, nonnegotiable measures to resolve problematic situations. Such situations are characterized by two features: their potential for harm and the need to solve them urgently before they develop that potential. Hence, the actual use of coercion or the threat of using it allows police to put a quick, non-negotiated, and conclusive end to problematic situations (e.g., keeping people away from the scene of a fire for their own protection and to allow firemen to do their job).

The main duties of police officers are to prevent crime and enforce current laws. Doing both of these things helps to ensure the health and safety of the communities that they are supervising.

The exact tasks that police officers carry out depend on the geographical location that they are employed in as well as the departments that they find employment through. For example, some cops are known as beat cops; these types of officers patrol the same area day after day. Other officers are known as narcotics officers, meaning they serve on a drug task force team. Others are on bomb squads.

With so many different types of police officers, each type has its own set of requirements that a person must fulfill before becoming that type of cop. Good candidates for people wanting to pursue a career as a police officer are those who are in good physical shape as well as those with good communication skills. In addition, police officers cannot have any type of extensive criminal history.

POLICE AND SOCIETY

There is a remarkable historical, geographic, and organizational diversity in the activities of people who are, or have been, defined as police. Police work has developed considerably from what it was centuries ago. As populations grew and informal institutions of socialization and social control—such as the family, schools, and the church—decreased in effectiveness, police became increasingly necessary. However, no uniform worldwide system of policing ever emerged.

Numerous factors help to explain the diversity of police activities and systems. The types of crime typically committed in a society and the methods used by criminals play a great part in determining a police force's activities. For instance, if criminals use firearms, the police are likely to be armed, or if criminals use computers to commit crimes, the police may establish a special unit dedicated to investigating cybercrimes. History also helps to explain this diversity; e.g., former colonies tend to keep the policing system established by their colonizers. Population plays an important role as well; policing rural areas and villages vastly differs from policing large cities. Foremost among the factors that determine a country's system of policing, however, is the political culture of the society—e.g., whether it is open and democratic or closed and totalitarian—and the state's conception of police accountability.

Policing Small Communities

Most people willingly obey most laws, whether a police officer is present or not. They comply with the laws because they consider them fair and because they believe that in the long run it is in their interest to observe them. In small communities in which most citizens know each other, people who live up to the community's shared ideals are rewarded with the esteem of their fellow citizens. If they break the law or fall short of other people's expectations, their lives often become more difficult because they are shamed, shunned, or ostracized by the rest of the community and are less likely to receive assistance in times of trouble. In all societies this system of informal rewards and punishments is the most potent aid to law enforcement, but it is strongest in small communities. The forces that order life in a small community thus make the task of the police much easier. Police action is needed only when such informal controls have proved insufficient.

This is why rural and sparsely populated areas are often policed by a single centralized—and often militarized—police force, even in countries that have a decentralized police system. A single police organization operating under a unified command is more cost-effective and more operationally efficient than a bevy of independent small-town police forces. Since the territory to cover may be very large and characterized by difficult terrain, police in such regions must have the long-range mobility and adaptability that are characteristic of military forces. In addition, the countryside has historically been policed by military organizations, as police forces were initially created in urban settings. (The great exceptions to this model are the United Kingdom and the United States, which have long resisted police centralization.)

Policing Large Societies

In larger and more complex societies, informal institutions of social control are generally weaker, and, as a result, formal institutions are generally stronger. The relative weakness of informal controls is attributable to a number of factors. In large societies people often deal with strangers whom they will never meet again and in such circumstances there may be fewer informal rewards for honesty or fewer informal penalties for dishonesty. Such communities tend also to be more technologically advanced, which leads to the adoption of new laws, such as those regulating the licensing and operation of automobiles and those concerned with commerce conducted on the Internet. Because some of these new laws may not have the same moral significance as older laws criminalizing violence, theft, or fraud, people may feel less of an obligation to obey them. Moreover, when new laws are created, crime increases almost necessarily.

There is thus a danger that people who are convicted of having violated a new law may feel aggrieved and in the future be less willing to cooperate with the police or to obey the law when they are not being observed. Finally, as societies grow, it becomes more difficult for people to place the public interest ahead of their private interests in circumstances where the two may conflict. An employer who catches an employee committing an offense within the workplace, for example, may choose not to notify the police because he fears that the firm's production, profit, or prestige would suffer if the offense was publicly exposed.

Police and the State

A country's political culture helps to determine whether its police forces are organized nationally or locally. The desire for efficiency lends itself to the establishment of centralized police forces, which can take advantage of coordination and savings in training, organization, and service delivery. However, such forces face the problem aptly summarized by the Latin question Quiscustodietipsoscustodes? ("Who guards the guardians?").

In some democratic countries, particularly the United States and, to a lesser extent, Great Britain, citizens have traditionally believed that the existence of a national police force would concentrate too much power in the hands of its directors. They have believed that local communities could not hold a national police force accountable for abuses of power, and they have feared that the national government could use such a police force to keep itself in power illegitimately. For those and other reasons, some democratic countries favor organizing police forces on a local basis. Decentralization brings the police closer to the community, and it often succeeds in tailoring policing to the specific needs of a community. However, a decentralized police apparatus tends to hinder the flow of intelligence between the various components of the system. Another drawback of a system of accountability to local government is that the narrow relationship between the police and their political overseers may facilitate the corruption of both parties. The need for police accountability is made evident by the great power that police forces wield over the lives, liberties, safety, and rights of citizens. Governments empower police to compel individuals to comply with the law; they allow officers to stop, search, detain, cite, and arrest citizens and to use physical and sometimes deadly force. If police use those powers improperly, they can abuse the civil rights of the very citizens they are supposed to protect. Thus, it is critical that police be accountable for their policies and behavior. In democratic countries, accountability is ensured mainly by three means. First, police forces are made subordinate to elected representatives (as in the United States, where mayors or state governors oversee the police, and as in Belgium, where a town's burgomaster is also the chief of police) or to special elected officials (e.g., the police and crime commissioners of England and Wales). Second, the courts are entrusted to safeguard the respect of due process by the police. Third, official bodies are appointed to hear and act upon complaints from citizens against the police.

Police and Public Safety Psychology

Police and public safety psychology is concerned with assisting law enforcement and other public safety personnel and agencies in carrying out their missions and societal functions with effectiveness, safety, health, and conformity to laws and ethics.

It consists of the application of the science and profession of psychology in four primary domains of practice:

- Assessment.
- Clinical intervention.
- Operational support.
- Organizational consultation.

Specialized knowledge: Police and public safety psychology requires, at a minimum, distinctive knowledge of the essential functions of police and public safety organizations and personnel, working conditions unique to their respective positions, common and unusual stressors in public safety work, normal and abnormal adaptation to occupational stress and trauma, research related to resilience and recovery in public safety personnel, and the unique aspects of confidentiality and testimonial privilege when providing services to public safety personnel and/or agencies.

Problems addressed: The common problem areas addressed through graduate courses, structured pre/postdoctoral placements, CE courses, and/or supervised employment include:

- Issues related to assessment (e.g., pre-employment and fitness-for-duty evaluations).
- Clinical interventions (e.g., critical incident debriefing and counseling).
- Operational support (e.g., hostage negotiation and criminal investigation support).
- Organizational consultation (e.g., management consultation, training, organizational development).

Population served: The primary populations served by police and public safety psychologists are law enforcement and public safety agencies, as well as police and public safety personnel and their families. Skills and procedures: The skills and procedures required of police and public safety psychologists are specific to the domain of practice.

Police Brutality

Police brutality is a form of police misconduct in which officers engage in an excessive use of force. The definition of "excessive use of force" is a bit fluid, but it is generally taken to mean force well beyond what would be necessary to cope with a situation. For example, a police officer who beat a nonviolent protester with a baton would probably be accused of excessive use of force, under the argument that the officer probably could have dealt with the situation much less violently.

Several nations around the world have laws which specifically address police brutality. Under these laws, complaints about the excessive use of force must be taken seriously, and investigated by a commission or district attorney. In fact, as human rights organizations have discovered, many complaints about excessive use of force by police officers are not investigated, and if they are, the finding is usually that the police officer acted appropriately. Only rarely are police subjected to disciplinary action as a result.

Researchers have suggested that the failure to prevent and act upon reports of brutality is probably related to the insular culture of police forces. Because the police are authorized and expected to use force when necessary, some investigators find it difficult to fault an officer for acting aggressively in a policing situation. Situations on the street can change rapidly and they are difficult to control, making it easy to justify a use of force that might seem excessive. Some police forces now routinely record all interactions with civilians so that these records can be reviewed in the event of an investigation.

This form of police misconduct can present in a number of ways. The most obvious form of brutality is physical. Pain holds, nerve gas, batons, pepper spray, and guns, for example, can all be used for the purpose of physical intimidation or to actually hurt people. Police brutality can also take the form of verbal abuse or psychological intimidation.

In many societies, police brutality and the profiling of minorities are closely intertwined. Members of the dominant race, religion, class, or ethnic group are, for the most part, treated with respect by the police, while minorities may find themselves targeted by officers. Many of the nations that attempt to legislate excessive force also have laws about minority profiling, but these laws are difficult to enforce, especially in societies where the bulk of the population holds negative views of minorities.

Police brutality has taken place for almost as long as humans have used police forces. Some periods have been more marred by violence than others. Nazi Germany, for example, was infamous for its brutal policing tactics, as was the United States during the Industrial Revolution, when violent police forces were used to intimidate labor activists and striking workers. The 1960s civil rights movement in the United States was also accompanied with brutality, especially in the case of mixed-race marches, and in the wake of the 11 September terrorist attacks in the United States, worldwide policing has become significantly more aggressive. Protests at international conferences and meetings held by organizations like

NATO, the WTO, the World Bank/IMF, and the Group of Eight (G8) have been met with some very violent policing tactics. In nations where there are few to no laws about excessive force, reports of its use to quell minority groups, protesters, and strikers are widespread.

CHALLENGES IN POLICE PSYCHOLOGY

Police psychology, also referred to as "police and public safety psychology," was formally recognized in 2013 by the American Psychological Association as a specialty in professional psychology. The goal of police psychology is to ensure law enforcement is able to perform their jobs safely, effectively, ethically, and lawfully. In police psychology, or, as it's correctly termed, "police and public safety psychology," psychology professionals assist police officers and public safety officials in doing their jobs, treating the physical and mental health of officers, victims, witnesses, public safety personnel, family members of police officers, and others. These professionals also help ensure that police departments and officers adhere to strict codes of ethics, are qualified and competent, and have the assistance they need to help keep the public safe.

Police officers and law enforcement staff are routinely exposed to dangerous situations that threaten their own personal safety, working in an environment that has a variety of negative mental health effects, not only on the officers and staff, but also on their families. Moreover, police officers spend their days in frequent encounters with some of the most violent members of society: the mentally ill, drug addicts, and criminals, who are more likely to need mental health services. Additionally, because policing is such a dangerous career, officers and staff are heavily screened before they receive the gun and badge that go with the job.

This is where psychology comes in. At its most basic, police psychology is the use of psychological principles in situations that involve public safety officials and police officers. According to the Doe Report, "Police psychology is the application of behavioral science and mental health principles to the concerns of police officers, their families, the department, and the community. Police psychologists perform a wide range of functions, which can be divided into several broad categories."

Those categories include clinical and mental health services, including stress debriefings after critical incidents, trauma interventions after shootings, individual and family therapy, substance-abuse counseling, and department-wide stress management. Operational assistance and support services may be necessary for extreme circumstances and specialized cases, such as crisis negotiation, hostage situations, criminal profiling, investigation, undercover and special assignments, and victim intervention. Police psychologists also play an administrative role in that they help human resources departments determine which applicants might make the best officers, liaise between the police and the public, provide expert testimony, and supply leadership and training. In every role, a police psychologist's job is to use psychological principles to make the work easier and provide clarity to every situation.

Steps to Becoming a Police Officer

Almost all police departments require that their officers hold a high school diploma. Some even require that an associates or bachelors degree be obtained.

For the most part, to become a police officer, a person will have to complete somewhere between two to four years of studies at an accredited college in addition to completing a police academy training program. It is important to note that the more advanced education and training a person has, the more successful he or she will likely be in becoming a police officer.

When applying for a job at a police department, most departments require a person to pass a civil service examination. The administration of this exam is conducted by the police department that a person is seeking employment through. In addition to this test, a person will be required to take part in a physical exam which tests the hearing of a person as well as his or her strength and agility. After passing this test, a person is then required to take part in a lie detector exam, and also a drug test. It is after all of these tests are passed that a person begins his or her training at a police academy.

If a person is seeking a job at a police department that requires him or her to possess a degree in psychology, there are many schools that offer such a degree. For example, the University of Kentucky has a great Associate's of Psychology degree program that can be completed in as little as 15 months. For people who want to earn their degree online, American InterContinental University has a great online Psychology degree curriculum.

Obtaining a degree in psychology is very advantageous for people wanting to become a police officer because it provides them an in-depth knowledge relating to why criminals act the way they do. It also helps officers know how to effectively deal with criminals.

Police Psychologist

A police psychologist performs a range of duties; however, every police psychologist's primary purpose is to shed light on the inner workings of the human mind in situations when it is not apparent. They apply psychological principles when working with people inside and outside police departments, gather evidence and data to inform recommendations, clarify witness testimonies, advise officers during interrogations, and, in general, offer insight into the hidden compartments of the human brain when called upon to do so.

To perform their jobs at an optimal level, police psychologists need a variety of specialized skills and knowledge, including:

- Thorough grasp of basic psychological principles
- Understanding of the functions of police departments and public safety administrations
- Working conditions and stressors unique to law enforcement careers
- Normal and pathological responses to stress and trauma
- Confidentiality of officers, victims, witnesses, and others
- Discretion with sensitive information and identities
- Excellent observation and analytical skills
- Patience and compassion without judgment, especially when dealing with criminals or situations of misconduct
- Good communication skills, both oral and written
- A healthy dose of skepticism, which is necessary when working with those who are not always being completely honest

- A strong sense of ethics and morality
- Good organization and record-keeping skills
- Timeliness — necessary to complete continuing education hours and licensing and certification requirements

Police psychologists can perform a variety of roles within law enforcement. The most common tasks of police psychologists include:

- **General counseling of police officers:** Police officers experience a lot of on-the-job stress. A recent study showed that this stress puts officers at a higher risk for suicide and for developing medical conditions such as metabolic syndrome, Hodgkin's lymphoma, and brain cancer.[1] To help officers cope with and avoid the health consequences of stress, police psychologists offer counseling services designed specifically for the needs of law enforcement.
- **Helping police officers learn to deal with life-or-death situations:** According to investigative reporting by The Washington Post, 987 people were shot and killed by U.S. police in 2017.[2] While shootings occur in only a small fraction of police encounters with civilians, minimizing police shootings is a priority for police departments around the nation. Police psychologists help with this effort by training police officers to properly assess/identify potential threats and respond in ways that protect the lives of police and citizens.
- **Helping police officers avoid or overcome PTSD:** From responding to murder scenes and fatal traffic accidents to subduing violent criminals, police officers often witness and/or experience traumatic events. As such, it shouldn't be a surprise that studies show anywhere from 19% to 34% of police officers suffer from post-traumatic stress disorder (PTSD). Since PTSD is potentially debilitating, police psychologists work with officers on strategies for handling traumatic events and for overcoming the symptoms of PTSD.
- **Helping police departments hire good officers:** Experts in policing believe ideal police officers exhibit initiative, a sense of ethics, respect and knowledge of laws, communication skills, common sense, civility, a service mentality, humility, a controlled temper, and a thirst for new knowledge.[4] By assisting with the interview process and developing written tests that assess character and personality, police psychologists help police departments find and hire officers who possess the right traits.
- **Assisting in interrogations and negotiations:** Not everyone in police psychology focuses on the mental health and stability of police officers. Some help the police solve crimes and prevent tragedies. For example, police psychologists who specialize in interrogation help interview and/or interpret the interviews of suspects and victims. Other police psychologists, who are trained in negotiation, help defuse hostage situations.

Police Psychology Roles: Public Safety and Law Enforcement

Police psychologists have a wide range of duties, but they're most commonly hired to perform one of four tasks: assessments, fitness for duty evaluations, clinical interventions, and operational support. Police psychologists have been used for decades to screen candidates who apply for jobs as police or public safety officers. Obviously, police departments must apply very high standards when hiring new personnel, but in actual practice, this is easier said than done. Since the mid-20th century, law enforcement departments have availed themselves of psychologists to assess the suitability of potential candidates. Police psychologists recommend those candidates who appear to be a satisfactory psychological match and rule out those who are inappropriate – or who may even be dangerous in the position.

Evaluations for fitness for duty take place in a wide range of workplace settings, such as construction or medicine, but in no situation are these evaluations more important than in law enforcement. Officers who take time off, suffer a physical or mental setback, or who perform poorly must be examined to determine whether they are able to resume their duties. Sometimes, they are not mentally or physically sound, possibly because they are incapable of going back to work after a distressing incident, or because they are experiencing difficulties in another area of their lives that compromises their ability to behave safely and professionally.

Police psychologists also are frequently called in for clinical interventions. Because traumatizing events are much more likely to occur in police work than in other jobs, police psychologists stay busy, offering short-term behavioral treatments to help traumatized police officers cope with their experiences. They also may intervene to help shell-shocked victims or vulnerable witnesses assist in investigations, and they frequently assist family members of both officers and victims in learning how to respond to stressors in a healthy manner.

Lastly, police psychologists are called upon to provide operational support. For instance, they often assist with the paperwork involved in the staffing, interviewing, hiring, evaluating, and training process of law enforcement officers.

Police Psychology Jobs and Job Description

Typically, police psychologists are employed by police departments or other public safety agencies, but state and federal government agencies also may utilize their services. Alternatively, police psychologists may go into private practice or consulting, either as lone practitioners or alongside other police psychologists.

While day-to-day duties vary widely, a police psychologist's primary role is to work with police officers, public safety staff, families, victims, witnesses, members of the legal and judicial system, and others involved in or affected by law enforcement. Typical duties on any given day may include:

- Training officers in basic psychology
- Conducting interventions after a crisis
- Providing counseling for shock, trauma, grief, and bereavement
- Offering cognitive behavioral therapy to officers, staff, witnesses, and more
- Helping officers manage stress, especially in undercover situations
- Diagnosing and treating mental health disorders
- Providing wellness coaching
- Forming peer support teams
- Preparing officers for the rigors of the field
- Assessing candidates for hire

- Assisting with crisis or hostage negotiations
- Crafting criminal profiles
- Performing "psychological autopsies," in which the police psychologist formulates a profile of a suicide victim
- Predicting the outcomes of various situations and therapeutic approaches

This list is incomplete, but it indicates the breadth of typical situations a typical police psychologist may encounter over the course of a single day, week, or month.

Police Psychology Degrees and Education

While a doctoral degree is not required to work in the field of police psychology, you cannot practice as a police psychologist without a Ph.D. The doctoral degree signifies that the applicant has undertaken extensive training in both psychological principles and police work. The doctoral program must be accredited by the American Psychological Association, and at least 100 hours of education must be earned that are directly related to police and public safety psychology.

Candidates are required to complete a post-doctoral internship or fellowship in police psychology, as well as one to two years of supervised training by a practicing police psychologist, for a total of 3,000 hours of direct work experience in a police psychology setting.

Most universities do not offer a degree in police psychology, which means that many students first acquire both an undergraduate and graduate degree in psychology to provide a sound background in the field. A master's degree in fields such as applied criminology, forensic psychology, or mental health counseling, for instance, allows the student to secure entry into a reputable doctoral program, which also may include studies in clinical psychology or forensic psychology. Students who wish to make police psychology their career path should choose a degree program with a focus on law enforcement.

Police Psychologist Licensing and Certification

The rules for police psychologist licensure are very strict. While no specific license to practice as a police psychologist is required, those who wish to use the title "psychologist" in any state must first earn a master's degree, after which they can apply for a license. Licensure requires successful completion of an exam administered by the applicable state's licensing board. All U.S. states are governed by the Association of State and Provincial Psychology Boards, and licensure requires passing the Examination for the Professional Practice in Psychology (EPPP). The EPPP is a 225-question exam that tests students on the foundational principles of psychology, behavior, assessment, diagnosis, and other core subjects.

After passing this test and earning a license, the candidate can apply for a doctoral program, or, if he or she has already completed the program, for board certification in Police & Public Safety Psychology, also offered by the American Board of Professional Psychology. To receive certification, the candidate must graduate from the Ph.D. program and complete the supervised internship.

Psychosocial Risk Factors at Work

Police officers are highly likely to suffer from work-related stress due to the obligations and tasks of their work, such as providing help, mediating conflicts between citizens, organizing traffic or reporting offenses. These tasks imply that the police officers are exposed to traumatic situations, and that being more likely to present with health problems as a result. Lack of resources in moments of pressure, such as lack of time and human or material resources, are related to a worse perceived health. In order to explain the occurrence of work-related stress, the theoretical models most used in research have been The Demand Control Social Support model and the Effort Rewards Imbalance model. These models state that workers experience stress, on the one hand, when he/she perceive excessive work demands and little control over them, and, on the other hand, when they note an imbalance between the efforts invested in their job and the rewards obtained in return. These models identify certain components, called psychosocial risk factors (for example, perception of: lack of control over tasks, excessive work demands, lack of organizational support, few rewards), a prolonged exposure to which is related chronic stress or burnout. The demands labor resources model has also been used in recent years to explain the occurrence of work-related stress. This model indicates that there are underlying psychological processes that play an important role in the development of work pressure and motivation. The progressive process of deterioration of health, poorly-organized jobs or chronic work demands (such as overload or emotional demands) consume the physical and psychological resources of the workers and can deplete their energy. Labor resources have a potential motivator of the intrinsic and extrinsic nature, which lead to efforts toward the achievement of objectives. On the contrary, the transactional model points out to the importance of cognitive processes and the perception of the person, in addition to individual differences as key elements in the development of stress. Thus, it could be said that the reaction to stress is highly personalized. Researchers have pointed out to the relevance of individual differences to explain how a person perceives and deals with a stressful situation. This idea is perhaps best represented in occupational psychology by the construct known as hardy personality, which describes the predisposition to show resistance to the detrimental effects of stressors and effectively adapt to meet the demands of the environment. In general research, hardy personality has been one of the studied individual variables that have been the most-related to work stress, partly due to the rise of positive psychology within the field of Work and Organizational Psychology.

The lack of social support within the organization is one of the variables that have best explained stress in police officers. The feeling of perceived support from peers and superiors is crucial for these professionals. In addition, police officers are at high risk for cardiovascular disease if they perceive low control, high demands, or pressure to carry out tasks and poor support. Likewise, the perceived imbalance between the efforts invested and the rewards received is related to work stress. Some studies have found that police officers who perceived low control, little organizational support, and few rewards had a greater number of symptoms associated with mental disorders such as depression, compared with those police officers who did not perceive those stressors adversely. These variables (perception of excessive job demands, low control, little support, or few rewards) are psychosocial risk factors. These are defined as the organizational and psychosocial factors of organizations that can leads maladaptation, tension, or psychophysiological stress responses and are likely to adversely affect health. Examples include low participation in decision making within the organization, lack of control over work, unplanned work schedules, overwork, physical or social isolation, perceived excess job demands (or very few), or job uncertainty.

Influence of Police Related Media, Victimization, and Satisfaction

The mission of law enforcement involves police performing five distinct responsibilities: preserving the peace, protecting people and property, investigating crimes and arresting offenders, preventing crime from occurring, and enforcing laws. By the 1970s, community policing was a focus of police departments and involved law enforcement collaborating with communities to assist them with unique problems in an effort to fulfill the mission. Unfortunately, law enforcement–minority relations continue to be problematic in the twenty-first century, which makes it difficult for police to fulfill their mission and hinders the quality of life of all parties involved. One of the reasons the relationship between law enforcement and minority groups may be strained is because minority groups (i.e., behavioral minority groups and racial minority groups) tend to report psychological and emotional abuse as a routine part of their interactions with police. Though unhealthy dynamics may occur between law enforcement and minorities in general for a variety of reasons, there is a substantial history of negative attitudes toward law enforcement held by African Americans when compared to other racial and ethnic groups. For example, Pastore and McGuire (2001) found that White Americans perceive policing as fair and balance, while some racial minorities view policing as oppressive and life-threatening. Even more thought-provoking is that research also shows that White college students are less likely to feel victimized by law enforcement than African American college students.

Police perceptions are of extreme importance when studying the relationship between minority and law enforcement, because ultimately police cannot be effective without public support. A lack of support from the public would render the police unable to apprehend criminals, deficient of information to solve crimes, uninformed about crimes, and unable to recruit quality recruits with diverse backgrounds. African American students' perceptions of police should be explored in a collegiate environment given the projected demographic changes occurring in the coming decades (i.e., a dominant multi-cultural majority) and the scant research literature focusing on the perceptions of law enforcement held by African American college students.

There are many things that influence African Americans' public perception of police, including victimization experiences. Researchers have found that crime victimization and police victimization have the same impact on the victims. Police victimization is the act of police officers using their systematic power to unlawfully harass, oppress, and/or abuse citizens that leads to undue stress. In the 80s and 90s, police harassment simply meant that African Americans were more likely to be stopped and questioned by the police; however, more modern experiences have shown that African Americans have suffered beatings and even murder at the hands of police. There is very little literature that focuses on the impact of improper police conduct on African American college students' perceptions of police. In general, positive perceptions of police officers tend to be experienced by African Americans when their interactions with law enforcement are respectful and non-threatening. Negative perceptions of law enforcement may abound when an individual has contact with law enforcement that is characterized by rudeness, apathy on behalf of the officer, and a lack of desire to take care of the problem. Given the aforementioned research literature, perceived, and actual victimization experiences may differ based on the party that is completing the assessment (e.g., public and police officer) and the part of the interaction that is the focal point (e.g., what officers do vs. how they do it). When individuals are void of victimization experiences, they may be influenced by familial victimization experiences. Negative experiences that family members had with law enforcement may influence an individual's perception of law enforcement in ways similar to that of personal experiences.

When examining experiences with law enforcement one must take into consideration the notion of procedural justice and differing perceptions between law enforcement and the public at times. Procedural justice focuses on how law enforcement interacts with the public; it is a necessary precursor to perceived legitimacy, which influences police efficacy and public safety. Procedural justice consists of four components: voice, transparency, impartiality, and fairness. The voice component deals with residents being able to voice their perspective and be heard in the interaction. Transparency involves law enforcement authorities sharing processes, policy, and procedure throughout the interaction while maintaining confidentiality when necessary. Impartiality involves police making decisions based on legal facts and an objective evaluation of the situation. Fairness is about community members being treated with dignity regardless of their situation. It should be noted that the rejection of police behavior by the public may be based on fairness, as opposed to the law, given that the public's familiarity with the law is sometimes low. Ultimately, the notion of procedural justice affects individuals' confidence in police as shown in recent statistics highlighting 42% of White Americans having high confidence in their local police department in contrast to only 14% of Black Americans exhibiting that same level of confidence. In an effort to not stereotype or overly generalize, there are interactions with Black Americans and law enforcement that are characterized by a great deal of respect, satisfaction, and presence of procedural justice. Nevertheless, procedural justice must be considered in face to face interactions and multimedia that depicts law enforcement given that it may influence attitudes toward law enforcement.

Multimedia, specifically television programming, deserves much exploration in the assessment of African Americans' perception of law enforcement because media influences perceptions of law enforcement when individuals lack personal experiences. Law enforcement officers are often portrayed in news coverage programs, crime-based reality television shows, crime dramas, and newspapers. The way that law enforcement is depicted across these media tends to vary. Law enforcement is often depicted in news programs positively due to an overview of a crime and a focus on an arrest that usually portrays the law enforcement officer as the heroine. Crime-based reality television shows are factual, tend to focus on actual crime, and overemphasize the arrests made by law enforcement officers; given that law enforcement usually has complete control over how they are depicted, they are often seen as heroic in crime-based reality television shows, even when using excessive force as a means to pursue justice. Television crime dramas are fictional, but may be based on true stories at times, and depict law enforcement officers in a positive light. In some of these shows, law enforcement officers act as vigilantes and violate civil liberties and laws to pursue justice. Additionally, most crimes that are presented in crime dramas are solved, which is not true to real life but necessary for a plot line that needs a resolution for entertainment purposes. Individuals watching a show to be entertained will be less likely to be influenced by what they see than an individual who is watching a broadcast for information. Additionally, perceived realism and the purpose behind watching a broadcast seems to be a key component of media influence. Some research has posited that college students' perceptions are less affected by mass media depicting law enforcement due to a focus on equity and fairness and acquired criminal justice knowledge.

If the information about law enforcement communicated via television indicates that procedural justice has been neglected, then this is likely to have a negative impact on the public's perception of law enforcement. However, if the media depicts law enforcement positively, such as is often the case with television news and crime-based reality television, increased confidence in law enforcement is likely to result when individuals do not have an arrest record or were not victimized.

Historically, an example of this can be seen in the drop of law enforcement approval ratings of Los Angeles citizens following the widespread coverage of the 1991 videotaped beating of Rodney King and the 1979 fatal shooting of Eulia Love). Additionally, the coverage of police misconduct in the deaths of Michael Brown in August 2014, Tamir Rice in November 2014, Alton Sterling in July 2016, Freddie Gray in April 2015, and many others have far reaching consequences on American citizens' mental health, emotional health, physical health, spiritual health, and perceptions of law enforcement.

THE CONTRADICTION OF POLICE PSYCHOLOGY

Police psychology, the practice of psychology in police settings, has been part of American policing since the late 1960s and has traditionally been a clinical endeavor by clinical psychologists. Although many large police agencies and some medium-sized ones employ full-time clinical psychologists, most agencies contract for part-time work with clinical psychologists who often maintain separate private practices. The practice of psychology in police settings has also been a research, consultation, and training endeavor by psychologists who have backgrounds in, for instance, experimental, social, and industrial-organizational psychology. Therefore, generally, police psychology is a field of practice in which psychologists of different training investigate and apply psychological knowledge to police settings and problems. (Here, this does not include other law enforcement settings and professionals, such as sheriffs, marshals, or correctional officers, who at times perform job tasks similar to police officers.) Psychological services for the police have traditionally involved evaluating police applicants, educating and training police officers, evaluating job tasks and duties, and carrying out fitness-for-duty assessments.

Evaluating Police Applicants

Since the 1960s, organizations and commissions such as the President's Commission on Law Enforcement and the Administration of Justice, the Commission on Accreditation for Law Enforcement Agencies, and the International Association of Chiefs of Police have recommended that police agencies evaluate the psychological fitness of police applicants. Today, most police agencies recognize and use a psychological evaluation as one part of the selection of police officers. Typically, licensed clinical psychologists carry out the evaluation. Some psychologists use a "select-in" evaluation strategy, whereby they look for applicants who demonstrate the qualities necessary to be successful on the job and recommend that police agencies accept them for law enforcement training. Other psychologists screen out applicants who demonstrate undesirable characteristics and recommend that police agencies no longer consider employing them. Many psychologists use both screen-out and select-in evaluation strategies, by which they screen out psychopathology and select in ideal police characteristics. Both focus on screening for suitable applicants.

Evaluations typically involve administering a battery of psychological tests, carrying out a personal interview, giving situational tests, and making a selection recommendation.

Psychological test batteries administered by psychologists have included intelligence tests, personality tests, projective tests, and situational tests. Intelligence tests, such as the Stanford-Binet Intelligence Test, measure applicants' cognitive abilities. Scholarly research has linked intelligence tests with success on the job and in recruit training. Psychologists use personality tests to measure the relatively stable characteristics or traits of applicants. Commonly used tests are the Minnesota Multiphasic Personality Inventory (MMPI), the California Psychological Inventory (CPI), and the Inwald Personality Inventory (IPI). These tests are self-report, paper-and-pencil personality inventories.

Research has shown empirical support for their usefulness in predicting what police applicants might say or do on the job—for example, being late or absent, using drugs, violating police procedures and rules, and using excessive force. Few psychologists continue to use projective tests, which ask applicants to respond to unstructured situations or stimuli, such as the Rorschach Inkblot Test. Less frequent among psychologists is the use of situational tests, in which police applicants engage a role-playing exercise usually representative of job-related work conditions. There has been little empirical evidence supporting the use of projective and situational tests in screening police applicants for law enforcement training.

Psychologists supplement test scores from a battery of psychological tests with information obtained from a personal interview, a common component of the psychological evaluation. Psychologists use a personal history questionnaire to gather information on applicants' background (e.g., family, work, health, and any criminal behavior). Their interview, in part, usually involves a structured question format. Psychologists, however, often ask probing questions that follow up applicants' responses and sometimes ask questions that their police agency clients request. Personal interviews with police applicants help psychologists interpret and validate test data sources.

Educating and Training Police Officers

The police have the responsibility to keep the peace, maintain order, enforce laws, and safeguard the well-being of the community. This kind of duty to act involves the possibility of danger all the time, puts police officers at risk, and requires education and training. Critical issues in police education and training to which psychologists have given considerable attention are negotiating hostage and barricaded-suspect (HBS) situations, handling people with mental illness, conducting criminal investigations, and managing job-related stress.

Negotiating Hostage and Barricaded-Suspect Situations

Most police agencies have and employ critical incident teams, sometimes called special response teams (SRT) or special weapons and tactics (SWAT) teams, to resolve or assist in resolving high-threat or special-threat conditions, such as HBS situations. Police use of critical incident teams has evolved since the highly publicized HBS situation during the 1972 Olympic Games in Munich, West Germany. The first police approach to handling an HBS situation was an assault, which involved officers primarily using forceful options, often with lethal consequences for suspects. Sometimes, suspects' family members subsequently took legal action against the police.

In the early 1970s, psychologists and sworn personnel developed verbal tactics as alternatives to the assault option. Such tactics focused on police officers extending incident time to de-escalate the situation and talking suspects into surrendering. Police records have shown that critical incidents teams successfully resolve most HBS situations without injury to participants when police officers negotiate verbally. When police agencies used clinical psychologists to negotiate such situations, the rate of success without injury to participants increased.

HBS negotiation training is available at the Federal Bureau of Investigation (FBI) academy in Quantico, Virginia. The FBI's Crisis Negotiation Unit delivers training to all FBI negotiators and other law enforcement negotiators. There are also private companies that develop and deliver specialized training in negotiation skills. Trainers are usually experienced police negotiators who are sometimes psychologists. Police agencies that employ full-time clinical psychologists sometimes use them to educate and train their critical incident team negotiators and work at times with them to resolve, or assist in resolving, HBS calls for service. Negotiation activities primarily focus on containing suspects, negotiating with them, uncovering the personal factors motivating their behavior, and extending incident time, which gives suspects the opportunity to vent their emotions and make sensible decisions. Negotiation training typically emphasizes developing active listening skills through role-playing. Scholarly research on the effectiveness of negotiation training is in its infancy. A recent preliminary finding showed that FBI agents significantly improved their active listening skills following participation in the FBI's National Crisis Negotiation Course. Generally, however, there is much research that needs to be done in order to evaluate the effectiveness of crisis negotiation training.

Handling People with Mental Illness

The police are having more contacts with people with mental illness. Researchers have estimated that between 5% and 10% of police-citizen contacts involve people with mental illness. Contacts often occur in the home, family members sometimes call for police services, and the police usually resolve calls without incident. Some researchers have suggested that the dismantling of state mental hospitals, the changing mentally ill population, the tightening of requirements for receiving mental health support, and the offering of limited psychological services are possible explanations.

The police are receiving education and training in the handling of people with mental illness. They recognize that mental illness is not a crime and that people having mental illness live in their communities, have professional vocations, and call for police services. The police also know that empirical investigations have found a link between mental illness and criminal behavior. For example, persons who suffer from bipolar disorder or schizophrenia are more likely to express antisocial behaviors that society criminalizes. Most mentally ill offenders are under the influence of alcohol or drugs when they commit crimes. There is some increased risk of mentally ill individuals becoming violent.

Although people who have a mental illness may commit a crime, be a victim of crime, or report a crime, police responses to encounters with them have improved with training. Police personnel, psychologists, and other mental health professionals have developed training curricula that includetopics such as symptomatology of mental conditions, non-arrest and arrest options, and community police responses. They have developed and made available model police policies for contacts with people with mental illness. These policies have helped police administrators standardize the nature of their departments' response while giving the police flexibility to meet the needs of people with mental illness.

Conducting Criminal Investigations

Psychologists have studied the procedures and tactics used by the police in criminal investigations. They have produced psychological knowledge and have helped the police apply it to criminal investigation techniques such as eyewitness identification. For example, a police detective has a crime suspect and asks an eyewitness to identify him or her by viewing photos. The detective shows the eyewitness eight photos one at a time (sequentially) rather than all at the same time (simultaneously) to reduce the chances of misidentification caused by the eyewitness comparing photos and trying to decide which one looks most like the suspect. Chances of misidentification are less when the detective does not know the actual identity of the suspect, tells the eyewitness that the suspect's photo may or may not be present, gives the eyewitness no feedback during or after the identification procedure, and asks the eyewitness about his or her level of confidence in the identification.

What psychologists have known about police interrogation tactics is that some of them lead to false confessions. For example, a police detective has a suspect of a crime and interrogates him or her for several hours. An interrogation is a stressful experience for the suspect. In a state of high stress, some suspects are highly suggestible and might come to believe that the accusations made by the detective are true. Other suspects may confess if the detective threatens punishment or makes promises during the interrogation— even if the suspect knows that he or she is innocent. In other cases, the desire for attention or fame, especially in a highly publicized crime, might motivate the suspect to confess despite having done nothing wrong.

Police detection of the lies told by suspects during interrogation has received considerable research attention by psychologists. The police know that uncontrollable physiological arousal often accompanies a suspect's lying. For example, a police detective has a suspect of a crime and uses the polygraph technique (or device) in interrogation. The polygraph examiner asks the suspect several non-crime-related questions that generate emotional responses (e.g., about past behaviors) and several crime-related questions. Both provoke physiological responses, but the crime-related questions provoke more physiological responses than the non-crime-related (or control) ones, which suggests that the suspect is guilty. Most courts do not accept polygraph results as evidence. Psychological research has suggested that the rate of accurately detecting deception is low and the rate of false positives is high. The police, however, continue to use the technique with others and try to convince suspects that they cannot beat the device and that they should admit the fact of having committed a crime.

Hypnosis is another investigative technique available to the police. Usually psychologists, psychiatrists, or trained forensic hypnotists conduct interviews using hypnosis. They use the technique mostly to obtain information from eyewitnesses or victims and rarely to obtain information from suspects. There is little empirical evidence to support the belief that hypnosis elicits reliable memories.

Criminal profiling is a set of investigative techniques used to identify the characteristics of suspects most likely to have committed a crime. For example, a police detective analyzes a crime scene, investigates the personal history of the victim, considers motivating factors, links the nature of the crime with similar behaviors of criminals, and finally generates a hypothesis about the suspect's sex, age, race, education, marital status, personality, and other personal characteristics. Specialized training in criminal profiling is available at the FBI Academy. Police profilers use behavioral science techniques along with other techniques of criminal investigation. They use criminal profiles to focus investigations in part on particular types of suspects while continuing investigative efforts on all possible suspects. How effective is criminal profiling? Some research suggests that professional profilers do better at extracting information from crimes and making predictions about suspects than do nonprofessionals.

Managing Job-Related Stress

Police stress is a reaction (or effect) caused by unfavorable physical, psychological, or social forces. Reactions may include physical, cognitive, behavioral, and affective changes in police behavior. Police stress may stem from law enforcement work, personal life, the criminal justice system, the police organization, or the public. Stress related to law enforcement work has received considerable research, training, and counseling attention, especially incidents involving force by and against the police, such as officer-involved shootings.

Police agencies are educating and training their officers to manage job-related tasks that can be stressful. Training curricula include recognizing stress reactions and learning skills to manage their potential harmful effects. Police agencies routinely provide their officers and families with information about job-related stress and mental health support. They establish peer support teams composed of officers and psychologists or other mental health professionals. Post-incident debriefings are common following critical police incidents. They serve as an early crisis intervention effort, facilitate discussion with officers, assist in restoring normalcy in officers' lives, and help police administrators identify officers who need professional mental health support. Peer support teams are usually part of the post-incident debriefing.

Evaluating Job Tasks and Duties

Psychologists with training in industrial-organizational psychology have contributed mostly to the study of police officers at work. A job analysis determines what responsibilities the police have, what tasks they perform, what knowledge and skills they possess, and what results they achieve. Analysis methods primarily involve reviewing the literature on policing, reviewing departmental literature (e.g., operational manuals, rules and procedures, policies, and general orders), observing the police at work (e.g., ride-alongs and training), conducting interviews with police personnel, and administering survey questionnaires. This battery of techniques produces an exhaustive list of job duties, such as crime prevention and law enforcement, and job tasks, such as making arrests and writing reports. Police agencies use information from the job analysis to make informed decisions about organizational operations such as police selection and promotional procedures.

A job analysis is lengthy and expensive. It requires organizational cooperation and commitment at all levels; it validates pre-employment standards and selection procedures. The Americans with Disabilities Act puts police agencies on notice that they must link their pre-employment standards and selection procedures with job-related behaviors. Staying current and consistent with job analyses gives police agencies some protection against claims of discriminatory selection procedures.

Carrying Out Fitness-for-Duty Assessments

Police agencies have a responsibility to monitor the psychological fitness of their officers. They have a right to order psychological evaluations of officers who develop patterns of problematic job-related behaviors. Misconduct might take the form of abusing authority, using excessive force, misusing drugs and alcohol, and engaging in criminal behavior. Police agencies must collect and document information on the problem behaviors they wish to correct. Documentation might include performance evaluations, pre-employment psychological screening reports, disciplinary actions, medical or counseling records, and other types of relevant reports that support a fitness-for-duty evaluation. Officers who go through a fitness-for-duty evaluation must give written consent.

Only licensed or certified psychologists (or psychiatrists) who have clinical experience can carry out a fitness-for-duty evaluation. The police agency requesting the evaluation is the client and not the officer going through it. Large police departments that have in-house psychologists usually have them perform the evaluation. However, a dual relationship occurs when in-house or outside psychologists counsel or have counseled an officer whom the police agency refers for a fitness-for-duty evaluation. Most police agencies contract with outside psychologists to avoid the conflicts that such dual relationships produce. Police departments must make every effort to avoid dual relationships. The Psychological Services section of the International Association of Chiefs of Police recommends that psychologists have training and experience in psychological testing and police assessment techniques and that they have knowledge of police job-related functions and the legal issues surrounding employment practices. An assessment of job-related mental fitness usually involves reviewing background information, administering a battery of psychological tests, conducting a clinical interview, generating a report, and making recommendations. The scope of the assessment is breadth and depth of psychological fitness, with the aim of identifying the absence or presence of personal characteristics essential for performing job-related behaviors that the officer falls short of doing. Outcome recommendations first specify "fit" or "not fit." Police chiefs or other police stakeholders (the client) may request additional recommendations, such as mental health counseling, remedial training, or other remedies.

POLICE OFFICER PERFORMANCE IN A SIMULATED CRITICAL INCIDENT

The work of police officers is challenging and dangerous. Police officers are required to operate effectively in the face of physical danger, taxing hours, and institutional burdens. There is a wealth of literature to suggest that the pressures of police work are severe and multifaceted, leading to physical, emotional, and social consequences. Unfortunately, these negative effects may contribute to the worsening of police officer mental and physical health by disrupting performance during critical incidents. In a critical incident, police officers are sometimes asked to make life and death decisions based upon their assessment of a given situation and the people within them. Mistakes made in these moments bear great consequences for all involved, and the pursuant emotional strain increases the risk of the police officer making mistakes in the future. The professional necessity of competent law enforcement performance during highly charged situations thus requires a better understanding of the factors responsible for performance within stressful encounters.

"Stress" refers to behavioral and physiological responses that are arousing and aversive, but importantly, whose effects are mediated by cognitive and dispositional factors within the individual. Following a stressor, there is a complex neurohormonal response that will fluctuate based upon the intensity, nature, and duration of the stressor, as well as several internal factors of the individual experiencing it. Empirical research distinguishes between acute stress – an ephemeral psychological or physiological response immediately following a stressor – and chronic, or persistent, stress. Although these are convenient theoretical distinctions, their application to understanding the effects of stress on police officer performance is muddled by the nature of police work that presents acute stressors frequently (i.e., multiple incidents a day), as well as sources of chronic stress, such as in anticipation of an incident, shift work, psychological trauma, or negative media coverage. A general theoretical model articulates the effects of stress on skill acquisition and performance follows a nonlinear function: moderate stress and arousal are often adaptive and can bolster performance, whereas high levels of stress and chronic exposure to stress sometimes impair cognitive function and behavioral performance. However, several factors moderate this relationship, including task complexity, and tasks that have multiple or high cognitive demands show a negative relationship with even moderate levels of acute stress. Negative effects of acute stress on individual performance of complex tasks are well documented, specifically those assessing memory, working memory and attentional control, and decision-making. Police officer actions during a critical incident stem from these cognitive processes, and therefore, it is useful to consider this theoretical framework when evaluating possible consequences of acute stress on police officer performance.

Several investigations have examined the effects of stress on job performance and decision-making of police officers. Police officers are a useful population for this area of study, because they are often required to make immediate decisions of great consequence across a variety of unpredictable situations. For example, an officer approaching a reportedly armed suspect must attempt to communicate with the suspect while simultaneously visually scanning for the presence of weapons, considering other threats within the environment (e.g., other potential suspects, nearby civilians who could be in danger), evaluating the suspect's potential escape routes, potentially coordinating movements with a partner, maintaining radio communication, and considering the nature of the suspect in question (e.g., the suspect's mental state, or if the individual is in fact the actual suspect). These extreme cognitive demands must also be done while the officer is likely to be highly emotionally aroused. In this context of demanding cognitive engagement and emotional arousal, the police officer will be required to make a split-second decision not only to potentially discharge their firearm but also to do so accurately. To add further complication to the matter, many critical incidents arise spontaneously during routine response calls, denying the officers the opportunity to plan or mentally rehearse.

Investigations into the matter have identified numerous factors that contribute to police officer performance during stress. These factors include decision-making styles, dispositional factors organizational training and culture, and situational characteristics.

Perhaps most critically, acute physiological arousal of police officers has been highlighted as a significant contributor to performance under stress. Acute arousal provides a surge of awareness and energy, increased vigilance to threat, increased responsiveness, and may contribute to successful recovery post-incident. In contrast, other functions are found to be impaired during acute arousal, including disrupted visual processing of peripheral information, declines in executive functioning, and difficulty in utilizing environmental feedback. Taken together, the cognitive processes and behavioral performance that are required in police work appear to be differentially affected by acute stress, and those functions that characteristically have higher cognitive demands appear to be vulnerable to disruption. One common example of this is the tactical decision to discharge a weapon, and officers under high acute stress conditions or reporting high trait anxiety are more likely to discharge their weapon and have poor shot accuracy. Fatigue, either due to acute or chronic stressors, further alters behavioral choices, including tactical decisions to shoot or pursue a suspect. Whereas acute stress or anxiety may impair complex and intentional behaviors, defensive behaviors and tactical actions that have been practiced to achieve automaticity appear to be less impaired. Accordingly, intervention studies among police officers have attempted to harness the benefits of physiological arousal, while minimizing its potentially deleterious effects. This intervention research suggests that with extensive practice and repetition, police officers can call upon well-rehearsed tactical procedures under duress, thereby translating physiological arousal into decisive and effective tactical responding.

Equally important as tactical decisions, an officer ability to effectively communicate is essential to resolving a critical incident safely. Verbal and nonverbal communication are other examples of behaviors that stem from complex and demanding cognitive processing, for which there is evidence of semantic and declarative memory functions to be impaired by acute stress at both very high and very low levels. Acute physiological arousal (as measured by indices such as cortisol) is predictive of impaired communication skills with some research suggesting that nonverbal communication (e.g., eye contact) can be predicted by physiological stress levels even prior to the encounter. In police officers, high acute stress and high trait anxiety predict poor verbal communication during an arrest.

Based upon the reviewed evidence, there is seemingly a paradox of police officer performance under stress – aspects of awareness and vigilance are bolstered, whereas behaviors that rely on complex cognitive processes, including communication, are disrupted and well-rehearsed, proceduralized skills are seemingly spared. All of these functions are relevant to police officer performance and decision-making ability during critical incidents directly have consequences to officer and public safety. Therefore, it is imperative to understand the effects of police officer physiological arousal (i.e., acute stress response) on tactical and communication skills during a critical incident. In the extant literature, few studies have considered these specific domains of police performance in the field, which hampers translation of the research to effective training interventions. A study that continually monitored police officer heart rates while on duty concluded that arousal was highest just prior to and during a critical incident, and officers did not fully recover before ending their shift, which underscores the need for research simulations that enjoy high ecological validity. We aim to address this limitation in the current study by examining the relationship between acute physiological arousal and police officer tactical and communication skills during a simulated critical incident that was modeled after a real-life occurrence.

We evaluated police officer physiological arousal with complementary indicators taken from the cascade of biological responses following threat and stress. Cortisol is secreted from the pituitary-adrenocortical axis, and because it is one of the most critical hormones to increase short-term resilience to stress, it is a common target for field assessment of stress response. Cortisol gradually increases following a stressor, reaching peak levels within 20–30 min and remains elevated for approximately an hour post-stress. Stress activates the sympathetic nervous system as evident by elevated heart rate. Increased heart rate indicates greater arousal, and moderate rather than extreme increase and rapid recovery to baseline rate indicate an adaptive response. In addition, there are secondary effects of stress. For example, stress increases blood viscosity as an adaptive response to reduce the risk of fatal hemorrhage following a fight. As a natural countermeasure, the anticoagulant, antithrombin, is released throughout the body's vasculature, especially where large blood vessels bifurcate or blood flow is turbulent and there is increased risk of clotting. Thus, increased antithrombin is an ideal response during a stressful encounter to minimize the risk of stress-induced blood clotting. A 5–10% elevation in antithrombin has been observed following stressful psychological tasks in a laboratory, with return to basal levels within 45 min post-stress. In the present study, we use change in cortisol and antithrombin from pre- to post-incident and maximum heart rate during the incident as indicators of individual physiological arousal.

With the use of these indicators of physiological arousal, we tested the hypothesis that greater stress response differentially affects police skills that rely on complex cognitive functions. Specifically, we hypothesize that greater increase in antithrombin and cortisol, as well as higher maximum heart rate, will predict lower scores on verbal and nonverbal communication with the suspect, which are conceived to have high cognitive demands. In contrast, elevation in physiological arousal indicators will predict better tactical skill, which is considered to rely predominantly on procedural memory

Critical Incident Simulation

The critical incident simulation was modeled after a real-life scenario that had resulted in the death of a police officer. The real-life incident was analyzed in detail, and the critical incident simulation was designed in consultation with police officers who were experts in police training. The critical incident simulation included multiple calls and potentially hostile encounters in order to elicit physiological arousal that is common to police officers.

The protocol for the incident was standardized across participants, and the critical incident and all associated physiological data collection were completed 8–10 am during the police training academy session. Each officer was equipped with a set of handcuffs, a loaded paintball gun, an extra round of ammunition, a closed radio system, and an unmarked police car. Officers were instructed to perform usual patrol work and were dispatched in pairs, consistent with typical protocol. Following deployment, the officers received three dispatch calls prior to the critical incident scenario. The first call requested assistance with an individual suspected of selling illicit drugs at the police academy building. Before arriving at the scene, the officer received a second call indicating that the suspect had moved to the shooting range where he was demonstrating aggressive and hostile behavior toward the public. Officers pursued the suspect to the shooting range, and before arriving, they received a third call that redirected the officer to investigate a suspicious vehicle at a restricted military airfield. Before completing the call, the officer was called off again and redirected to investigate the critical incident – the scene of a post office robbery. Police officers were directed to the critical incident approximately 90 min after deployment.

Dispatch informed the officer that a post office had been robbed, the suspect had fled the scene, and the identity of the informant who had reported the incident was unknown. The officer was instructed to meet the building maintenance manager inside an exterior door, which had been damaged during the robbery. These instructions were designed to lower the police officer expectations of the degree of danger in the call, creating a surprising hostile encounter.

Upon arrival at the scene, the police officer observed the informant (an actor) standing 60 yards away from the building in an open field, and the informant was pointing at the damaged exterior door. The officer then walked 15–20 yards to approach the door. Without warning, two masked and heavily armed suspects (actors) exited the building. The suspects took aim at the police officers, and the first suspect immediately fired a shot from his paintball weapon. The second suspect turned right and stopped. The second suspect only spoke English, and although participating officers were fluent in English, they were not instructed of this requirement prior to the incident. The actors portraying the suspects were instructed to follow the police officers' clear, unambiguous orders when they reasonably comprehended the meaning (i.e., in a language they understood or communicated via body language and hand signals). The simulation ended when the police officer handcuffed the suspects. The critical incident was completed within approximately 30 min (within 2 h of deployment in total).

Police Skill Assessment

Police officers performed the critical incident simulation in pairs, but performance was rated individually. An independent police officer, who was an expert in the subject matter, observed the critical incident simulation from a rooftop vantage point. Each police officer was rated in eight domains: tactics, verbal communication, nonverbal communication, material management/dexterity, self-control, control of the suspect, control of the public, and confidence in incident management safety. Each domain was rated on a scale ranging from "poor" (0) to "excellent" (100). Scores across the domains were summed to calculate Total Performance Rating, which ranged from 0 to 800, and higher scores indicated better overall performance. Total Performance Rating is a summary measure that is comparable to a job performance rating a police officer may receive in the academy or on duty. Here, the measure was used to assess effects on general performance in a preliminary analysis. The hypothesized differential effects of physiological arousal were tested with specific scale ratings for verbal and nonverbal communication and tactical skill.

Physiological Arousal Indicators

On the day of the critical incident simulation, the police officers fasted in the morning. Blood samples were collected prior to the critical incident simulation, following which the officers ate a standard breakfast meal before deployment to the simulation scenario. A second blood sample was collected immediately following simulation completion, with no more than a 15-min delay. Circulating antithrombin and cortisol in blood serum were measured using standard laboratory tests. Increase in each of these biomarkers is consistent with a healthy, adaptive response to stressful situations. To measure change in circulating antithrombin and cortisol, the difference of post-incident measure from pre-incident measure was calculated, and positive change scores indicated an increase. Heart rate was used as an indicator of psychophysiological arousal. Officers wore a portable monitor to measure heart rate before and after the simulation, as well as continuously throughout the incident. The baseline heart rate measure was collected during the simulation before the dispatch call for the critical incident, and final heart rate measurements were taken within 10 min of simulation's conclusion. Because heart rate was expected to recover quickly in this sample of healthy cadets, maximum heart rate during the incident was used as a proxy indicator of maximum arousal during the critical incident. In secondary analyses, change in heart rate from pre- to post-incident was also tested as a predictor of skill rating.

Physiological Predictors of Police Officer Performance

The realistic critical incident simulation provided a strong analogue to real-world performance. The officers were forced to respond to a rapidly changing environment, shifting objectives, and uncertainty regarding potential threats. The simulated critical incident appears to have induced stress similar to a real-life experience. As evidence of the simulation's efficacy, police officers demonstrated increased heart rate during the scenario and trends for elevated antithrombin. The result was an ecologically valid and rich assessment of police officer performance across multiple domains: tactics, verbal communication, and nonverbal communication, for which skill ratings were differentially predicted by physiological arousal. In the present sample, elevated antithrombin emerged as a significant predictor of police officer performance. Antithrombin plays a central role in countering the body's chemical cascade mechanisms that are involved in creating blood clots during trauma; thus, increased antithrombin has been considered an adaptive anticoagulant response that is desirable during stress. Observed elevation in antithrombin and other anticoagulants persists for an extended time after the stressor has been removed, presumably for its benefits to reduce the risk of blood clot from trauma that may be favored in evolution. As an index of physiological arousal, greater increase in antithrombin predicted higher Total Performance Rating. Total Performance Rating (the sum across multiple skill ratings) is comparable to the assessments police officers would receive in training and when on duty and represents a summary of job performance across multiple skill domains. The result is consistent with the expectation of healthier physiological responses predicting better performance in the field. Several laboratory studies have demonstrated that moderate levels of physiological arousal are adaptive and positively correlate with skill acquisition, accuracy, and long-term retention. The Total Performance Rating reported here includes multiple types of skills, some that are complex and explicit (i.e., verbal communication), some that are conceptually related to proceduralized or implicit skill (i.e., tactical skill), as well as less complex skills (i.e., materials management) and self-referential ability (i.e., self-control, confidence). In this manner, the Total Performance Rating provides a nonspecific summary of job performance, and it is in this measure that we identified a positive correlation between physiological arousal and performance.

Yet, when specific police skills were considered distinctly – verbal and nonverbal communication that are complex skills and tactical skill that included well-rehearsed behaviors – increased antithrombin was not universally positive. Specifically, greater increase in antithrombin was negatively associated with verbal communication, and a nonsignificant, but positive, association with tactical skill and nonverbal communication. Our hypothesis was partially supported, finding evidence of deficits in verbal communication, although the effects on nonverbal communication and tactical skill were not statistically significant.

Considering elevated antithrombin as an indicator of the police officer stress response, it is plausible that skills that were more effortful were differentially affected. This is consistent with another study that reported high acute stress and high trait anxiety negatively correlated with verbal communication by police officers during an arrest. Verbal communication is cognitively demanding, requiring attentional and processing resources that, during a critical incident, would be also in use by visual scanning and working memory as the officer assessed the scene. When under psychological and emotional stress, effortful and explicit cognitive functions, like those required for verbal communication, tend to falter. Stress-related impairments to declarative memory, which we speculate may have contributed to poor verbal communication in this study, is consistent with the evidence of inaccurate officer reporting in post-incident reports and debriefing that is associated with stress response and fatigue. In this study, the cognitive demands for verbal communication were likely heightened because the Swedish officers were required to speak to the suspects in a language they were fluent in, but not native to. To our knowledge, the effects of acute or chronic stress on verbal communication in police officers during a critical incident have not been well studied. As communication is a critical strategy in resolving an incident without lethal force, further research in this area may identify targets for training intervention.

In contrast to the negative effect on verbal communication, nonverbal communication and tactical response were weakly, but positively, correlated with increased antithrombin. It is possible that both skills relied more upon procedural knowledge and thereby were more resilient to physiological arousal in the stressful encounter. Officers can train for a variety of scenarios, emphasizing the use of core tactics that will be employed in a multitude of situations (e.g., how to hold a firearm, the techniques for subduing a subject to apply handcuffs). These specific techniques can be drilled and repeated to the point of automaticity, thereby reinforcing procedural memory. Similarly, common nonverbal cues can be rehearsed and become like habits. Bearing this interpretation, prior intervention studies that have used repeated rehearsal have found that behavioral skills, such as tactical self-defense, are resilient to the effects of acute stress. However, other observational studies report a negative effect of acute stress on tactical behaviors, such as hand-cuffing and arrest procedures and the use of force while controlling a suspect. Considering the available evidence, it is plausible that with intentional training, rehearsed tactical skills and nonverbal communication may be resilient to acute stress during a critical incident. Although the details of a situation will change, these well-rehearsed techniques can be relied upon during a stressful event, unlike verbal communication that cannot be easily stereotyped.

Effective communication during a police encounter will necessarily depend upon the utterances of the individuals involved. Determining basic verbal commands that can be rehearsed to aid automaticity, even during stressful encounters, may be a useful target for future cadet training programs. However, proceduralized skills by nature are inflexible and there may be a risk of an officer relying too much on such skills when under duress. Much as tunnel vision may unduly restrict situational awareness, an over-reliance on proceduralized communication skills may interfere with the breadth of verbal engagement that is sometimes required in a critical incident. As an alternative, police officers could instead rehearse techniques to increase flexibility and awareness during stressful situations, thereby allowing for the cognitive freedom to engage in improved verbal performance.

If we extend this evidence to police officer decision-making and performance in the real world, there are two important implications. First, successful decision-making among police officers relies upon several distinct skill domains, across which the officer may be differentially successful. Returning to the previous example of approaching a potentially armed suspect, an officer may be quite successful in positioning himself/herself as to avoid attack and may also be successful in identifying the presence of a weapon. However, failure to verbally engage with the suspect and deescalate the situation could undo the successes achieved in the other domains. Second, articulating an ideal physiological response for police officers is quite complex. The police officer health, personal history, and baseline anxiety may modify their ideal physiological responsiveness. Furthermore, the psychophysiological needs for quick reaction times and visual scanning may not be entirely congruent with the needs required to address an individual in a calm, authoritative manner. Experiments and interventions focusing on one performance domain (e.g., decisions to shoot) as a measure of decision-making may wish to consider the addition of alternative performance domains to address this complexity.

The present results identify the importance of physiological responsiveness as a predictor of police officer performance in response to critical incidents. However, not all physiological indicators of stress were associated with performance – we did not find evidence of maximum heart rate during the scenario or change in cortisol correlating with performance. A constrained elevation in heart rate is ideal for performance and is of particular importance during critical decision-making moments within an encounter. In this sample, heart rate was elevated to indicate arousal in the scenario but did not predict individual differences in police skills. Similarly, the release of cortisol is theorized to be beneficial during dangerous situations, providing an increase in vigilance and arousal. It is further believed that an elevation in cortisol levels during stressful experiences will subsequently assist in returning the body to a state of homeostasis, thereby facilitating successful recovery.

Following this evidence, we expected a moderate increase in cortisol during the training scenario to predict better performance, but here we found a nonsignificant trend for decrease in this sample. The statistical trend indicating decrease in cortisol may be an artifact of measures that were taken in the morning (8–10 am), as cortisol is naturally high in the early circadian rhythm and decreases with waking time. The failure of cortisol to emerge as a significant predictor of performance may also reflect the complex nature of the hormone and its effects. Excessive cortisol activation has been associated with negative outcomes, both physical and emotional. Furthermore, there is evidence to suggest that the relationship between cortisol and cognitive function may be moderated by several variables, including previous trauma. In the present context, the role of anticipatory anxiety may be particularly important. When inducing cortisol via anticipatory stress, studies suggest that individuals become riskier in their decision-making and less accurate overall. Thus, although cortisol activation may prove adaptive for some, for others (particularly those with high anticipatory anxiety), the hormone may prove a hindrance. The current study design precludes tests of possible moderators of the effects of cortisol or heart rate, and therefore, we cannot presently test this hypothesis. Future studies of larger samples that include detailed personal and health histories would be positioned to evaluate the importance of individual factors in police officer decision-making under stress.

The reported evidence should be interpreted with consideration of its limitations. First, the analyses are reported from a small sample of cadets, which was sufficient to detect some hypothesized effects to significance, but tests of cortisol and heart rate may be underpowered. Further, we were unable to effectively test possible nonlinear relationships between physiological markers and performance ratings in a sample of this size nor was the sample sufficient to power a larger model testing differential effects across all of the performance domains that were rated during the simulation. This warrants a larger follow-up study to address these important research questions. Second, the sample was selected to include male cadets and does not represent the diversity of the international community of police officers. Nonetheless, we report on physiological markers of stress that are well validated and typical police skill domains, and therefore, the results here can be applied to understanding the effects of physiological arousal and stress on police performance across communities. Physiological response to acute stress and associated behavioral consequences varies as a function of age and sex, which we cannot consider here due to the selection of only male cadets and age was not reported in the study. Third, the analyses are correlational and based upon observational data and therefore cannot comment on causality. The physiological response to psychological and emotional stress is well established, and we take advantage of this knowledge in this study design, but we do not directly manipulate circulating biomarkers. Fourth, the sample was drawn from a parent study that included a behavioral intervention of imagery and skills training 1 year prior. The sample in the present report represents both the control (50%) and intervention conditions (50%), selected at random. We do not test possible intervention-related differences in the present analysis, which were not hypothesized, and the small sample size is expected to be insufficient for such a test. The degree to which intervention may modify the differential effects of stress on communication is left to future studies to address. Finally, the simulation was designed as an analogue to an actual event and was developed to be conducted within a police academy training setting. This setting, though adding some ecological validity, provided logistical constraints. For example, all testing was done in the morning hours and possible time-of-day effects that are relevant for circulating cortisol could not be examined. Further, under different simulation parameters, with a team of multiple raters with complementary areas of expertise (e.g., an expert in police tactics in addition to an expert in communication) could have provided a more nuanced evaluation of police officer performance.

REFERENCES

1. Baumeister, R. F., Bratslavsky, E., Finkenauer, C., and Vohs, K. D. (2001). Bad is stronger than good. Rev. General Psychol. 5, 323–370. doi: 10.1037/1089-2680.5.4.323

2. Birzer, M. L. (2008). What makes a good law enforcement officer? Phenomenological reflections from the African American community. Law Enforc. Pract. Res. 9, 199–212. doi: 10.1080/15614260701797488

3. Callanan, V. J., and Rosenberger, J. S. (2011). Media and public perceptions of the law enforcement: examining the impact of race and personal experience. Polic. Soc. 21, 167–189. doi: 10.1080/10439463.2010.540655

4. Chermak, S. M., McGarrell, E., and Gruenewald, J. (2006). Media coverage of law enforcement misconduct and attitudes toward law enforcement. Int. J. Polic. 29, 261–281. doi: 10.1108/13639510610667664

5. Craig, R. J. (2005). Personality-guided forensic psychology. Washington, DC: American Psychological Association.

6. Mbuba, J. M. (2010). Attitudes toward the police: the significance of race and other factors among college students. J. Ethnic. Crim. Justice 8, 201–215. doi: 10.1080/15377938.2010.502846

2 POLICE PATROLLING

INTRODUCTION

Police patrolling refers to the active, routine, and systematic movement of police officers through their assigned areas to deter and detect criminal activity, provide a visible presence, and offer a sense of security to the community. This fundamental aspect of policing aims to prevent crime, enhance public safety, and build trust between law enforcement and citizens. Patrols can be conducted on foot, by vehicle, bicycle, or even on horseback, depending on the environment and objectives. The practice of patrolling serves multiple purposes: it allows officers to respond quickly to incidents, fosters community relations by making officers more accessible, and helps gather intelligence on potential criminal activities.

There are various types of patrolling, such as proactive, reactive, random, and directed patrols. Proactive patrols focus on preventing crime through a constant and noticeable police presence, often in high-crime areas. Reactive patrols, on the other hand, involve responding to specific incidents as they occur. Random patrols are unpredictable and can cover various areas within a jurisdiction, enhancing the unpredictability of police presence and potentially deterring crime more broadly. Directed patrols are based on data and intelligence, directing officers to areas where crime is statistically more likely to occur. Effective police patrolling requires strategic planning, informed by crime data and community feedback, to allocate resources where they are most needed. Technological advancements have further enhanced patrolling efforts; for instance, GPS and real-time data analysis help optimize patrol routes and improve response times.

Community policing models often integrate patrolling as a core component, emphasizing the importance of interaction and partnership between police and the community. By engaging with residents, attending local events, and maintaining an approachable demeanor, officers can build rapport and trust, which are crucial for effective law enforcement. Moreover, police patrolling is not just about law enforcement; it also involves providing aid and assistance, such as helping lost individuals, offering first aid, or supporting public events. Despite its many benefits, patrolling can also present challenges, including resource limitations, the physical and mental demands on officers, and potential negative interactions with the public. Effective training, support, and community engagement are essential to overcoming these challenges.

PATROLLING: THE POLICE SCIENCE

Police patrols play an important role in public service by responding to incidents, deterring and preventing crimes. It can give a sense of security to people who need protection and discourage those who may commit crimes in the absence of a patrol. Police patrolling is an indispensable component and function of police departments. The goals and objectives of police patrol include crime prevention, criminal apprehension, law enforcement, order maintenance, public services, and traffic enforcement. However, since police resources are limited, there is an understandable interest in patrol strategies and operations that provide safety at minimum cost.

Typically, a city is partitioned into command districts or precincts. Each command district usually has a headquarters and a commanding officer to manage and supervise the police patrol operations. Each command district is further divided into several beats or sectors. Police can effectively manage their operations through the design of the command districts and the choice of patrol strategies of the police units within those districts. There are three major types of patrol strategies for patrol officers: active patrol, random patrol, and directed patrol. In active patrol, patrol officers should use every opportunity to discover, detect, observe, and interdict the unusual event. Random patrol means patrol routes should be random and varied so that the patrol behaviors will not be predicted by potential criminals. In directed patrol, patrol officers pay more efforts to hotspots of crime so they can respond quickly and reduce the crimes in hotspots. In practice, patrol officers may choose one strategy or combine them to accommodate the specific conditions in their area. Another important patrol principle is beat integrity. Patrol officer is expected to remain within assigned patrol district. Beat integrity can be absolute or relative, depending on the number of patrol units assigned and the size of the patrol district and the activity within the area. For absolute beat integrity, patrol officers should remain in the assigned patrol district at all times. In relative beat integrity, patrol officers remain largely within the patrol area and leave it only for good reason, such as back up another officer or respond to a call for service (CFS) incident in another patrol district. When there is a CFS incident, many police departments use the principle that "the nearest police car responds to the call", which belongs to the case of relative beat integrity.

Police patrol district design or region design is one of the important resource allocation strategies of police department. The deployment of patrol force through designated patrol districts is a standard management method to enhance the deterrent capability of uniformed patrol force. Better districting plans can lead to lower response times, officers' familiarization with their assigned area, more efficient utilization of personnel, equalized distribution of workload, uniform police visibility, enhanced officer safety, balanced police response to calls and officer accountability. For small and medium-sized cities, patrol district design determines the patrol boundaries for each patrol unit, for example, police car. For large cities, patrol region design usually starts from higher level of resource allocation. Larger patrol districts for several patrol units are determined first then these districts are further divided for each patrol unit. Patrol districts should be designed in a rational and systematic manner. Several factors need to be considered when designing patrol districts: 1) the size of the area to be patrolled should not exceed the limit that a single officer can cover, depending on types of the area (urban, suburban or rural), 2) natural or man-made barriers, (e.g., rivers, railroad tracks, interstate highways, valleys), 3) workload indicators (e.g., CFS, criminal incidents, traffic patterns), 4) significant area characteristics (e.g., local neighbor hoods, major shopping centers). Different cities have different CFS and crime pattern. CFS incidents or crime events are more likely to happen in some area than other areas. So, the police patrol resources should be spatially allocated based on the characteristics of cities.

Police Patrol Goals and Objectives

Police patrol officers are charged with ensuring the safety and wellbeing of specified areas within a police precinct. This area is known as the "beat" the officer is responsible for patrolling, on foot, on bike, with a partner or in a solo capacity. By patrolling the same areas on a regular basis, officers get the lay of the land, get to know area residents and business owners, and becomes better able to judge when something is unusual or off.

Police patrols serve a variety of purposes, all with the underlying objective of keeping a particular area of a municipality safe and crime-free. Patrol activity may include the following activities:

- Monitoring suspicious or unusual activity
- Responding to calls for assistance or investigation
- Issuing citations for traffic or parking violations
- Investigating abandoned vehicles
- Dispersing unauthorized, non-permitted crowds
- Trouble shooting issues such as traffic lights being out, missing children or senior citizens

Police officers on patrol may be flagged down or called by citizens for any number of issues.

- Well checks
- Medical emergencies
- Power outages
- Vandalism
- Suspected gang activity
- Trespassing
- Domestic issues
- Fights and disturbances
- Animal reports (lost pets and wild animals)
- Criminal activity
- Robbery

- Mugging
- Assault

Some issues patrol officers may be able to diffuse or address on the spot, others require calls for backup or referral to other appropriate government or civil service agencies.

There are myriad goals of a patrol officer which vary according to circumstances, and are often different every day. In addition to doing their jobs effectively, police patrol officers must also ensure their own safety and the safety of their partners and the general public when responding to criminal activity. Some of the key objectives include:

- Professional, lawful approach to law enforcement
- Careful documentation/reporting of alleged criminal activity
- Assisting citizens by responding to emergency calls in a timely fashion or providing referral to other appropriate agencies
- Ensuring no criminal activity is taking place during shift
- Reading Miranda Rights
- Arresting offenders without injury or incident
- Safely transporting detained suspects
- Logging detailed reports
- Maintaining the integrity of crime scenes and aiding in the collection of evidence
- Testifying in court, as required

In short, the over-arching goal of a police patrol officer is to ensure the health and safety of the communities she serves while carrying out the lawful mission of the law enforcement agency the officer represents.

Basic Police Patrol Duties

Patrolling a municipality to preserve law and order is the essence of good policing. Police officers are expected to skillfully perform a number of important duties each and every shift. The top five police patrol functions include crime prevention, community policing, accident investigations, and prisoner transport and traffic enforcement.

Technological innovations like two-way radio, cell phones and computer terminals in patrol cars have dramatically expanded police agencies' reach. However, most officers rely on acute observation and gut feelings to get their jobs done. A new officer's inability to read body language can increase the risk of injury or death, while mastering those cues can give the officer confidence to manage dangerous situations.

- **Crime Prevention.** Uniformed police officers are assigned beat patrol duties in specific geographic areas, which they check for signs of possible criminal activity. Officers also conduct searches and cite, warn or arrest any offenders that they confront. Many of these activities occur as follow-up investigations of citizen complaints and emergency calls. These roles tend to be more compartmentalized at larger departments, where officers who show sufficient experience may serve on special bike, canine, horseback and motorcycle patrol units.
- **Community Relations.** To patrol a neighborhood effectively, police

officers must also win residents' trust. As the U.S. Department of Justice, or DOJ, explains, patrols offer an ideal opportunity for achieving this goal. This strategy, known as community policing, has become an increasingly popular approach since the 1980s. Instead of staying in their cars, officers continually talk with businesses, community leaders and residents. This approach can be implemented through beat patrol duties that include regularly walking or riding bikes through the neighborhoods. They also attend public town hall meetings to discuss issues affecting citizens in the neighborhood.

- **Accident Investigations.** Investigating accidents is another time-consuming task mentioned in the typical job description for police officers. Patrol officers are expected to direct traffic, examine the scene of an accident, interview witnesses, provide first aid for any injured victims, and take written statements from drivers. Other essential duties include clearing any obstructions or wreckage and directing or rerouting traffic.
- **Traffic Enforcement.** Parking and traffic enforcement provides one of the biggest chances for officers and residents to interact, as noted by the Bureau of Labor Statistics, or BLS. For most drivers, the most likely outcome is a verbal warning or written citation. In other cases, however, traffic stops might end with a stolen car's recovery or a fugitive's arrest. To protect themselves, officers watch for extreme nervousness, furtive movements, and lack of eye contract. Many departments actively teach this strategy, which heightens the officer's ability to guard against injury by reading behavioral cues.
- **Prisoner Transport.** Patrol obligations aren't limited to the neighborhood in which the officer works. When prisoners must testify in legal proceedings or need hospital treatment, an officer must escort them and make sure that they're being properly guarded. Other jurisdictions may assign officers to watch jail trustees as they work in public and then search inmates after returning them to their cells.

Police Patrol District Design

Performance measurements and related problems

There are two common performance measures used for police district design: the average response time and the variation of workload. Quick response to citizen calls for service can 1) improve the chances of catching the offender at the scene or nearby 2) increase the changes of identify and locate witnesses, 3) provide immediate gathering of physical evidence, 4) provide immediate lifesaving first aid, 5) enhances the reputation of police department, 6) creates citizen satisfaction with the police. The spatial distribution and allocation of police cars to districts affect both performance measures. In a 1971 study of the New York Police Department more than half of all dispatches were inter-sector dispatches (between districts). Usually, the nearest police car responds to the CFS incident so it may cross the patrol boundaries to respond.

The average response time for these inter-sector responses was approximately 40% greater than that for intra-sector responses and the average travel distance was about 53% greater. This large proportion of inter-sector cases indicates that the district design may not be efficient with regard to the first measure, response time.

Approaches to Police District Design

Manual methods

Historically, the geographic patrolling boundaries were drawn by hand based on police department's knowledge and experience of the total area and the availability of the police resources. Police department also considered the natural boundaries, such as the hills or rivers, the locations of hotspots of crime as well as the administrative boundaries, such as neighborhoods and communities. The limitation of the hand drawn boundaries is that the human is limited in the number of options they can consider and in their formal evaluation of the alternatives. Each alternative represents a different possibility in terms of workload and response times, but assessing these by hand can be very time consuming. The assessment is particularly difficult since both workload and response times are stochastic. This inability to measure the efficiency of the districting alternatives means that manual methods are not appropriate and good computer-based methods are required in order to create district that can positively impact high-level decision making by the police.

Operations research and GIS methods

The first OR application was to use p-Median clustering minimize the total weighted travel distance to service the expected calls. In 1979, Aly and Litwhiler used an interchange heuristic method to allocate police briefing stations to districts. In 2002, a simulated annealing approach, to search for a good partitioning of the police command districts by assessing the average response time and variation of workload of police officers with a simulation called PCAM. GIS methods can be also used in police district design. A maximal covering formulation to determine optimal police patrol areas. This approach produced good alternatives for police districts design. However, the criteria for evaluation were based on static calculation of distances, weights of incidents, and queuing model statistics. Police patrols are highly dynamic activities. It is difficult to use static approaches to find effective answers for most police.

Problem complexity

Computational complexity

A convenient formulation for the police district design problem is as the aggregation of smaller geographic units into larger units that form the districts. This problem has a rich history in mathematics and operations research. This problem reduces to the graph-partition problem with the constraints of contiguity and compactness. One example of graph-partitioning is the political redistricting problem. The census blocks are partitioned into districts such that each district has equal population. There are two constraints on the problem solution: contiguity and compactness. The polygons within each district must be spatially contiguous so that all members of district can connect with one another without leaving the district. Compactness provides for shorter travel times between members of the district. Evaluation of compactness depends on the distance metric used. For Euclidean distance a circle is the most compact shape, while for Manhattan distance a square is most compact. The graph partitioning problem has been shown to be NP-hard.

Another formulation for districting uses graph theory. In this formulation, the regions or geographic units as nodes and the adjacency between regions as edges connect the nodes. For each node, there is a weight representing attributes of the region, for example, population. The objective of districting is to maximize or minimize the function of the weights between different districts. For example, we could use the absolute difference as the function and minimize the difference in population between districts. For the police districts we want to minimize the difference in forecasted activity between districts since this will minimize the difference in travel or response time. We could also minimize the difference in workload between districts. This formulation of the districting problem can be reduced to the problem of "Cut into Connected Components of Bounded Weight", which is also NP-hard.

As with all optimization problems we can employ either exact or heuristic methods. Exact methods systematically exam districting plans explicitly or implicitly. Since the problem is NP-hard, we can use explicit methods only for small districting problems that have limited practical applications. Heuristic methods, such as, simulated annealing, genetic algorithms, and stochastic gradient ascent can find local optima for the districting problem. These local optima can provide good operating solutions for police departments.

Evaluation Complexity

The police patrol district design problem has greater complexity than the computational issues mentioned in Subsection "Computational complexity". Consider the graph-theoretic formulation of the districting problem. In this formulation some function of the region weights is used as the optimization criterion. For example, the sum of the absolute difference in populations between all pairs of regions can be used. In the police districting problem the evaluation is more complicated than a simple sum of average differences. To evaluate the response time we need to compute the travel times for the incidents within each district that require police attention. The locations and times of these incidents are stochastic and must be modeled by an empirical distributions based on current incident data. Further the travel times depend on the characteristics of the road networks in the regions and the environment conditions, e.g., weather and traffic congestion. None of these factors can be conveniently modeled by single variable functions of the region weights.

The workload metric has similar complexities. Since the actual workload depends on travel times, the complexities described above hold for workload. Additionally the types of incidents and their spatial distribution within and across the districts affect workload. The type of incident is also stochastic and cannot be calculated by single variable functions typical of districting problems. The complex evaluation need for districting requires an approach that can produce accurate estimates of response time and workload for different districting designs.

Approach to Police Patrol Districting

The approach we have developed for the police districting problem begins by generating alternative districting plans. Subsection "Generation of alternative districting plans" gives details of the parameterized algorithm to generate the alternative plans.

To evaluate these alternatives we have developed an agent-based simulation. We use the simulation to measure district performance using two metrics: average response time and workload. The simulation we use reveals important complexities in the choice of districting plans.

Generation of Alternative Districting Plans

The generation of districting plans is based on atomic geographical units. There are some existing geographical units such as police beats or census blocks. Usually, these geographical units consider administrative boundaries, important roads, or some natural boundaries (mountains, rivers). The redistricting procedure can start from these units and re-group them into several districts. When developing districting plans for large areas containing hundreds of such geographical units, police beats or census blocks are good choices for atomic units. However, some cities only have 20 or 30 census blocks. Police beats or census blocks are not small enough for optimal patrol boundaries. In such case, grid network can be used instead.

The city can be divided into several hundreds of grids and they are small enough to be atomic units. Clearly, more atomic units represent more possible districting plans. Such representation is more suitable for systematic and scientific study of districting problem. The output districting plans based on grid boundaries can be adjusted according to existing boundaries such as important roads, administrative boundaries and natural boundaries.

The main idea of our districting algorithm is similar to the Constraint-Based Polygonal Spatial Clustering (CPSC) algorithm. The two main steps of the algorithm are 1) select seed polygons (one atomic geographical unit) and 2) select the polygon in neighborhood to be added to the existing cluster until all units are assigned to districts. The major difference of our redistricting algorithm is the selection of seed for each district. Rather than totally randomizing the locations of the seeds, we locate the seeds on several concentric circles over the urban region (see Figure 1).

The underlying intuition is that there is a general trend that downtown area of city has more population than suburbs. So the CFS incidents and crime events are also more likely to happen in central region of city. In the concentric circles model, central region of city has more seeds than suburbs and the patrol districts in downtown area tend to be small, which may facilities quick response and reduce workload variation. When selecting the seeds, the minimum distance between these seeds should be greater than a threshold to allow space for the districts to grow.

Then, each seed alternates in acquiring adjacent atomic units until a stopping criterion is reached. The stopping criterion is that the sum of CFS probabilities of units in the district is greater than a user selected bound. During the growing process, the districts or existing cluster of polygons select one adjacent unit to develop. If there are several alternatives, it chooses the one that can maximize the compactness score. Some randomness can be added to this procedure.

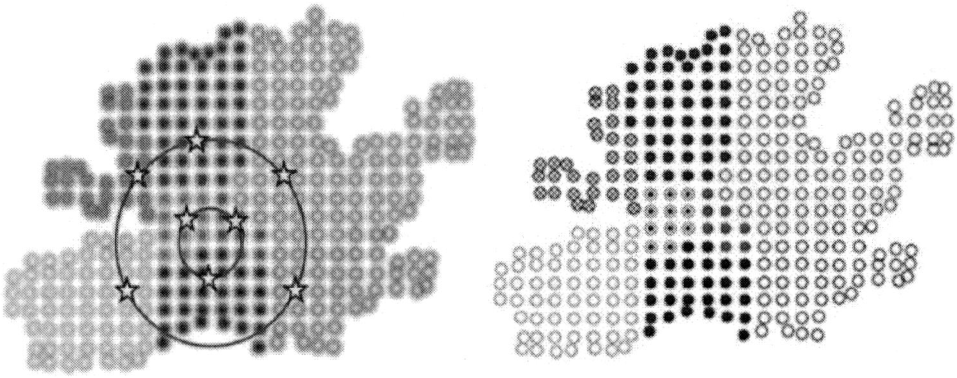

Figure 1. Seeds selection of police districting for Charlottesville.

Source: https://media.springernature.com/lw685/springer-static/image/art%3A10.1186%2F2190-8532-2-7/MediaObjects/13388_2012_Article_30_Fig1_HTML.jpg?as=webp

The difference between random growth and compact growth can be seen in Figure 2. The district can randomly choose one adjacent unit to develop. After a number of iterations of development, all districts stop growing because the stopping condition is met or because there are no more adjacent units for growth. Usually, there are still some unassigned units in the peripheral region of the city. They are assigned to the adjacent districts based on compactness principle. Then, the districting plan is adjusted to balance the CFS probabilities in each district and smooth the boundary between districts.

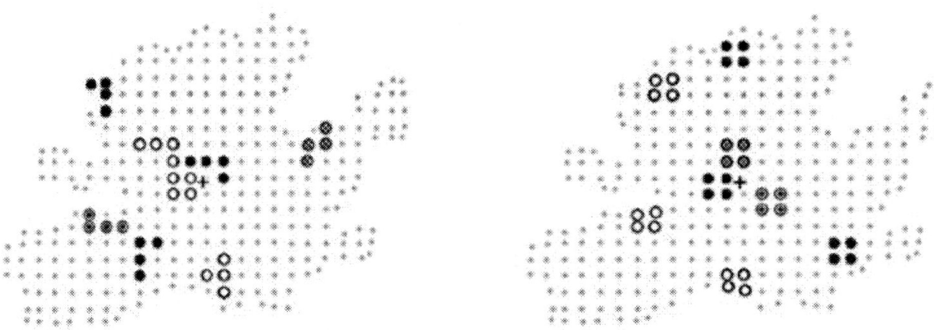

Figure 2. Random growth vs. Compact growth.

Source: https://media.springernature.com/lw685/springer-static/image/art%3A10.1186%2F2190-8532-2-7/MediaObjects/13388_2012_Article_30_Fig2_HTML.jpg?as=webp

The locations of the seeds for districts determine the framework and basic structure of the districting plans. The relevant parameters for starting the growing process are: 1) the center of the concentric circles, 2) the number of circles, 3) the radius of each circle, 4) the number of seeds on each circle. Additional parameters determine the course of district growth. Examples are: 5) the stopping criterion, 6) the number of growth iterations, 7) growth randomness vs. compactness, 8) the number of iterations that balance the CFS probability between districts, 9) the number of iterations that smooth the boundary between districts. Therefore, a districting plan can be described and represented by a set of districting parameters. Once a districting plan is generated, some measurements can be quickly calculated without detailed simulation evaluation, such as compactness of plans and the variation of CFS probability of all districts. These intermediate measurements of districting plans can be used to select top proportion of plans for further simulation evaluation.

Relation between Parameters and Response Variables

Without prior knowledge about how districting parameters affect final response variables, we randomize these parameters to generate some plans, quickly calculate the intermediate measurements, and take some time to get final responses through simulation evaluation. Then we build statistical models to study the relation between them, especially how districting parameters and intermediate measurements affect the final performance variables. The districting parameters can be adjusted to generate more plans that may have better performances. Since it is time intensive to use simulation to evaluate these plans, they can be ranked by the combined weighted score of the intermediate metrics. The weights are adjusted based on the relation between intermediate variables and final performance variables.

Evaluation of districting plans using simulation

Because the assessment of response times and workloads requires the incorporation of multiple factors that interact in complex ways we cannot use closed form expressions. Also, field experiments in the law enforcement and safety management are clearly not feasible because of the risks and costs, not to mention, the public relations problems. This means that evaluation of the police patrol districting plans requires a high fidelity simulation. A feature key needed in this simulation is the ability to accurately represent behaviors of the police in response to calls-for-service. Agent-based simulations afford the ability to effectively represent these behaviors.

Agent-based simulations capture of the behaviors of objects in an environment, such as police patrols in city, through the use of decision rules. These decision rules govern the interactions between objects in the simulation. For example, when a police car object interacts with a road object the rules specify the rate of transition to the next road object. These rules can also represent static properties of the object, for example the speed limit, and the dynamic properties of the environment, such as weather, construction, and traffic conditions. Other example rules used in our simulation include:

- The nearest police car to a new CFS responds to that CFS;
- The responding police car takes the shortest path to the location of the CFS;
- If a police car is servicing a CFS then it is no longer available to respond to a new CFS;

- If the nearest available police car is in a different district it will cross the district boundary and respond to the CFS.

The interactions between multiple objects governed by the rule sets in the simulation produce emergent behaviors or properties that cannot be predicted before running the simulations. For our purposes the most important emergent properties are the response times to CFS and police workloads. These properties are the metrics that allow us to score the effectiveness of different patrol districting plans. Neither of these properties can be accurately anticipated a priori using only a districting plan and the numbers of CFS within the districts. As we indicated in Subsection "Evaluation complexity" if we could simply develop districting plans that equalize the expected CFS in each district then our problem reduces to the graph-partitioning problem. Although graph-partitioning is NP-hard; nonetheless, there are available heuristics than can be applied.

Instead the police districting problem has evaluation complexity in addition to the computational complexity of the graph-partitioning problem. In fact, when we use our high fidelity simulation to evaluate police districting plans that minimize the difference in CFS between districts they actually do worse than some other plans. The same is true for workload. The ability to discover these emerging properties is an important feature of the agent-based simulation we built and a critical requirement in the assessment of competing districting plans.

We implemented the simulation using Java Repast. Java Repast is an open source, agent-based modeling and simulation platform. It uses object-oriented model and has a source library of classes for creating and running agent-based simulations and for displaying and collecting data from these simulations. Geographic data, such as the data expressed in shapefiles, can be imported into the Java Repast model. Using these geographic data the behaviors and movements of the agents can be controlled according to rule sets that exploit these data. For example, the shapefile data layer on secondary roads can have attributes that provide speed limits in different segments of this layer.

We built our police patrol simulation model as an extension to Malleson'sRepastCity prototype. The inputs to our simulation model consist of the shapefiles of the city, the patrol district plan, the police patrol allocation plan and a data set of CFS times, locations, and severity (this last attribute determines the distribution of the service time for the CFS). The shapefiles for the city include primary and secondary roads, major highways, and obstacles or impediments (e.g., construction or road work).

In order to simulate the time and spatial pattern of actual CFS and maintain the randomness of the city environment, the time between incidents and the locations are randomly chosen based on the distribution of actual CFS. Rather than use a bootstrap approach which would resample from actual CFS, we instead use an empirical fit of the distributions of the CFS in space and time. We then chose CFS values based on random draws according to these distributions.

Police cars are on patrol in their districts until they are dispatched by a CFS. Their patrol routes are randomly chosen from the network of roads in their assigned districts. An incoming CFS will generate the dispatch of the nearest police car and that car will follow the shortest route to the location of the CFS. In following this route it will use the maximum safe speed for the route which is greater than or equal to the speed limit on the route. After the police car reaches the CFS location, the police car will remain at that location for the service time of that CFS. We obtain this service time as random draw from the service time distribution for the type and severity of the particular CFS. The service time distributions are empirical distributions found from the data set of actual CFS. When the service time ends the police car returns to its patrol route and again becomes available for dispatch to the next CFS.

We run the simulation for chosen number of runs or for a selected amount of simulation time. For each CFS in a run we record

- The time and location of the CFS;
- The identity of responding police car;
- The time of dispatch for the responding police car;
- The time of arrival at the CFS location for the responding police car;
- The time of departure from the CFS by the responding car (i.e., the time of arrival plus the service time);
- The travel distance of the responding car.

Using these data we can calculate the average response time and workload for each run and, hence, for each districting plan.

BEATS AND PATROLS

The principles governing the dispatch of constables on beats are, firstly, that the SHOs and Beat officers should be held responsible for reporting crime and supplying information about the movements of bad characters and secondly that constables should not, as a rule, visit villages, except under definite orders, for a definite purpose or unless the village lies on their way to or from any duty. There shall be day and night beat arrangements every day.

Beats and patrols are fundamental components of law enforcement strategies, aimed at maintaining public safety and order through proactive and visible policing. A "beat" refers to a designated area or route that a police officer regularly patrols. This concept, originating in the 19th century, is rooted in the notion of community policing, where officers become familiar with the neighborhoods they serve, fostering relationships with residents and businesses. The primary purpose of a beat is to create a consistent police presence, which can deter crime through visibility and enable officers to respond more swiftly to incidents within their assigned areas. Beats can vary in size and complexity, ranging from small urban blocks to larger rural districts, and are often determined based on factors such as crime rates, population density, and geographic features.

Patrols, on the other hand, encompass the broader activities undertaken by police officers as they traverse their beats. Patrols can be conducted on foot, by bicycle, motorcycle, or in vehicles, depending on the terrain and the nature of the area being policed. The objectives of patrols are multifaceted: they include crime prevention, the maintenance of public order, the enforcement of laws, and the provision of assistance to the public. Patrol officers are typically the first responders to emergencies, making their role crucial in the initial assessment and management of incidents. They engage in activities such as monitoring high-crime areas, conducting traffic stops, responding to calls for service, and performing community outreach.

Effective patrol strategies are essential for optimizing police presence and ensuring efficient use of resources. These strategies can include directed patrols, where officers focus on specific issues such as drug activity or gang violence, and random patrols, which aim to create an unpredictable police presence to deter criminal activity. The integration of modern technology, such as GPS tracking, data analysis, and real-time communication systems, has enhanced the efficiency and effectiveness of patrol operations. Data-driven approaches allow law enforcement agencies to identify crime hotspots and allocate resources more strategically, thereby improving the overall safety of the community.

The relationship between beats and patrols is synergistic; while a beat provides the framework for an officer's area of responsibility, patrols are the operational activities carried out within that framework. The success of this system relies heavily on the officer's familiarity with their beat, which can lead to more effective policing through better local knowledge and stronger community ties. Community engagement is a critical aspect of this relationship, as it builds trust and cooperation between the police and the public. When residents feel connected to and respected by their local officers, they are more likely to report crimes and collaborate in community safety initiatives.

Selection of Areas and Villages to be visited

The Station House Officer, shall determine what areas or village should be visited for the purpose enumerated in clause No.1577 and how frequent the visits should be and also which criminals must be watched by the Police alone, which by the Police as well as by the members of the community liaisoning groups such as the members of neighborhood watch scheme.

Villages to be regularly visited should be conveniently grouped and a beat book (Form No. 41) kept for each group. Separate beat books will be kept for use when constables are deputed upon the occasional duties already specified.

Beat Constables are required to bring the signature of a respectable inhabitant of the village in proof of their visit to a village. For the purpose of checking beat books, a book in Form No. 41 (A) shall be kept in the station, in which shall be entered the usual signatures of the village officers and of any respectable villagers selected to sign in beat books.

Point books in Form No. 41 (B) shall be supplied to selected respectable inhabitants. It shall be the duty of beat constables and officers checking beats to sign and date their names in the point books whenever they visit the villages. Beat constables shall obtain the signature of the point book holder in the beat ticket. Checking officer, Sub-Inspectors and Inspectors shall also see whether constables who have visited the village subsequent to the previous check have signed the point books.

Bad character – check register – maintenance of

(a). A check register of all K.Ds., habitual offenders and suspects, inclusive of those residing in the limits of outposts shall be maintained in each station

(b). The bad characters who are in jail and not likely to be released during the year, can be entered at one stretch in the opening pages of the register. The bad characters who are present, out of view or in jail but likely to be released during the year shall be entered beat-war thereafter. In the cases of bad characters in jail, entries regarding the period of imprisonment and the dates of their probable release shall be made against each.

(c). Close watch bad characters should be written, KDs first and then suspects in red ink, followed by non-close watch bad characters in blue or black ink, in the same order. All those entries should be beat-war.

(d). The date of the expiry of the History sheet shall be noted in the remarks column against each bad character.

(e). Such a register will be maintained in out-posts also, for characters living in their respective jurisdiction when the out-posts are for the purpose of checking KDs, suspects and habitual offenders.

(f). Names of notorious rowdies ordered by an officer of and above the rank of Superintendent of Police to be watched, shall also be entered in this register.

Road Patrols

It is incumbent upon the Police to ensure the safety of the roads and strict attention must, therefore, be paid to road patrolling. Unduly severe work should not be demanded from night patrol men. They should be sent out with definite orders which may be varied, as circumstances permit, with respect to the time to be passed at particular spots. It should always be possible to arrange for a patrol to take some rest at a named place. If possible, two constables or one constable and one Home guard should patrol together or a constable should be accompanied by more members of neighborhood watch scheme or village group. It is often useful for patrol constable to look up bad characters in villages not far from the road side. To secure the due performance of road patrolling, constant checking is absolutely essential, and offences of and above the rank of Superintendent of Police must see that all subordinate officers, from Inspector downwards, perform their fair share of this duty.

System of Work in Town Areas

The whole of the Police of a town areas with the exception of Sub-Inspectors, station writer, standing guard and men for traffic regulation duty will be divided into two or more groups to perform beat duties with a view to covering many town areas at a time. The time of duty will be suitably allotted by the SHO. The checking officers including the special night rounds officer shall cover all areas of the town during nights and check the beat constables. The arrangements will be made to cover the areas during day time so that the men on night duty will be given rest. During day time one HC and two men of Traffic Police Station shall perform traffic patrol duty to prevent road side encroachments and Traffic rule violations (5). The Sub-Inspector or other officer in charge of the station for the time being, will make a note of orders and instructions to beat men in the general diary in regard to matters which will be carefully prepared with due regard to the requirements of the station therein will be noted:-

- the notorious rowdies who require to be looked up and the times when they should be checked;

- localities where nuisances are committed and the times when such nuisances are usually committed;
- bazaar-streets which incessantly require to be cleared of obstruction and the hours during which they are liable to obstructions;
- cases of missing children;
- notices of important cases requiring the vigilance of beat men; and
- particular localities to be specially visited for prevention of mischief or other crimes, specifically bag lifting in the busy areas.

Beat men will, as they come on duty, make a point to get to know the orders and instructions recorded in the general diary for their information and guidance through the officersincharge of the G.D. They will issue detailed orders to the men on those matters and will also note in the general diary later on that duties assigned to them were duly performed. Beat Constables sent out to attend to obstructions or nuisances in particular localities or any other work may be instructed if they find out obstructions or nuisances, etc., or when they have done the work allotted in the places to which they were sent, to patrol through them smartly and return at once to the station to be in waiting or to be sent out to other places. Constables without definite work are not to loiter about the streets. Instructions for Constables in regard to work to be attended to by them should be noted in the beat book, pocket note book and the general diary. The Constables will note in their pocket note / beat books the time of their departure from and return to the station, giving reference to their notebooks for details of work done. Any shortcomings noticed by officers should be noted in their pocket note / beat books, on the return of Constables to the station. It is the duty of the Head Constable to receive from the Constables their note-books and to see that these are properly written up. They must then and there question them as to short comings, etc., and take any action that may be called for. They will then write up the general diary. The note-books must be in the station and the SHO will be responsible for their custody under lock and key. The general duty Head Constable will take charge of the notebooks whenever the SHO happens to be absent from the station.

Night Patrols

One or more batches of patrol-men mixed with crime team men in mufti should be sent for night rounds to important junctions, streets or lane corner, where house-breakers are likely to pass from their sphere of operation. Such patrol men including the mufti men should hide themselves in unobservable parts of the locality, alert and ready to pounce up on night hawks. These might, with advantage, be shifted from one corner to another for specified periods on each night and need not necessarily be kept on for the full period of five hours in one place. They shall be also able to spot their checking officer when they pass. (Specified directions as to the locality and time at each spot, should be noted in Tamil in the books concerned before the men are detailed). Other available men may be given a specific short length of streets to go round, noting the exact streets. Such blocks to be traversed by patrols should be changed from night to night. The greatest care must be taken to limit the extent of these patrol-men, not be used for other works continuously. Bad characters should not be checked by night by the Police unless they are actually under suspicion of being engaged in night crime. Regular enquiries in the day time are what are required. Sub-Inspectors shall go on night round on successive nights, the Inspector of Police also doing this duty at frequent intervals to be specifically laid down. If the circle Inspector has rural areas also, he shall check night patrols in these areas by means of surprise visits as frequently as possible.Sub-Inspectors in charge of town stations should personally detail night patrols giving full and specific instructions on the above lines in the general diary. When the duty Head Constable have become familiar with the above principles, they may be allowed to detail night rounds, subject to constant supervision and check by the Sub-Inspectors.

Town men should have a clear day off at regular intervals of not less than six days. As far as Head Constables are concerned, there are in all town stations a sufficient number of Head Constables. Duties should be rotated among Head Constables in such a way, every Head Constable gets rest. In regard to Constables the strength available will be evenly utilized for beat and patrol duties except writer and court PCs.No one of his off-duty day may leave his headquarters without permission. If, in the public interest, any Head Constable or Police Constable is not given a day off duty in any week he shall be given rest in later stages. The SHO will be responsible also for letting the men off for meals or for reasonable periods of relaxation under record in the general diary. When he goes himself for meals or relaxation he will hand over under formal record in his general diary to the Head Constable. Petty petitions will be handed over to the Head Constables for disposal.

General Instructions While Performing Beat and Patrol Duties

Villages and areas should be selected basing on the following criterion and frequent beats served.

- Important village, where recently frequent crimes reported, kds/bcs reside and where there an acute factions;
- Unimportant village; and
- Deserted village, which is far off or which is geographically isolated.

The SHO, Head Constable and all Constables should know each beat and all areas and routes. Meeting beats should be arranged between the adjoining stations and the Beat constables should be required to halt in the meeting villages or places or junctions, where necessary. In such cases, the beat constables should sign in the beat books of their counterparts with date and time. Special betas should be arranged for extraordinary occasions as and when the "Bravo Scheme" is operated in a particular area including the adjoining areas and the borders. Beat Constables should be instructed to visit railway stations, bus stands and the places where trucks halt and go.

With regard to performance of beat and patrol duties, the entries shall be made inthe following registers.

- Sample signature book
- Beat book
- Pocket note book / second pocket note book
- Point book / patta book
- KD/BCs (Exconvicts) – check register
- History sheets, if any
- Village roster

- Duty roster
- General diary

The beat constables should gather the following information and report to the Station House Officer, who should check the signatures in the sample signature book in the station and study the information and take appropriate action. For example, if a bad character is reported to be absent from his village, the Station House Officer will issue an enquiry roll Form "A" to the Station House Officer to whose jurisdiction the bad character is reported to have gone.

- The beat PCs should watch dangerous criminals or gangs which require surveillance.
- They should ascertain any definite piece of information and serve processes.
- They should find out whether any crime has occurred in the beat.
- They should intelligently gather information about the visit of any bad character, suspicious strangers, wandering gangs and new tenants in a particular area of a village.
- They should make enquires about the movements and doings of exconvicts / KDs / rowdies / suspects / budding criminals and whether they have been spending money lavishly or incurring expenses beyond his normal means.
- They should find out whether there are any receivers of stolen properties in the village and whether any known receiver has been contacted by any bad character or strangers.
- They should make enquires about liquor shops, illicit distillation of liquors / IMFL, unlicensed weapons, gatherings and panchayat, activities of political parties, usury, factions or ill-feelings in respect of lands, temples, processions, festivals, religious or communal disputes, stone throwing likely to give rise to riots, provocative wall-posters and other matters affecting the public peace.
- They should collect information about the delivering of lecturers, holding of meeting of political nature or otherwise.
- They should enquire in particular villages whether bad characters have been or rare, in the neighbourhood.
- They should maintain a watch in the arrack shops particularly in the bordering arrack / liquor shops about the visits of suspicious persons.

Duties of supervisory officers in relation to beats:-

- CIs / SIs / HCs should check beat PCs by surprise.
- They should at random compare the entries of dates and hours in the beat book with those in the point books. Such verification should be made even when the Station House Officer or Head Constable goes to a village or to any place in a beat or any other work, such as petition enquiry or investigation.
- The CIs/SIs should also make enquires with residents / villagers other than point book holders about the beat constable's presence on the days noted in the beat book.
- The SHOs should be able to check all the beats in the limits at least once a month. The ASIs / HCs should do so more often.

- Officers of and above rank of Circle Inspector visiting or inspecting a station should not only see whether beat villages have been properly selected, but also ensure that beats are being regularly served and checked. The fact of having done so should be embodied in the inspection notes together with the instructions, if any, given to the SHOs

PATROLLING AND CRIME PREVENTION

Police patrols play an important role in public service by responding to incidents, deterring and preventing crimes. It can give a sense of security to people who need protection and discourage those who may commit crimes in the absence of a patrol. Police patrolling is an indispensable component and function of police departments. The goals and objectives of police patrol include crime prevention, criminal apprehension, law enforcement, ordermaintenance, public services, and traffic enforcement. However, since police resources are limited, there is an understandable interest in patrol strategies and operations that provide safety at a minimum cost. Police patrol officers are charged with ensuring the safety and wellbeing of specified areas within a police precinct. This area is known as the 'beat' the officer is responsible for patrolling, on foot, on a bike, with a partner or in a solo capacity.

By patrolling the same areas regularly, officers get the lay of the land, get to know area residents and business owners, and becomes better able to judge when something is unusual or off. The deployment of the patrol force through designated patrol districts is a standard management method to enhance the deterrent capability of the uniformed patrol force. Better districting plans can lead to lower response times, officer's familiarization with their assigned area, more efficient utilization of personnel, equalized distribution of workload, uniform police visibility, enhanced officer safety, balanced police response to calls and officer accountability. Patrol has three parts: answering calls, maintaining a police presence to deter crime, and probing suspicious circumstances. A presumed advantage of patrol is that police car cruising randomly through city streets supposedly create the feeling that the police are everywhere. The patrol officers detect, deter, and guard against personal attacks, loss of assets, criminal activity and acts of terrorism by their high visibility, observations and inspections.

Importance of Patrol

It is widely believed that if the presence of the police is highly visible, criminals and violent mobs will remain off the streets for fear of detection or arrest. When planning patrols that are conducted with the deterrence of criminal activity as their chief aim, ensure that times and routes of the patrol are varied and unpredictable. Particularly in a peacekeeping mission, patrols can be used to determine the position, volume, armament of local military facilities, police or rebel factions. This may be particularly useful intelligence, should violence erupt or in conjunction with agreements made under the peace process by the various factions. Patrols can be used to support an investigation, where a crime has been committed. Patrols can be used to interact with the local population to see if further information can be obtained about the investigation or may be asked by local police to assist with an area search for evidence. The process whereby a patrolling mission is organized and conducted can be defined in four phases; the planning phase, the practical preparation, the conduct of the patrol itself and the debriefing

Types of Patrols

Patrols can be conducted by many different means, depending on the environment, the existing equipment and requirement of the mission. Of the many different types of patrols; here is a list of the main ones:

- Foot patrols: It is perhaps the most effective way of patrolling as the police officers can interact directly with the local population. However, they are restricted to a small area as the police will need to be able to return to their base on completion of the patrol unless it is a long-distance foot patrol, in which case there will be a need for greater planning and preparation. The reliability and range of the radios should be taken into account when considering the distance to conduct foot patrols.
- Vehicle patrols: These give the patrol the ability to travel further and cover more ground. However, they will be restricted to what the officers see from their vehicle unless they can stop and patrol for part of the way on foot. A combination of foot and mobile patrol is most effective for outlying towns and villages, where the unit can travel there by vehicle and then patrol the town on foot. The commanding officer needs to put in place a reporting system whereby the patrolling officers indicate where they stopped, who they met and which information/observations they managed together.
- Air patrols: They are less common in peacekeeping missions due to the restricted amount of air facilities. However, drones (remote-controlled pilotless aircraft) or helicopters can be used. Helicopters can also be used in conjunction with foot patrols by transporting a unit to a remote location and then dropping them off for a patrol, collecting them either at the same location at a later time, or a different location such as the end of the foot patrol route.

Purpose of a Patrol

The purpose of police patrols is to have a constant, vigilant police presence on the town. This accomplishes several things. First and foremost, if there is a crisis or a need for a police presence, such as an accident or criminal activity, patrolling ensures that police are constantly mobilized and ready to respond to emergencies. Beyond that, there is a psychological effect of patrolling. The presence of police officers, or even the knowledge that they can arrive quickly, will deter a lot of criminal activity or help citizens feel safe. By keeping police on patrol, they help improve the safety of the region naturally just by their presence in addition to the obvious benefit of emergency preparedness. This presence helps keep the public safe and feeling secure

Police patrols serve a variety of purpose, all with the underlying objective of keeping aparticular area safe and crime-free. Patrol activity may include the following activities:

- Monitoring suspicious or unusual activity.
- Responding to calls for assistance or investigation.

- Issuing citations for traffic or parking violations.
- Investigating abandoned vehicles.
- Dispersing unauthorized, non-permitted crowds.
- Gathering information.
- Repression of prevention of criminal activities.
- Support investigations.
- Apprehend or otherwise bring offenders to justice.
- Liaison.
- Community policing.
- Keep contact with isolated detachments.
- Intelligence gathering.
- Planning and operation plan.

Role of Officers on Patrol

- Getting Information: Observing, receiving, and otherwise obtaining information from all relevant sources. · Resolving Conflicts and Negotiating with Others: Handling complaints, settling disputes, and resolving grievances and conflicts, or otherwise negotiating with others.
- Identifying Objects, Actions, and Events: Identifying information by categorizing, estimating, recognizing differences or similarities, and detecting changes in circumstances or events.
- Making Decisions and Solving Problems: Analyzing information and evaluating results to choose the best solution and solve problems.
- Communicating with Supervisors, Peers, or Subordinates: Providing information to supervisors, co-workers, and subordinates by telephone, in written form, e-mail, or in person.
- Communicating with Persons Outside Organization: Communicating with people outside the organization, representing the organization to customers, the public, government, and other external sources. This information can be exchanged in person, in writing, or by telephone or e-mail.
- Evaluating Information to Determine Compliance with Standards: Using relevant information and individual judgment to determine whether events or processes comply with laws, regulations, or standards.
- Documenting/Recording Information: Entering, transcribing, recording, storing, or maintaining information in written or electronic/magnetic form
- Monitor Processes, Materials, or Surroundings: Monitoring and reviewing information from materials, events, or the environment, to detect or assess problems.
- Performing General Physical Activities: Performing physical activities that require considerable use of your arms and legs and moving your whole body, such as climbing, lifting, balancing, walking, stooping, and handling of materials.
- Establishing and Maintaining Interpersonal Relationships: Developing constructive and cooperative working relationships with others, and maintaining them over time.

- Assisting and Caring for Others: Providing personal assistance, medical attention, emotional support, or other personal care to others such as coworkers, customers, or patients.
- Updating and Using Relevant Knowledge: Keeping up-to-date technically and applying new knowledge to your job.
- Analyzing Data or Information: Identifying the underlying principles, reasons, or facts of information by breaking down information or data into separate parts.
- Processing Information: Compiling, coding, categorizing, calculating, tabulating, auditing, or verifying information or data.
- Training and Teaching Others: Identifying the educational needs of others, developing formal educational or training programs or classes, and teaching or instructing others.
- Interpreting the Meaning of Information for Others: Translating or explaining what information means and how it can be used.
- Organizing, Planning, and Prioritizing Work: Developing specific goals and plans to prioritize, organize, and accomplish your work.
- Performing Administrative Activities: Performing day-to-day administrative tasks such as maintaining information files and processing paperwork.
- Thinking Creatively: Developing, designing, or creating new applications, ideas, relationships, systems, or products, including artistic contributions.

UNPACKING THE POLICE PATROL SHIFT

As a core pillar of the criminal justice system, the police have existed at the forefront of scholarly and public attention for decades. Given the implications of their work, such interest is well-justified. From a scholarly perspective, the police are highly visible representatives of the criminal justice system and related to both social and crime control. From a practical perspective, the police impact the lives of people and the safety of communities. Not all entities within the policing institution, however, are equally implicated in these matters. Most salient among these discussions are the patrol officers: the uniformed, public-facing, and frontline personnel responsible for conducting the voluminous, street-level work of police. Yet, despite this importance, the nuance of patrol work has arguably received less empirical attention than some related topics, such as the structure of police organisations and the effects of police on crime. Considering the diverse role of police, it is critical that research tackles the pressing questions of what patrol officers do, when, and for how long to then inform related conversations about their work.

To contribute to this aim, we draw upon computer-aided dispatch (CAD) data for a random sample of 60 patrol shifts to explore the practices of patrol officers working in a Canadian police agency. Our observations present a more mundane and nuanced depiction of policing than sometimes presented in public narratives. Handling calls for service, most of which are classified as low priority and not crime-related, comprises only a modest proportion of officers' time on patrol. Other activities include being available to handle calls for service, working from headquarters, engaging in meal breaks, and completing administrative and other operational tasks. Given the reliance of modern police on electronic data to map and assess their practices, our use of these data to observe patrol officers exhibits wide, international relevance. We discuss such relevance in light of its practical considerations and methodological implications.

The Role of the Patrol Officer

Patrol officers are the backbone of police. They comprise the largest proportion of all officers in many police agencies. As frontline responders, they are directly responsible for responding to calls for service, including emergencies and non-emergencies, and investigating crime. In less direct capacities, they are tasked with representing the institution through their uniformed presence, preventing crime, and engaging in the additional tasks of police, like managing fear, providing social service referrals, and confirming the welfare of people. The consequences of the work of patrol officers is significant.

Nearly all public-police interactions and crime investigations start at the patrol-level, and the activities and decisions of even the most junior patrol officer exhibit the potential to shape the trajectory of an entire event and the outcomes for all affected people. The ability for patrol officers to effectively balance their responsibilities, including for reactive and proactive policing, can also impact a whole sleuth of policing outcomes, from response times to crime rates to clearance rates.

Research has long argued that much police work does not regard crime, but rather social order and peacekeeping functions. Consistent with this argument, recent research that explored police calls for service from across the United States found that "traffic-related problems, everyday disputes, worries of suspicious behaviors, disorders, disturbances, and general requests for help and assurance" comprised the majority of calls for which officers are dispatched. If patrol officers are handling these calls, then it would suggest that their work is diverse as a function of these diverse requests. But patrol work is not only about handling calls for service.

Many crime control efforts are directly implicated in the work of patrol officers. For example, hot spot policing, of which has been the subject of enormous scholarly attention, most often involves patrol officers spending time patrolling high crime areas referred to as "hot spots." As one case in point, Koper (1995) argued that the optimal length for patrol stops is 11 to 15 min. Other kinds of proactive police work, including traffic-related enforcement, also typically falls upon the shoulders of patrol officers, who sometimes engage in traffic stops when not handling calls for service. A similar logic can be presented for proactive drug- and weapons-related enforcement as well, which frequently manifest in the form of officer-initiated stops.

However, the fact that patrol officers, whose work can be fluid and dynamic, are often tasked with engaging in these activities as well as handling calls for service implies that they must manage their time in a way that allows for competing demands to be addressed. This is especially the case when performance metrics for patrol officers include both reactive and proactive policing outputs. As generalists, patrol officers must not only exhibit some competency in most areas, but also must be available to complete many different tasks.

Measuring the Work of Patrol Officers

Assessing the activities of patrol officers is no easy feat. Although much patrol work is public, insofar that it is frequently conducted in public spaces and in the purview of members of the public, it is not necessarily accessible, at least from an empirical perspective. To fully understand the work of patrol officers, one must observe the work of such officers: not just at a single call for service, not just for a few hours, but for an extended period of time and at different times.

Researchers tackling patrol-related questions have largely employed two approaches. First, is the ethnographic or field study approach that has placed researchers in the seat of patrol cars. By physically riding alone with police, researchers are able to manually observe the work of patrol officers and its intricacies in tremendous detail. Second, is the secondary data approach that has situated researchers at the epicentre of police records. By post hoc assessing the activities of patrol officers via secondary data, researchers are able to assess patterns in public demands on police as well as the activities of officers. For example, researchers can assess the frequency of different call-types and their dispositions as well as the number of some proactive activities conducted by patrol officers.

Like all research methods, each of these approaches presents benefits and weaknesses. Whereas field research may provide a richer and more holistic assessment of the practical work of patrol officers, it can be time-intensive and costly, which can limit the number of shifts that can be reasonably observed. It can also present the risk of reactivity, whereby officers change their activity as a function of being monitored. Whereas secondary data analyses offer a greater ability to compile larger volumes of data over longer periods of time, at lesser costs, and without concerns about reactivity, secondary data generally do not offer a comparable depth of information about individual officers or their shifts. Because of data limitations, including privacy concerns if the data are publicly available, these typically quantitative examinations are frequently conducted in the abstract: researchers are often forced to study macro-level trends as opposed to more micro-level behaviours. For example, researchers may quantify the number of traffic stops conducted or types of calls for service attended during a day/week/month/year, but may not be able to disentangle how many stops were conducted and how many calls were attended by how many different individual officers and in the context of which specific shifts.

As part of the present research, we supplement existing literature by employing more of a hybrid approach to "electronically" ride-along with police for a random sample of 60 patrol shifts. Specifically, we pose the following questions: (1) How can CAD data be leveraged to measure the activities of patrol officers?; (2) What do CAD data suggest about the activities of patrol officers in terms of substance and time?; and (3) What are the challenges of using CAD data for research purposes and how might such challenges inform future researchers' use of these data? As we outline below, the data that we draw upon and the analyses that we conduct are rich in volume and nuance. We also focus on the shift as our unit of analysis. By testing these questions at this unit using these data, we are able to provide a comprehensive snapshot of patrol officer activity as well as highlight the methodological implications of using electronic records to study patrol work.

These contributions are especially important given the salience of current debates surrounding policing and how the work of patrol officers could, should, or ought to look in an era of reform.

In lieu of analysing shift logs for all officers for all possible patrol shifts, which would be neither practical nor necessary, we analyse a random sample of 60 patrol shifts associated with 28 different officers from 2019. The variation in the number of shifts per officer was the result of our below described sampling strategy and the finite number of officers assigned to the patrol section.

Standard patrol shifts at this police agency are 12 h long and subdivided by time of day. The regularly scheduled "day shift" commences at 7:00am and the regularly scheduled "night shift" commences at 7:00 pm. All patrol officers work a four shift rotation, whereby they complete two day shifts followed by two night shifts before receiving four rest days. As a function of this shift pattern, each patrol officer works across different times and days of the week each week. All officers patrol alone at this agency, with one officer per vehicle (unless training).

In order to ensure that we represented all shift times, days of the week, and months of the year in our sample, we employed a stratified random sampling strategy to select our shifts. First, we randomly sampled three weekday (i.e., Monday–Thursday) and two weekend (i.e., Friday–Sunday) dates within each month. Next, we randomly selected shift times for each identified date, ensuring that we retained at least one day shift and one night shift for both weekday and weekend dates within each month. Finally, we randomly sampled an officer for each identified shift whose electronic data we then compiled. Because our unit of analysis is the shift, we did not consider officer particulars as part of our sampling process. See Table 1 for a summary of our sample of shifts.

Table 1. Summary of patrol shifts in our sample (N = 60)

Variable	**# Shifts**	**# Officers**
Time of day		
Day	29	–
Night	31	–
Day of week		
Monday	11	–
Tuesday	7	–
Wednesday	7	–
Thursday	11	–
Friday	13	–
Saturday	7	–
Sunday	4	–
Month		
January	5	–
February	5	–

March	5	–
April	5	–
May	5	–
June	5	–
July	5	–
August	5	–
September	5	–
October	5	–
November	5	–
December	5	–
Shifts per officer		
1	–	12
2	–	7
3	–	4
4	–	3
5	–	2

Shift Logs and Status Codes

Each shift log began when the patrol officer signed into the CAD system and concluded when they signed out of the CAD system. While signed into the CAD system, all documented activities of the officer were electronically recorded in the form of two-digit status codes. These status codes are generated by officers via their in-car computers and/or dispatchers via their dispatch software. For example, an officer can use their in-car computer to mark themselves at their headquarters ("HQ"). An officer can also use their in-car computer to mark themselves as conducting a foot patrol ("FP") or roadblock ("RB"). Dispatchers, namely those working in the capacity of radio-operators, can also update status codes on behalf of officers. For example, dispatchers can mark officers as available ("IS"), engaged in a traffic or person stop ("TS" or "PS," respectively), or providing cover for another officer ("CU"), among others.

Given that status codes reflect the type of activity that a patrol officer is engaged in at any documented point in time (at least in a rudimentary form), we can use them as a measure of officer activity. Moreover, given that updates to officers' status codes are date- and time-stamped within the CAD system, analysing them and their textual remarks allows us to post hoc estimate the amount of time that officers spent on each activity. For example, if the shift log indicates that the officer conducted a person stop ("PS") at 1:05 pm and then initiated a meal break ("62") at 1:09 pm, we would estimate that the officer spent four minutes on the person stop. Similarly, if the shift log indicated that the officer initiated a roadblock ("RB") at 11:03 pm and then became available ("IS") at 11:43 pm, we would estimate that the officer spent 40 min at the roadblock.

In their raw form, patrol officers used a total of 23 different status codes during our sample of shifts. With that being said, many status codes are similar in substance and therefore we grouped them into broader categories that effectively captured their shared theme. For example, we grouped all status codes related to calls for service into the shared category of "calls" and all status codes related to administrative tasks into the shared category of "administration." This resulted in a final list of eight different status code categories, which we retained for our analyses (see Table 2).

Table 2. Status code categories and their descriptions

Status code category	Status code	Description
Available	IS	In-service
Unavailable	NA	Not available
Headquarters	HQ	Headquarters
	DT	Detachment
Administration	CT	Court
	MT	Meeting
	RW	Report writing
	SD	Special duty
	TN	Training
Calls	DP	Dispatched
	ER	Enroute
	OS	On-scene
	TR	Transporting
Stops	PS	Person stop
	TS	Traffic stop
Other operational	CU	Cover unit
	EF	Enforcement
	FP	Foot patrol

	IN	Investigation
	OV	Out of vehicle
	RB	Roadblock
Meal breaks	61	Coffee break
	62	Meal break

In addition to the date and time, status codes also provide information about the call-type of a call for service that a patrol officer has been assigned if their status code changes while electronically attached to a call. Exploring the types of calls for service that patrol officers respond is of much empirical interest, and, therefore, we use this information to estimate the prevalence and demands of different call-types. We recognise, however, that call-type classifications are not without their limitations. As argued by Simpson and Orosco (2021), calls for service data can exhibit at least some measurement error. Not only is the information initially provided by callers to dispatchers often ambiguous and nebulous, but the public's reasons for requesting police can be complex and dynamic, making the process of classifying events into specific call-types difficult. Further complicating such process is the fact that calls can change over their lifespan as new information is brought to the attention of police, which can lead to changes in classifications over time. This applies to service-oriented requests as well. As one case in point, Pearce and Simpson (2022) observed that requests for police to conduct wellness checks are not always initially classified as the expected "Check Well-Being" call-type (a similar finding was observed by Ratcliffe (2021) for public health calls more broadly). If calls are not accurately classified and/or updated in the CAD system, then relying upon such classifications to interpret the nature of calls could present challenges.

Observations from "Electronically" Riding Along with Police

In this first section of results, we describe the activities of patrol officers and their temporal patterns. Consistent with the police agency's mandate, the average duration of shifts in our sample (as recorded by the CAD system) was 11.5 h. The shortest shift in our sample had a duration of approximately four hours and the longest shift had a duration of roughly 15.5 h. Shorter shifts were often a function of officers' pre-scheduled leave, including for vacation and/or administrative functions, like the need to attend court in the morning immediately following a night shift. In contrast, longer shifts were typically the result of unanticipated needs, including handling high priority calls for service at the end of the shift. Rather than use raw minutes engaged in different activities as part of our analyses, which would not account for this variation in the active amount of time on duty, we thus use percentages to assess the amount of time that officers engaged in different activities: $(min_{activity} / min_{shift})*100$. See Figure 3 for a depiction of activities by shift.

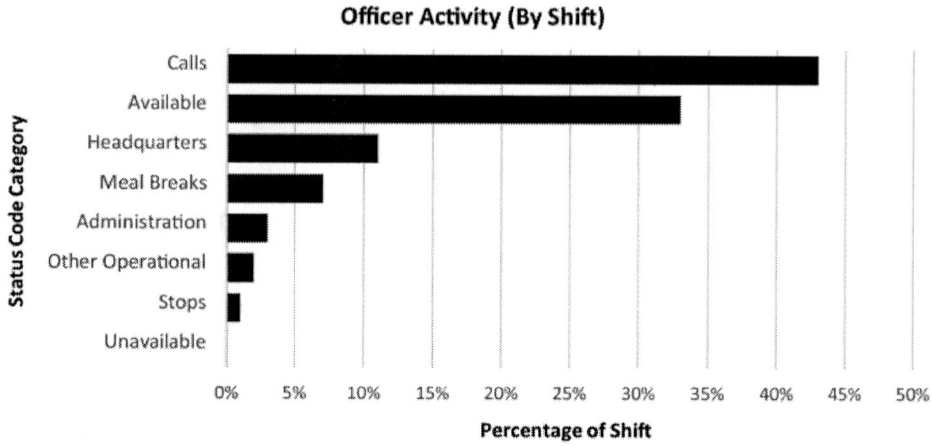

Figure 3. Percentage of patrol shift engaged in different activities (by shift).

Source: https://media.springernature.com/lw685/springer-static/image/art%3A10.1186%2Fs40163-022-00178-9/MediaObjects/40163_2022_178_Fig1_HTML.png

At an aggregate level, patrol officers handled 354 different calls for service of 55 different call-types during our sample of shifts. Of such calls, more regarded non-crime than crime-related call-types. In fact, the most frequently occurring call-types included: "Alarm" (11%), "Suspicious Person" (7%), and "Abandoned 911" (6%). Of the calls for service in our sample, 12% were assigned the highest priority level of 1, 26% were assigned the mid-level priority of 2, and the remaining 62% were assigned the lowest priority levels of 3 or 4. These findings indicate that much patrol work may be mundane, insofar that it does not involve the kinds of action and thrill traditionally depicted in policing media. Across our sample, officers were electronically attached to calls for service for a total of 292 h. The average duration of calls for service from initial dispatch to closure in the CAD system was 50 min.

At an individual level, patrol officers handled an average of six calls for service during each shift, with a minimum of one call and a maximum of 12 calls. However, as we discuss below, not all calls require equal investments from officers. For example, some calls are concluded faster than others because they do not result in criminal charges (e.g., for a bylaw complaint). Sometimes calls are also cancelled before officers arrive on-scene, if, for example, the problem in question resolves itself without officer attendance (e.g., for a hazardous complaint). And, other times, a suspect may not be located once an officer arrives on-scene (e.g., for a suspicious person complaint).

Consistent with such logic, the amount of time that officers spent electronically attached to calls for service during their shift ranged from as low as 15 min to as high as 579 min. Moreover, calls for service which required more time frequently involved crimes, typically because they required more formal investigation and associated report writing. Within the crime context, calls related to violent crimes averaged longer durations than those related to property crimes. Although we recognise that measurement error exists in call-type classifications, and therefore they must be interpreted with some caution, differences in durations indicate that different calls for service may require different levels of investment by officers. See Table 3 for a summary of call-type demands by prevalence and duration for the top 10 most frequently occurring call-types attended by officers during our sample of shifts.

Table 3 Call-type demands by prevalence and duration for the top 10 most frequently occurring call-types attended by officers during our sample of shifts

Call-type	% Total calls	Median duration of calls
Alarm	11	21 min
Suspicious person	7	24 min
Abandoned 911	6	20 min
Assist general public	5	35 min
Property	5	21 min
Disturbance	4	42 min
Theft	4	31 min
Traffic complaint	4	27 min
Check well-being	4	39 min
Suicidal person	3	68 min

As outlined above, the raw amount of time spent handling calls for service may not always be an ideal measure of the demand of such calls on patrol officers. Given that shift durations can vary, the percentage of time spent electronically attached to calls for service during the shift may be a more helpful measure. On average, patrol officers spent approximately 45% of their shift electronically attached to calls for service on day shifts and 41% on night shifts. Of such time, most was spent while the officer was marked as on-scene at calls, although we discuss the challenges of using different status codes as they pertain specifically to call handling below. These results imply two conclusions.

First, only a modest proportion of an officer's shift appears to be spent actively handling calls for service. This infers that officers spend their remaining time on other activities. Second, some variation may exist with respect to the amount of time spent handling calls for service as a function of shift. This underscores the importance of time in understanding patrol work: riding along with police during the day may produce a different image of patrol work than riding along with police during the night.

Other activities

The observation that patrol officers generally spent less than half of their shift handling calls for service begs questions about their other activities. As shown in Table 4, the average patrol shift is comprised of many different activities that are not specifically related to call handling.

Table 4. Percentage of patrol shift engaged in different activities (by shift time)

Status code category	Percentage of shift		
	Day shift %	Night shift %	Difference %
Calls	45	41	4
Available	27	38	11
Headquarters	13	8	5
Meal breaks	8	6	2
Administration	4	3	1
Other operational	2	2	0
Stops	1	2	1
Unavailable	0	0	0
	100	100	

During day shifts, patrol officers were recorded as being available, on average, for approximately 27% of their shift. Although we cannot confirm the specifics of what officers physically did during such available time (a point that we revisit later), we assume based on operational experience that much of this time was spent conducting routine preventive patrols. On average, officers conducted one traffic or person stop per day shift (with a range of zero to five stops), which comprised approximately 1% of their shift time. Officers also spent approximately 4% of their day shift engaged in administrative duties and 2% engaged in other operational activities, like conducting foot patrols, roadblocks, and/or directed enforcement. On average, officers spent approximately 13% of their day shift working at their headquarters and 8% engaged in meal breaks. Finally, officers conducted an average of 20 vehicle license plate queries via their in-car computers (a proxy for police proactivity), with a minimum of zero and a maximum of 122 queries.

During night shifts, patrol officers were recorded as being available, on average, for approximately 38% of their shift. Officers spent approximately 3% of their night shift engaged in administrative duties, 2% on other operational activities, and 8% working at their headquarters. Officers also spent approximately 6% of their night shift engaged in meal breaks. In terms of proactivity, officers conducted an average of one traffic or person stop per night shift, which comprised approximately 2% of their shift time. Officers also conducted an average of 13 vehicle license plates queries via their in-car computers during night shifts.

We observed few obvious differences between weekday and weekend shifts among our sample. For example, we found similar patterns in the number of activities during shifts, the number of calls for service handled during shifts, and the priority levels of such calls (although there were proportionally greater numbers of calls classified as the "Alarm" call-type on weekdays and the "Assist General Public" call-type on weekends). We also found similar patterns in how patrol officers spent their time during shifts, with the exception of time spent handling calls, which appeared to be greater on weekends. Finally, we found that officers conducted more license plate queries, on average, on weekends than weekdays.

Patterns of Activities Among Shifts

As described above, the average patrol shift is comprised of many different activities. Not only do patrol officers engage in different activities during their shifts, but they also frequently engage in such activities during different parts of the shift. For example, officers always began their shifts at their headquarters. In many instances, and when call volume allowed, officers then engaged in a meal break, often in the form of coffee with their colleagues. In roughly 40% of instances, an officer's meal break was immediately followed by their response to their first call for service of the shift. During peak hours, and following clearance of each call for service, officers normally became available for only a short period of time before being dispatched to another call.

However, during non-peak hours, and especially during night shifts, officers were frequently recorded as being available for prolonged periods of time before status code changes. During night shifts, officers also frequently engaged in a final meal break immediately before the conclusion of their shift, typically in the form of a visit to a local cafe.

At a more micro-level, changes in patrol officers' activities were generally consistent with the linear nature of police work. For example, officers were normally dispatched to a call for service before being marked as enroute to such call and then eventually on-scene at that call. Proactive activities, like conducting traffic or person stops, were generally followed by indication that the officer was available again for a call for service.

Officers also always terminated their shift with the unavailable status code. In this way, status codes can offer an interesting alternative to observing the activities of officers, albeit with limits, without needing to physically ride-along with them and manually record their activities.

Finally, different shifts across our sample exhibited different levels of activity. Whereas some shifts had a plethora of different activities, other shifts had very few activities. Indeed, the range of activities recorded across our sample of shifts was 11 to 59 activities, with an average of 29 activities. Day shifts generally exhibited more activities than night shifts. With that being said, this variation in volume could be the result of many different factors, most of which we are unable to empirically assess as part of our research. For example, sometimes the number of activities may be a function of the officer working the shift: some patrol officers are simply more active than others and/or more accurately document their activities. Other times, the number of activities may be the result of organisational priorities. Depending upon calendaring and workflow, a shift may be dedicated almost entirely to report writing if an officer must catch-up on their work queue and/or complete overdue assignments. In other circumstances, the number of activities may be a consequence of the policing environment during that specific shift. Police activity varies as a function of people, and sometimes people proactively seek out less from the police and/or fewer people are active in the city, which in turn can limit the number of activities that officers could reasonably engage in during the shift.

Complications of "Electronically" Riding along with Police

The shift logs produced by the CAD data provided much insight into the work of patrol officers. Such insight, however, was not without its complications. These electronic police records presented many challenges for both use and interpretation, which are relevant to past and future use of these data in research. In this second section of results, we thus describe these challenges and their relevance for the use of these data for assessing research questions of an applied nature.

First, although comprehensive, two-digit status codes alone in their raw form did not always present a nuanced picture of an officer's activity. In some instances, additional remarks that accompanied such codes were necessary to obtain clarity. For example, an officer may accompany the on-scene status code with textual remarks about making a phone call to the complainant, which would indicate that they were metaphorically on-scene rather than physically on-scene. Officers may also use the same status codes to refer to multiple different activities, including for activities with their own status codes. For example, officers may use the status code for enforcement to describe their roadblock, which technically has its own status code. Officers may also engage in various definable activities while marked at headquarters, including report writing for previously handled calls for service, which too have their own status codes.

Second, apparent changes in patrol officer activities were sometimes the result of technological implications of different status codes rather than practical changes in officer activity. For example, if while electronically attached to a traffic-related call for service, an officer conducted a stop on the subject vehicle, and the radio-operator used the traffic stop status code to indicate such stop, then the officer would be electronically detached from the associated call for service. The shift log for such officer would therefore appear much more truncated than it was in reality: it would appear as if the officer was handling a call for service only to be cleared from such call for a traffic stop to then be again dispatched to that call following that stop, when theoretically the traffic stop was a part of the call.

Third, and relatedly, officers may sometimes conduct activities without formally changing their status code to document such activities. For example, officers may attend a colleague's call for service without electronically attaching themselves to that call or even forget to denote themselves on-scene at their own call. This speaks to the broader issue of assessing the exact number of officers present at an event at any specific time, of which there is little ability to do using this kind of methodological approach. Relatedly, an officer may speak to a pedestrian about their concern while still recorded at the scene of an unrelated call for service. Lastly, officers may engage in activities even while listed as being available, like eating, if they believe that they could be reasonably cleared from the activity to handle a call for service if dispatched. From this perspective, it is particularly challenging to interpret the available status code because it could represent so many different practical things: "being available" is not necessarily synonymous with "doing nothing," but potentially doing something undocumented.

Less of a complication, but more of an interpretational side-effect, these data also provide a glimpse into the complicated work of radio-operators. Given that many status code updates are completed by radio-operators, examining the nature of status code changes provides insight into the activities of radio-operators and the diversity among their styles of dispatching. For example, under ideal circumstances, officers should have a dispatched, enroute, and on-scene status code change for each call for service that they handle. However, in many instances, this was not the case: typically because radio-operators initially dispatched officers using the status code for enroute, thereby providing no information about the temporal gap from when an officer was initially dispatched to the call and when they actually began travelling to that call. This illustrates why researchers should apply some caution when relying upon what has now sometimes become publicly available response time information for calls for service. In some cases, radio-operators also left officers electronically attached to their calls for service while such officers completed the associated reports, whereas in other cases, radio-operators electronically cleared officers from their calls in favour of a dedicated status code for report writing. These distinctions made it difficult to breakdown how much "on-scene time" was officers actively responding versus passively writing about the call for service in question.

Relatedly, radio-operators sometimes electronically cleared calls for service from the CAD system immediately after the officer departed the scene of such call, whereas other times they electronically "stacked" the call to the assigned officer so that they could be re-dispatched at a later point in their shift to complete the associated report. In these instances, the total time that the officer was electronically attached to the call varied. Moreover, in the case of the latter, the shift log made it appear that the officer was re-dispatched to the call for re-response at a later time, when in reality the second dispatch was simply so that the officer could write the associated report via their in-car computer. As noted in the preceding paragraph, this too complicated our ability to confidently assess the specific amount of time that officers spent report writing (and, hence, again our use of the term, "handling").

REFERENCES

1. Curtin KM, Hayslett-McCall K, Qiu F: Determining optimal police patrol areas with maximal covering and backup covering location models. Netw. Spat. Econ 2010, 10: 125–145. 10.1007/s11067-007-9035-6
2. Larson RC: Measuring the Response Patterns of New York City Police Patrol Cars. 1971. New York City Rand Institute R-673-NYC/HUD
3. Taylor PE, Huxley SJ: A break from tradition for the San Francisco Police: patrol officer scheduling using an optimization-based decision support system. Interfaces 1989, 19: 4–24. 10.1287/inte.19.1.4
4. Altman M: The computational complexity of automated redistricting: Is automation the answer? Rutgers Comput. Technol. Law J 1997, 23: 81–142.
5. Knoppers BA, Miller HF: Computer simulation of police dispatching and patrol functions. International Symposium on Criminal Justice Information and Statistics Systems Proceedings 1972.
6. Bond, C., and D. Gow. 1996. Policing the beat: The experience in Toowoomba, Queensland. Crime Prevention Studies 7: 153–173.
7. Greene, J.R., ed. 2007. Patrol, types and effectiveness of. In The encyclopedia of police science, vol. 1, 898–899. New York: Taylor & Francis Group.

8. Melenka, N.K.M. 2016. Exploring the long-term impact of a Foot Patrol policing Initiative in North Vancouver, British Columbia, Canada. Masters Dissertation: Simon Fraser University.
9. Mitchell PS: Optimal selection of police patrol beats. J. Crim. Law 1972, 63(4):577–584.
10. Simpson, R., & Orosco, C. (2021). Re-assessing measurement error in police calls for service: Classifications of events by dispatchers and officers. PLoS ONE, 16(12), e0260365.
11. Pearce, J., & Simpson, R. (2022). The role of police in conducting wellness checks: Insight from a study of police data. Police Practice and Research, 23(4), 400–413.
12. Ratcliffe, J. H. (2021). Policing and public health calls for service in Philadelphia. Crime Science, 10, 5.
13. Koper, C. S. (1995). Just enough police presence: Reducing crime and disorderly behavior by optimizing patrol time in crime hot spots. Justice Quarterly, 12(4), 649–672.

3 POLICE ORGANIZATION AND ADMINISTRATION

INTRODUCTION

Police organizations are structured to ensure effective law enforcement and public safety through a hierarchical system of ranks and specialized units. At the top of the hierarchy is the Chief of Police or Commissioner, who oversees the entire department and sets strategic priorities. Below the chief are various ranks such as Deputy Chiefs, Captains, Lieutenants, Sergeants, and Officers, each with specific responsibilities and areas of command. Specialized units within a police organization, such as homicide, narcotics, traffic, and community policing, focus on particular types of crime or community issues, providing expertise and targeted responses. This hierarchical structure ensures clear lines of authority and communication, allowing for efficient coordination during routine patrols, investigations, and emergency situations. The organization also includes support roles like dispatchers, administrative staff, and civilian employees who contribute to the overall functionality of the department. Effective police organizations are characterized by strong leadership, clear policies, continuous training, and a commitment to community engagement and ethical standards.

In the field of administration, police have an important role to play. In India, Police is the coercive arm of the State, which is entrusted to perform the basic duty of the State that is maintenance of law and order. Therefore, law and order administration has acquired significance at the Central, State, Range, District and Sub-District level in rural and urban areas. Rapid growth of population, industrialization, urbanization, and growing political consciousness led to law and order problems. Agrarian and tribal revolts, political caste and communal violence, labor and student unrest and terrorism are indications of law and order problems. In all societies, particularly in developing societies, these conflicts and tensions are inevitable and many manifest in different forms. Freedom and independence will not have meaning unless these basic issues are properly attended.

Police are one of the most ubiquitous organizations of the society. The policemen, therefore, happen to be the most visible representatives of the government. In an hour of need, danger, crisis and difficulty, when a citizen does not know, what to do and whom to approach, the police station and a policeman happen to be the most appropriate and approachable unit and person for him. The police are expected to be the most accessible, interactive and dynamic organization of any society.

Their roles, functions and duties in the society are natural to be varied and multifarious on the one hand; and complicated, knotty and complex on the other. Broadly speaking the twin roles, which the police are expected to play in a society are maintenance of law and maintenance of order. However, the ramifications of these two duties are numerous, which result in making a large inventory of duties, functions, powers, roles and responsibilities of the police organization.

THE ORGANIZATION OF POLICE

Police forces are usually organized and funded by some level of government. The level of government responsible for policing varies from place to place, and may be at the national, regional or local level. In some places there may be multiple police forces operating in the same area, with different ones having jurisdiction according to the type of crime or other circumstances. For example in the UK policing is primarily the responsibility of a regional police force; however specialist units exist at the national level. In the US policing there is typically a state police force, but a municipality may have its own police force. National police agencies also have jurisdiction over serious crimes or those with an interstate component.

Origin of Police Organization

The origin of police organizations dates back to ancient civilizations where maintaining public order and enforcing laws were essential functions of governance. In early societies, such as Mesopotamia and Egypt, rulers employed guards and officials to oversee compliance with laws and protect citizens. In ancient Rome, the Cohortes Urbanae served as a city police force responsible for maintaining order within the city.

The concept of a modern police organization began to take shape in the 18th and 19th centuries in response to the growing complexities of urban life and increasing crime rates. The Metropolitan Police Act of 1829, introduced by Sir Robert Peel, established the first modern and professional police force in London, known as the Metropolitan Police Service. This force was organized along military lines, emphasizing discipline, a hierarchical structure, and the use of uniforms to make officers easily identifiable. Peel's principles of policing, which emphasized crime prevention, public cooperation, and ethical conduct, became foundational to police organizations worldwide.

In the United States, early policing efforts were more localized, with constables and watchmen employed in towns and cities. However, as urban areas expanded, the need for a more organized and professional police force became evident. The establishment of the New York City Police Department in 1845 marked a significant development in American policing, adopting many of the principles and structures from the British model.

Throughout the 20th century, police organizations evolved further with the advent of new technologies, investigative techniques, and a greater focus on community policing and civil rights. Modern police organizations now operate within a complex framework of legal, social, and political considerations, continuing to adapt to new challenges and societal expectations.

Characteristics of Police Organizations

The Police Act of 1861 largely governs Indian police forces. The Police Act gives each State Government the power to establish its own police force. In addition to the Police Act, other legislation such as the CrPC also regulates the police system. Based on the Police Act of 1861, the Indian police have three basic characteristics:-

- The police force is organized, maintained and directed by several States of Indian Union;
- The Indian police system is horizontally stratified like military forces organized into different cadres; and
- The police in each State are divided vertically into armed and unarmed branches.

The Indian police organizational setup has virtually remained the same since past century. It is ironical that the Police Act of 1861 has hardly changed due to changes in an around them. Despite the new democratic, secular, socialistic, welfare and humanitarian values vouched for in the Constitution after independence in 1947, the Indian police, by and large follows the philosophy of Para-militarism. The constitution of India provides that the police is the state subject. It is therefore for the state to maintain peace and security within their territorial jurisdiction. There are, however, certain situations which authorize the Centre to intervene in the law and order problems of the State because the Centre is under a duty to protect the States from internal disturbances. Primarily it is the duty of the State govt. to maintain the civilian police force. Besides the state police force there are certain police force establishments at the Union level, such as the Border Security Force, the Railway Protection Force, the Central Reserved Police Forces, or the Central Industrial Security Force.

The police set up in India is essentially divided into following broad categories:

- The general police which looks after the general police work and assist in crime investigation, detection crime control and it's also involved in law and order maintenance and enforcement of law.
- The special arm force are paramilitary force which are there to assist the general police in maintaining the law and order and performing specialize duties like border securities large scale riots, election duties, VIP and Industrial security, disaster relief and general public order maintenance.

Apart from these to basic categorization there are specialized police services which take care of particular policing jobs like:

- Railway police
- Intelligence Police agencies
- Traffic police
- Women Police
- Border Security Police
- Specialized Investigative Police Agencies

- Armed Reserves
- Specialized Security Agencies

Police: A State Subject

The police is a State subject and its organization and working are governed by rules and regulations framed by the State Governments. These rules and regulations are outlined in the Police Manuals of the State Police, Circular Orders and Standing Orders of the Director General of Police. The State Government exercises superintendence over the Police Force in the state. The head of police in the state is the Director General of Police, who is responsible to the State Government for the administration and for all functioning of the State Police and for advising the government on police matters.

States are divided territorially into administrative units known as districts. An officer of the rank of Superintendent of Police (S.P.) heads the District Police Force. A group of districts form a Range, which is looked after by an officer of the rank of Deputy Inspector General of Police. Some states have Zones comprising two or more Ranges, under the charge of an officer of the rank of an Inspector General of Police (I.G.P.). Every District is divided into Sub-divisions and each Subdivision is under the charge of an officer of the rank of Additional Superintendent of Police (A.S.P.) or Deputy Superintendent of Police (D.S.P.).

Each Sub-division is again further divided into a number of Police Stations, the number depending on its area, population and volume of crime. In some of the states there are Police Circles consisting of a group of Police Stations. Circle headed usually by an Inspector of Police. A Subdivision may have one or more Police Circle. The Police Station is the basic unit of police administration in the district.

Under the Criminal Procedure Code, all crime has to be recorded at the Police Station and all preventive investigative and law and order work is done from there. A police station is divided into a number of Beats, which are assigned to constables for patrolling, surveillance, collection of intelligence and other police works. In larger Police Stations as in cities and metropolitan areas the officer in charge is an Inspector of Police or even a D.S.P., while in rural areas or smaller police stations the officer in charge is usually of the rank of Sub-Inspector of Police. The State Police is divided into the Armed and the Unarmed Police.

The Unarmed Police or the Civil Constabulary is uniformed but unarmed, although the personnel may carry a short baton. It is the police with which the public comes in contact daily. It investigates crimes, patrol streets, regulates traffic, looks for lost children and generally extends police assistance to the people whenever it is called upon to do so. The primary function civil police are to maintain law and order and deal with crime in all aspects like prevention, detection and investigation. Even prosecution was in the hands of the Police earlier in many places but now performed by a separate prosecution staff.

The Civil Police include mainly District Police forces, supervisory structures at the Range, Zone and State Police Headquarters and specialized branches to deal with crime, intelligence and training problems. The District Police force also has armed reserves, which are used mainly to meet the requirement of armed guards and escorts. They are occasionally also deployed to meet any emergency situation, before the state armed police arrive to handle it. The armed reserves are treated as part of the district civil police.

The Armed Police is normally organized into battalions more or less similar to the infantry. There may be one or more battalions in the State. They are quartered at various places in the cantonments established at various places in the state and is, thus, concentrated in a few points. It does not have daily contact with the public. It does not respond to calls of assistance from individuals but orders from superior officers, which are issued when a situation involving public interest has arisen. It usually acts as a group and its personnel hardly exercise any individual discretion.

POLICE ADMINISTRATION

The nature of police work includes police crime control, order maintenance, social service roles and also Police discretion. The role of police inside the station is leadership, management and discharging the duties whereas outside the police need to maintain the political, labor relations, media relations, community, and inter-agency. They are mostly executive in nature and executive. Police tasks are identified for the operations, administration, and auxiliary service subsystems.

Leadership in the police organization relay on the functions, sources of influence, and leadership styles and leadership theories associated to it. Police patrol, call response, and investigatory strategies and operational and problem specific such as the hostage negotiation, domestic violence, riot control duty also falls under their duty. The organizational communication, police decision-making, and police information systems also play a vital role in police functioning.

The evolution and nature of police work are discussed, including police crime control, order maintenance, and social service roles. Police discretion also is considered. The internal (management and leadership) and external (political, labor relations, media relations, community, and interagency) roles of the police executive are described; executive styles are characterized; and executive qualifications (e.g., skills, knowledge, experience) are discussed. Police tasks are identified for the operations, administration, and auxiliary service subsystems. Aspects of group behavior and social systems are examined, and emergent system development and its consequences are delineated. Leadership in the police organization is discussed in terms of functions, sources, of influence, and leadership styles; and leadership theories are outlined.

Police patrol, call-response, and investigatory strategies are considered, and operational and problem-specific (e.g., hostage negotiation, domestic violence, riot control) tactics are discussed. Also examined are organizational communication, police decision making, data analysis, and police information systems. An overview of policies and procedures is provided. Individual, program, and organizational evaluation goals and methods are presented, together with descriptions of human development, structural design, and work process approaches to organizational improvements.

Police officers protect the lives and property of citizens. They maintain order, catch lawbreakers, and work to prevent crimes. In small towns they perform many duties. Larger cities have a more structured division of responsibility. Police officers may patrol the streets on foot or in squad cars; control traffic; or work as detectives investigating crimes. At the police station officers may be assigned to work in the crime laboratory or the records department. All officers file reports of incidents, and many testify at trials and hearings.

Police officers are supervised by senior officers. The chain of command is modelled after that of the armed services. In larger cities sergeants, lieutenants, and captains direct the work of squads or companies of officers. Police officers in large cities may work as patrol officers assigned to either traffic control or crime prevention, as detectives who investigate crimes, or as officers in the crime laboratory, generally report to police chiefs or commissioners. In small towns the chief of police may be the only ranking officer.

Role, Functions and Duties of the Police in General

The role and functions of the police in general are:

- To uphold and enforce the law impartially, and to protect life, liberty, property, human rights, and dignity of the members of the public;
- To promote and preserve public order;
- To protect internal security, to prevent and control terrorist activities, breaches of communal harmony, militant activities and other situations affecting Internal Security;
- To protect public properties including roads, railways, bridges, vital installations and establishments etc. against acts of vandalism, violence or any kind of attack;
- To prevent crimes, and reduce the opportunities for the commission of crimes through their own preventive action and measures as well as by aiding and cooperating with other relevant agencies in implementing due measures for prevention of crimes;
- To accurately register all complaints brought to them by a complainant or his representative, in person or received by post, e- mail or other means, and take prompt follow-up action thereon, after duly acknowledging the receipt of the complaint;
- To register and investigate all cognizable offences coming to their notice through such complaints or otherwise, duly supplying a copy of the First Information Report to the complainant, and where appropriate, to apprehend offenders, and extend requisite assistance in the prosecution of offenders;
- To create and maintain a feeling of security in the community, and as far as possible prevent conflicts and promote amity;
- To provide, as first responders, all possible help to people in situations arising out of natural or man-made disasters, and to provide active assistance to other agencies in relief and rehabilitation measures;
- To aid individual, who are in danger of physical harm to their person or property, and to provide necessary help and afford relief to people in distress situations;
- To facilitate orderly movement of people and vehicles, and to control and regulate traffic on roads and highways;
- To collect intelligence relating to matters affecting public peace, and all kind of crimes including social offences, communalism, extremism, terrorism and other matters relating to national security, and disseminate

the same to all concerned agencies, besides acting, as appropriate on it themselves.

- To take charge, as a police officer on duty, of all unclaimed property and take action for their safe custody and disposal in accordance with the procedure prescribed.
- To train, motivate and ensure welfare of police personnel

Requirements

Many police departments require that applicants be high school graduates; an increasing number expect some college education. Applicants usually must be at least twenty-one years of age and U.S. citizens. In many communities, applicants must meet minimum requirements for height, weight, eyesight, and hearing. Because most police departments fall under civil service regulations, applicants must pass written tests that measure their analytical skills. Rigorous physical examinations and background checks are also required. Senior officers screen applicants.

New recruits often participate in formal classroom training in police academies. After graduating they continue to train on the job with experienced officers for three to twelve months. In small communities there may be no formal training program. Officers are usually encouraged to continue their education by taking college courses in criminal justice. Those who want to be police officers must first take the civil service test. Many departments allow high school graduates and college students studying criminal justice to start out as cadets or trainees while still in their teens. If they meet all the requirements, cadets may be appointed to regular police work when they turn twenty-one. For promotion to higher rank, officers must take civil service tests. Good work records and special honors help officers get ahead. Police officers who have investigation abilities may advance to detective. Other positions include sergeant, lieutenant, captain, and inspector. The employment of police officers is expected to grow as fast the average for all jobs through 2014. Openings will depend on government funding and the number of experienced officers who retire or leave the profession. Competition for jobs will be stiff. The best opportunities will be found in urban areas. Police work can be dangerous and stressful. Officers often deal with violent criminals and may be injured or killed. They must make quick decisions while on duty, yet be tactful and patient with people who are in trouble or have been victims of terrible crimes and abuse. Police protection is provided twenty-four hours a day, so officers may work outdoors in all kinds of weather. Work shifts are usually rotated; however, officers are on call at all times for emergencies. Overtime may be required. Most police departments provide uniforms or uniform allowances. Many officers belong to labor unions.

The Nature of Police Work

The myth of police as crime-fighters has been conveyed to the American people through television dramas, comic strips, and newspaper articles. It conjures up in one's mind an image of a police officer doing a dangerous job that requires him or her to outshoot, outpunch, and outwit dangerous criminals. For most American police, there is little correspondence between this image and reality. In a major metropolitan area (where crime rates are the highest), half of the officers in the local department will not make a felony arrest during a given year. The total annual rate of weapon discharges per hundred police officers is in the range of two to six.

Major Functions of the Police Officials

Even though we refer to the police as law enforcement officers, the enforcement of criminal law (in other words, investigating crime and apprehending criminals) is only one of several functions that the police perform. The functions of the American police include providing basic social services, maintaining order, and controlling crime.

- In the area of social service, the police help people who need emergency assistance, whether it is giving first aid or finding lost children. Typically, over 50 per cent of the telephone calls to the police requesting assistance involve social service as compared with less than 20 per cent relating to crime.
- Among the order-maintenance activities are traffic control, crowd control, resolving domestic disputes, and moving prostitutes from the streets. The focus of order maintenance is on handling situations to preserve the peace rather than enforcing the letter of the law. The appropriate order-maintenance solution may be making an arrest but it often consists of some less formal action.
- In the area of crime control, the police engage in a range of activities, such as patrol and criminal investigation.

Major Responsibilities

- To identify criminal offenders and criminal activity and, when appropriate, to apprehend offenders and participate in later court proceedings.
- To reduce the opportunities for the commission of some crimes through preventive patrol and other measures.
- To aid individuals who are in danger of physical harm.
- To protect constitutional guarantees.
- To facilitate the movement of people and vehicles.
- To assist those who cannot care for themselves.
- To resolve conflict.
- To identify problems that is potentially serious law enforcement or government problems. ω To create and maintain a feeling of security in the community.
- To promote and preserve civil order.
- To provide other services on an emergency basis.

Factors Influencing Discretionary Decisions

The seriousness of the crime and the strength of the evidence affect an officer's decision to arrest. The more serious the crime and the stronger the evidence, the more likely an officer is to make an arrest. A suspect's demeanor also makes a difference. The more disrespectful and the less different a suspect act toward an officer, the more likely that officer is to use force.

Scope of Police Administration

The police administration in its present form was established long back. Through the decades, the system has not undergone any significant change.

The Indian police Act of 1861 continues to be the basis for police system in India. There are several Suggestions for its replacement by new legislation. The Police Administration is a top-heavy administration and there is a change of political leadership has created a serious credibility gap in this police leadership. Constitutionally, law and order is a State subject. But over the years the central police organizations like Central Reserve Police Force and Border Security Force have increased. Deployment of the police force in the States on occasions without informing them has created tensions in Centre-State relations. So, the study of Police Administration can lead to the address these gaps. In recent years terrorism and violence in different parts of the country are on the increase. The community expects the police to take steps to control the problem. .Police Commissions at the National and State levels have made several suggestions to make the police efficient, responsive and responsible. The reforms are required not only in organization, personnel, procedures but also in the attitudes of the people and the police officials. Whatever reforms were implemented they were done half-heartedly without understanding the socio-political milieu within which the police has to operate. Because of the adhoc and piecemeal nature of the reforms they did not have the intended effect. Reform should be continuous because no adhoc approach will give the intended results. By addressing all these factors, the study in police administration has wide scope in the present scenario.

POWERS AND FUNCTIONS OF POLICE

The police as law of enforcement officer are required to serve the community by protecting all persons against illegal acts which is consistent with high degree of responsibility required as per the law. The police functions are multi furious and multi dimensional. The powers given by the law to the police makes the police one of the most important elements in the initiations of criminal justice process and at the same time makes the police completely responsible as an agency working towards social cohesion and public peace. The functions of police in the modern democratic society have multiplied and the role expectation has also increased. Major functions of police can be listed through the following points:

- Promote and preserve public order;
- Investigate crimes and where appropriate, to apprehend the offenders and participate in subsequent legal proceedings connected therewith;
- Identify problems and situations that are likely to result in commission of crimes;
- Reduce the opportunities for the commission of crimes through preventive patrols and other appropriate police measures;
- Aid and cooperate with other relevant agencies in implementing appropriate measures for prevention of crimes;
- Aid individuals who are in danger of physical harm;
- Create and maintain a feeling of security in the community;
- Facilitate orderly movement of people and vehicles;
- Counsel and resolve conflicts and promote amity;
- Provide other appropriate services and afford relief to people in distress situations;
- Collect intelligence relating to matters affecting public peace and crimes

in general including social and economic offences, national integrity and security; and

- Perform such other duties as may be enjoined on them by law for the time being in force.
- To protect constitutional guarantees such as right of free speech and assembly.
- To assist those who can't care for themselves; the intoxicated, the addicted, the mentally ill, the physically disabled, the old and the young.
- To create and maintain a feeling of security in the community.
- Regulation and control of private morals and public decencies of life.

The primary functions of police is the prevention and detection of crime and to maintain public peace and order in the society. The rights and duties of the police to inflict punishment are limited. Since there job is to pick up criminals from the society they play vital role in bringing the offenders to the justice.

Patrolling and Surveillance

Patrolling is the visible police function for the purpose of general watch and word. Patrol and surveillance provide the most direct and effective means of preventing crime. A police beat is a given route or area to be covered by constable on patrol. In a town it usually means streets and building in a given locality while in a rural area it may comprise one or more villages or a stretch of road. Patrolling police officer keep a general watch over a particular beat in order to prevent crime. In insurgency area armed police units do routine patrolling either on foot or on vehicles depending upon the locality. Police patrolling is also an exercise in area dominance by the law enforcement agencies especially where there are acute law and order insurgency related problems. Surveillance is another important function of police which is based on anti-crime branch. Each police station generally has list of criminals and anti-social elements which required special watch. Surveillance activity involves various method of keeping such watch.

Preventive functions and Arrest

One of the important task assigned to the police is to make arrest of law breakers and suspected criminals and to take them into custody in order to prevent crime. The preventive powers of the police are contain in the code of criminal procedure which also defines legal elements of such power. The police may arrest a person on a warrant issued by a competent court. An arrest made on a warrant is in fact a case of arrest made by the Court through police. But at times, the circumstances may require the police to make an arrest without warrant. The police may arrest without warrant when they apprehend the commission of a crime or when they have reason to believe that crime has been committed by the suspected person.

The police can arrest and take into custody vagabonds, habitual rogues, persons with doubtful antecedents, of those who are conditionally released from jail or person for the sake of maintenance of law and order within their territorial jurisdiction.

Investigation by the Police

The purpose of the investigation is to collect evidence and to apprehend the culprit. The police can question any person suppose to be acquainted to be the facts and circumstances of the case. An investigation is defined as all the proceedings under the CrPC for the collection of the evidence, conducted by a police officer or any person authorized by a magistrate. The principal agency with the power under law to carry out investigation is the police force. An investigation is initiated after an registration of an FIR regarding a cognizable offence. The police may start investigation in the cognizable without the prior permission of the magistrate while in case of non-cognizable offence the permission of magistrate is needed. Thus, during the course of investigation, the police is empowered to make search, order production of documents, seize any suspicious property, call witnesses, require them to attend court and arrest persons suspected or having committed crime without warrant. After the investigation, a police report is prepared upon which proceedings are instituted before a Magistrate. The law requires that every investigation should be completed without undue delay. Nevertheless, delays do occur in the process of investigation for one reason or the other. The conclusion of a police investigation should be contained in a final report. At the completion of an investigation, the police should submit this report with all the details of the case to a magistrate. If the accused is to be prosecuted, this report is called a charge sheet or challan. If there is a charge sheet, it should list relevant charges along with the laws which have been contravened. After looking at the charge sheet, the magistrate decides to either (a) proceed with the case, (b) order further investigation of the case, or (c) dismiss the charges against the accused.

Essential Constituents of Investigation

During the course of investigation done by a police officer, following steps are generally taken which constitute a typical investigation

- The police authorities will proceed to the scene of an incident.
- They will ascertain the facts and circumstances of the case.
- They will attempt to discover and arrest the suspect(s).
- They will collect evidence relating to the incident through
  - examination of various people (including the accused), and
  - search of places and seizure of things considered necessary for the investigation and for production at trial.
- They will form an opinion about whether the material collected forms the basis of a case to placed before a magistrate for trial and, if so, file a charge sheet under S.173 CrPC.

The police powers and functions related to investigation involve search, seizure, questioning, interrogation, arrest, etc. The powers and functions involve however are not unlimited, these powers are well defined by law and procedure. The individual liberty and freedoms guaranteed under the constitutions limit the powers and functions of the police officers during the discharge of their duties.

Public Peace and Law and Order Management

The maintenance of public peace and law and order within a police jurisdiction is given high priority in police function. Thus criminal procedure court gives power to the police to use restrain civil force for dispersal of unlawful assembly the police may arrest people. In order to prevent public nuisance, writing or unlawful conduct. The police may initiate a process of taking security for keeping the peace. Police may also initiate process for removal of nuisance and for active maintenance of public order and social tranquility.

ROLE, FUNCTIONS AND DUTIES OF THE POLICE IN GENERAL

Functions of the police are necessary as that governs the society as a whole in maintaining the law and order. The duties include crime prevention, conflict resolution, and crime detection work. The functionaries of police and their working at the ranges, zones and districts, etc., help one to know the police force establishment. Commissioner ate system is practiced at the metropolitan cities in order to make the police functions effective at a greater level.

Police are one of the most ubiquitous organizations of the society. The policemen, therefore, happen to be the most visible representatives of the government. In an hour of need, danger, crisis and difficulty, when a citizen does not know, what to do and whom to approach, the police station and a policeman happen to be the most appropriate and approachable unit and person for him. The police are expected to be the most accessible, interactive and dynamic organization of any society. Their roles, functions and duties in the society are natural to be varied and multifarious on the one hand; and complicated, knotty and complex on the other. Broadly speaking the twin roles, which the police are expected to play in a society are maintenance of law and maintenance of order. However, the ramifications of these two duties are numerous, which result in making a large inventory of duties, functions, powers, roles and responsibilities of the police organization.

The role and functions of the police in general are:

- To uphold and enforce the law impartially, and to protect life, liberty, property, human rights, and dignity of the members of the public;
- To promote and preserve public order;
- To protect internal security, to prevent and control terrorist activities, breaches of communal harmony, militant activities and other situations affecting Internal Security;
- To protect public properties including roads, railways, bridges, vital installations and establishments etc. against acts of vandalism, violence or any kind of attack;
- To prevent crimes, and reduce the opportunities for the commission of crimes through their own preventive action and measures as well as by aiding and cooperating with other
- relevant agencies in implementing due measures for prevention of crimes;
- To accurately register all complaints brought to them by a complainant or his representative, in person or received by post, e-mail or other means, and take prompt follow-up action thereon, after duly acknowledging the receipt of the complaint;
- To register and investigate all cognizable offences coming to their notice through such complaints or otherwise, duly supplying a copy of the First Information Report to the complainant, and where appropriate, to apprehend offenders, and extend requisite assistance in the prosecution of offenders;
- To create and maintain a feeling of security in the community, and as far as possible prevent conflicts and promote amity;

- To provide, as first responders, all possible help to people in situations arising out of natural or man-made disasters, and to provide active assistance to other agencies in relief and rehabilitation measures;
- To aid individual, who are in danger of physical harm to their person or property, and to provide necessary help and afford relief to people in distress situations;
- To facilitate orderly movement of people and vehicles, and to control and regulate traffic on roads and highways;
- To collect intelligence relating to matters affecting public peace, and all kind of crimes including social offences, communalism, extremism, terrorism and other matters relating to national security, and disseminate the same to all concerned agencies, besides acting, as appropriate on it themselves.
- To take charge, as a police officer on duty, of all unclaimed property and take action for their safe custody and disposal in accordance with the procedure prescribed.
- To train, motivate and ensure welfare of police personnel

Social Responsibilities of the Police

Every police officer shall:

- Behave with the members of the public with due courtesy and decorum, particularly so in dealing with senior citizens, women, and children; Sec (57), Model Police Act 2006
- Guide and assist members of the public, particularly senior citizen, women, children, the poor and indigent and the physically or mentally challenged individuals, who are found in helpless condition on the streets or other public places or otherwise need help and protection;
- Provide all requisite assistance to victims of crime and of road accidents, and in particular ensure that they are given prompt medical aid, irrespective of medico-legal formalities, and facilities their compensation and other legal claims;
- Ensure that in all situations, especially during conflict between communities, classes, castes and political groups, the conduct of the police is always governed by the principles of impartiality and human rights norms, with special attention to protection of weaker sections including minorities;
- Prevent harassment of women and children in public places and public transport, including stalking, making objectionable gestures, signs, remarks or harassment caused in any way;
- Render all requisite assistance to the members of the public, particularly women, children, and the poor and indigent persons, against criminal exploitation by any person or organized group; and
- Arrange for legally permissible sustenance and shelter to every person in custody and making known to all such persons provisions of legal aid schemes available from the Government and also inform the authorities concerned in this regard.
- Preserve, promote and protect human rights and interests of weaker sections, backward classes, poor, weak and the downtrodden.

Crime Prevention and Preservation of Peace and Security

This would include:

- Gast and patrolling, including nakabandi, performing picket and ambush jobs, checking vehicles and frisking passengers
- Surveillance and checking of bad characters
- Preventive arrests
- Collection and transmission of criminal intelligence

Police Personnel

Superintendence over the police force in the state is exercised by the State Government. The head of the police force in the state is the Director General of Police who is responsible to the state government for the administration of the police force in the state and for advising the government on police matters.

States are divided territorially into administrative units known as districts. An officer of the rank of Superintendent of Police heads the district police force. A group of districts form a range, which is looked after by an officer of the rank of Deputy Inspector General of Police. Some states have zones comprising of two or more ranges, under the charge of an officer of the rank of an Inspector General of Police.

Every district is divided into sub-divisions. A sub-division is under the charge of an officer of the rank of ASP/Dy.SP. Every sub-division is divided into a number of police stations, depending on its area, population and volume of crime. Between the police station and the subdivision, there are police circles in some states and each circle is headed by an Inspector of Police. The police station is the basic unit of police administrative in a district. Under the Criminal Procedure Code, all crime has to be recorded at the police station and all preventive, investigative and law and order work is done from there. A police station is divided into a number of seats, which are assigned to constables for patrolling, surveillance, collection of intelligence, etc. The officer in charge of a police station is an Inspector of Police, particularly in cities and metropolitan areas. Even in other places, the bigger police stations, in terms of area, population, crime or law and order problems, are placed under the charge of an Inspector of Police. In rural areas or smaller police stations, the officer in charge is usually a Sub-Inspector of Police.

Patrol

A highway patrol is either a police unit created primarily for the purpose of overseeing and enforcing traffic safety compliance on roads and highways, or a detail within an existing local or regional police agency that is primarily concerned with such duties. They are also referred to in many countries as traffic police, although in other countries this term is more commonly used to refer to foot officers on point duty who control traffic at junctions.

Patrol Objective

The focus of a patrol is oriented by on the results which are expected from the headquarters that initiated it. There can be many reasons or aims of a patrol. Here we will look at some of the main reasons. Gathering information is probably the key point to both domestic and peacekeeping missions. By patrolling an area, a unit can ascertain the mood of the population, their acceptance of the presence of UN peacekeepers (or not), inhabitants' willingness to engage with the unit and willingness to share useful information. The level of trust that the unit manages to create with the population will significantly impact how much information can be gathered. Including female officers in such patrols is a good way to reach out women and children in the local population which might be reluctant to discuss with "men in uniforms". This is likely to contribute to an increased level of trust between the unit and the population. 'Information' has to be understood in the broadest meaning of the word. This could be anything from getting information about some citizen in need of help to operational intelligence related to politically motivated disturbances. It is essential to pre-define what is expected to be gathered on any given patrol. However, at the same time, it is critical for the officers to remain open minded, benevolent and curious.

In both domestic and peacekeeping missions patrols are used for crime prevention. It is widely believed that if the presence of the police is highly visible, criminals and violent mobs will remain off the streets for fear of detection or arrest. Extensive studies have shown however, that this is best realized through 'proactive patrolling'. The term 'proactive' in this context, means seizing the initiative and denying criminals the chance to assemble and strike. This is best done through interaction with the locals wherever and whenever an opportunity to talk with them arises. When planning patrols that are conducted with deterrence of criminal activity as their chief aim, ensure that times and routes of the patrol are varied and unpredictable.

Patrolling is also associated to one of the key missions for FPUs, meaning the protection of UN staff and facilities. This will imply, among other things, beyond the pure deterrence and visibility, cooperation with the UN security Service. For instance, having an evacuation plan taking into consideration where UN staff are accommodated, work and gather, is necessary.

In a non-executive mandate patrols can be used as a liaison exercise with the local police and can be conducted in support of them.

Particularly in a peacekeeping mission, patrols can be used to determine the position, volume, armament of local military facilities, police or rebel factions. This may be particularly useful intelligence, should violence erupt or in conjunction with agreements made under the peace process by the various factions.

In domestic policing, patrolling is a key part of Community Policing because without the police getting into the community and interacting with them, they may be seen as distant, aloof and disinterested. This is just as important in Peacekeeping missions where UN police must be seen to interact with the local population and take interest in their lives while maintaining their neutrality and impartiality.

In areas where the peacekeepers are thinly spread over a wide area, it is important to use patrols to keep contact with isolated detachments. Often this can be a lifeline providing resupply and occasionally reinforcements.

Finally patrols can be used to support an investigation, where a crime has been committed. Patrols can be used to interact with the local population to see if further information can be obtained in relation to the investigation or may be asked by local police to assist with an area search for evidence. In the same perspective, it may happen that the FPU during a patrol happen to be the first responders. In such a case, when the intervention is actually completed, FPU staff may have to put a cordon in place to contribute to the freezing of the crime scene. This requires a level of technical knowledge which will be described in a further lesson.

Functions of Patrol Police

- *Accident investigation*: Gathering evidence to determine the cause of a roadway accident.
- *Commercial vehicle enforcement*: Enforcing highway laws related to commercial transport, including weight limits and hazardous materials rules.
- *Education*: Providing public information, handouts, and displays to encourage safe driving and usage of the roads.
- *Emergency response*: Securing the scene of a traffic accident by using cones and flares as well as providing first aid to the injured.
- *Law enforcement*: Assisting local police in rural areas, and keeping an eye out for non-traffic violations.
- *Maintenance:* Observing and reporting damage to the roadways, and conducting hasty road surveys after disasters or the passage of inclement weather.
- *Traffic enforcement*: Enforcing laws and regulations intended to improve traffic safety, such as speed limits.

Phase of Patrol

Police patrols typically go through several phases, each with distinct objectives and activities. These phases ensure comprehensive coverage, effective response, and continuous adaptation to the needs of the community and the evolving nature of law enforcement. Here are phases of patrol:

Preparation Phase

- *Briefing/Shift Roll Call*: Officers receive information about recent incidents, wanted individuals, special assignments, and areas requiring extra attention. They also review any changes in policies or procedures.
- *Equipment Check*: Officers inspect and prepare their equipment, including vehicles, radios, weapons, and other necessary tools. Ensuring that all equipment is in working order is crucial for officer safety and effectiveness.
- *Route Planning*: Depending on the patrol strategy, officers may plan their routes and identify key areas to focus on based on crime data, community feedback, and departmental priorities.

Proactive Patrol Phase

- *Visible Presence*: Officers maintain a visible presence to deter crime and reassure the public. This can involve patrolling in vehicles, on foot, by bicycle, or other methods suitable for the area.
- *Community Interaction*: Engaging with community members, listening to their concerns, and building rapport. This phase is essential for gathering intelligence and fostering trust between the police and the community.
- *Surveillance and Monitoring*: Observing high-crime areas, potential hotspots, and locations with reported suspicious activity. Officers look for signs of criminal behavior and intervene when necessary.

Response Phase

- *Incident Response*: Responding to calls for service, which can range from minor disturbances to serious crimes in progress. Officers must assess situations quickly and take appropriate action, such as securing the scene, providing first aid, or apprehending suspects.
- *Investigation*: Conducting preliminary investigations at the scene, gathering evidence, interviewing witnesses, and documenting findings. This phase is critical for building cases and ensuring that incidents are properly recorded.
- *Traffic Control and Enforcement*: Addressing traffic violations, conducting stops, and managing accident scenes. Ensuring the safety and smooth flow of traffic is a key component of patrol duties.

Administrative Phase

- *Report Writing*: Completing detailed reports on incidents, arrests, and other activities. Accurate documentation is vital for legal proceedings and departmental records.
- *Communication*: Updating dispatch and supervisors on status, outcomes of incidents, and any ongoing concerns. Effective communication ensures that all relevant parties are informed and coordinated.
- *Follow-Up*: Depending on the nature of the incidents handled, officers may need to conduct follow-up investigations, contact victims or witnesses, and collaborate with detectives or other units.

Evaluation Phase

- *Debriefing*: At the end of the shift, officers may participate in debriefings to review the day's activities, share insights, and discuss any issues encountered. This phase helps in refining tactics and improving future patrol operations.
- *Feedback and Reflection*: Officers reflect on their performance, receive feedback from supervisors, and identify areas for improvement. Continuous learning and adaptation are crucial for effective policing.

Beat Police

Beat police typically patrol on foot or bicycle which provides more interaction between police and community members. Before the advent of personal radio communications, beats were organized in towns and cities to cover specific areas, usually shown on a map in the police station and given some sort of name or number. Officers reporting on duty would be allocated a beat by their sergeant and sometimes given a card indicating that the officer should be at a particular point at set times, usually half an hour, or forty-five minutes apart. The points would usually be telephone kiosks, police pillars or boxes, or perhaps public houses where it would be possible to phone the officer should he be needed to respond to an incident. The officer would remain at the point for five minutes and then patrol the area, gradually making his way to the next point. Beats in town centers would be relatively small areas but in the suburbs much larger. A shortfall in manpower would mean that one or more beats would be left unpatrolled at the discretion of the duty sergeant. Sometime during an officer's shift, he could expect a supervisory officer to meet him at one of the points. This ensured the beat patrol was being correctly carried out and was an opportunity to discuss problems. The supervisory officer would sign the officer or constable's pocket book, ensuring that it was up to date. It was expected that a constable would learn all about each beat he covered, even though they would not necessarily be the same one each shift. A new constable would usually be shown around the beats by an experienced constable who would point out important considerations. These would include vulnerable premises such as banks and post offices, perhaps showing the officer where a peephole would give a view of a safe. A constable was expected to learn where known criminals resided or resorted and which public houses might be the source of problems or keeping late hours.

The same principles extended to beats patrolled on bicycles or in motor vehicles. Even with radio communication, the patrol vehicle would be expected to visit and remain at certain points at particular times, enabling supervisors to meet up with the patrolling officer or to give a visible police presence at times when this was deemed particularly needed. Missing a point without good reason was regarded very seriously and was often the cause of disciplinary action against an officer. Beat officers were commonly used in the 1800s.

Outpost

The state government may declare one or more Police outposts to be attached to a mother Police Station. An officer in charge of outpost will be in the rank of Head Constable or Asst. Sub-Inspector of Police. Presently, the following (ten) outposts function in this territory. The duty of the officer-in-charge of the outpost, either Head Constable or Asst. Sub-Inspector is to supervise the work of his men, maintain the prescribed records and submit the daily general diary to the mother Police Station.

The HC or ASI, in charge of the outpost is not an officer in charge of a Police Station and is not empowered to record a "First Information", within the meaning of section 154 Cr.P.C., of a cognizable offence or to enter its substance in the First Information Report form. If information of a cognizable offence, therefore is lodged with the officer in charge of the outpost, he shall record the facts in his outpost, 'general diary' and report them as expeditiously as the circumstances of the case may require, to the Station House Officer (mother station).

The information referred to in section 154 Cr.P.C., the substance of which should be entered in the first information report form in such a case in the information first received by the Station House Officer which in many cases be the outpost Head Constable report. Head Constables or ASIs in charge of out posts have been empowered to hold investigation under section 174 (1) Criminal Procedure Code, 41 Cr.P.C. and simple investigation cases that occurred within the limits of the OPs. But, this will, however, not absolve the Station House Officer from any responsibility.

When the Sub-Inspector cannot arrive in time, the scene of crime in the OP limit should be preserved and protected by the HC / ASI who would also make certain ascertainment about the occurrence till the arrival of the Station House Officer.

REFERENCES

1. Bureau of Police Research & Development, Research Studies Compendium 1970-2006. BPR&D New Delhi 2006.
2. Mathur.K.M ,Police in India Problems and Prospects, Gyan Publishing House New Delhi 1991.
3. Paranjape.N.V, Criminology and Penology 13th edition, Central Law Publishing House Allahbad 2008.
4. Raghvan RK, Policing a Democracy, A Compartaive Study of India & USA, Manohar Publishing House New Delhi 1999.
5. Reiner Robert, The Politics of Police, Oxford University Press, Oxford 2000.
6. Sharma.P.D, Police and Criminal Justice Administration in India, Uppal Publishing House, New Delhi 1985.
7. Zender.Lucia, Criminal Justice, Clarendon Law Series, Oxford University Press, Oxford 2004.
8. Roy, Jay tilak Guha (ed.), (1999), Policing in Twenty First Century, Indian Institute of Public Administration, New Delhi.
9. Kamal Mishra, (2009), Police Administration in India, Mittal Publications.
10. M.B.Chande, (1997), The Police in India, Atlantic Publishers and Dist.
11. Bayley, D. H. (1994). Police for the Future. Oxford University Press.
12. Bittner, E. (1970). The Functions of the Police in Modern Society. National Institute of Mental Health, Center for Studies of Crime and Delinquency.
13. Cordner, G. (2016). Police Administration (9th ed.). Routledge.
14. Dempsey, J. S., & Forst, L. S. (2015). An Introduction to Policing (8th ed.). Cengage Learning.
15. Gaines, L. K., & Worrall, J. L. (2011). Police Administration (3rd ed.). Cengage Learning.
16. Goldstein, H. (1977). Policing a Free Society. Ballinger Publishing Company.
17. Greene, J. R. (2007). The Encyclopedia of Police Science (3rd ed.). Routledge.
18. Kelling, G. L., & Moore, M. H. (1988). The Evolving Strategy of Policing. U.S. Department of Justice, Office of Justice Programs, National Institute of Justice.
19. Kappeler, V. E., Sluder, R. D., & Alpert, G. P. (1998). Forces of Deviance: Understanding the Dark Side of Policing (2nd ed.). Waveland Press.
20. Langworthy, R. H. (Ed.). (1999). Measuring What Matters: Proceedings from the Policing Research Institute Meetings. U.S. Department of Justice, Office of Justice Programs, National Institute of Justice.
21. Maguire, E. R., & King, W. R. (2013). The Changing Nature of Crime and Criminal Investigations. In M. L. Dantzker & R. D. Hunter (Eds.), Research Methods for Criminology and Criminal Justice (3rd ed.). Jones & Bartlett Learning.
22. Peak, K. J. (2012). Policing America: Challenges and Best Practices (7th ed.). Pearson.
23. Reiss, A. J. (1971). The Police and the Public. Yale University Press.
24. Skogan, W. G. (2006). Police and Community in Chicago: A Tale of Three Cities. Oxford University Press.
25. Wilson, J. Q., & Kelling, G. L. (1982). Broken Windows: The Police and Neighborhood Safety. The Atlantic Monthly.

4 POLICE TECHNOLOGY AND TACTICS

INTRODUCTION

Police technology and tactics encompass a wide range of tools, methods, and strategies used by law enforcement agencies to prevent crime, ensure public safety, and maintain order. Modern police technology includes sophisticated equipment such as body-worn cameras, drones, automated license plate readers, and advanced communication systems. Body-worn cameras, for instance, are employed to increase transparency and accountability, capturing interactions between officers and the public. Drones are used for surveillance and search operations, providing aerial views that are invaluable during critical incidents or natural disasters. Automated license plate readers aid in identifying stolen vehicles and tracking suspects, enhancing the efficiency of patrol operations. Communication technology, including encrypted radios and mobile data terminals, ensures seamless and secure information exchange among officers and between agencies.

In addition to hardware, software advancements play a crucial role in modern policing. Predictive policing software analyzes vast amounts of data to identify crime patterns and predict potential criminal activities, enabling proactive measures. Geographic Information Systems (GIS) are used to map crime hotspots and allocate resources more effectively. Computer-Aided Dispatch (CAD) systems streamline the management of calls for service, ensuring quick and coordinated responses. Databases and information sharing platforms, such as the National Crime Information Center (NCIC), provide officers with access to critical data on criminal histories, warrants, and missing persons.

Tactics in policing have also evolved significantly, integrating technology with traditional law enforcement methods. Community policing is a strategy that emphasizes building relationships between police and communities to foster trust and cooperation. This approach involves officers working closely with residents, understanding their concerns, and collaboratively addressing issues. The adoption of crisis intervention techniques, particularly in dealing with individuals with mental health issues, is another important tactic. These techniques involve specialized training for officers to de-escalate situations and provide appropriate support.

The use of tactical units, such as SWAT (Special Weapons and Tactics) teams, represents a specialized response to high-risk situations, including hostage rescues, armed confrontations, and terrorist threats. These units are equipped with advanced weaponry and protective gear, and they undergo rigorous training to handle extreme scenarios. The integration of negotiation teams with tactical units is also a key aspect, aiming to resolve situations peacefully whenever possible.

Moreover, the implementation of data-driven policing has transformed law enforcement. By analyzing crime data, police can deploy resources more strategically, focusing on areas and times with higher crime rates. This method not only improves efficiency but also helps in reducing crime rates through targeted enforcement and preventive measures.

Despite the benefits, the use of technology and advanced tactics in policing raises ethical and privacy concerns. The deployment of surveillance tools like facial recognition software has sparked debates about civil liberties and the potential for misuse. Ensuring that these technologies are used responsibly and transparently is crucial to maintaining public trust.

POLICE TECHNOLOGY

Police technology refers to the wide range of scientific and technological methods, techniques, and equipment used in policing. As science has advanced, so too have the technologies that police rely upon to prevent crime and apprehend criminals. Police technology was recognized as a distinct academic and scientific discipline in the 1960s, and since then a growing body of professional literature, educational programs, workshops, and international conferences has been devoted to the technological aspects of police work.

Many examples of an incipient police technology date from ancient and medieval times. For example, the ancient Egyptians used detailed word descriptions of individuals, a concept known in modern times as *portrait parlé* (French: "spoken portrait"), and the Babylonians pressed fingerprints into clay to identify the author of cuneiform writings and to protect against forgery. Nevertheless, early technology was quite crude, such as the medieval methods of trial by ordeal and trial by combat, in which the innocence of suspects was established by their survival. A more humane medieval method, and a step toward modern concepts, was compurgation, in which the friends and families of a disputant took oaths not on the facts but on the disputant's character. Formalized police departments were established in the late 17th century in continental Europe, and since that time technologies have developed rapidly—transforming police work into a more scientific endeavour.

Yet police technology differs greatly in type and sophistication from country to country. It is generally more sophisticated in countries that are wealthy and that produce or import a high level of technology. (However, undemocratic countries tend to invest a great share of their gross national product in police technology, even when they are poor.) Police technology also depends on the physical setting and the political environment where police work is done. Urban policing relies more on technology than small-town and rural policing, and the degree to which a police force is militarized has a strong impact on its weaponry. Finally, some newer crimes, such as cybercrime, can be fought only by using an extensive array of technology that exceeds the scope of police technology proper.

Mobility

To be effective, police forces must be in close proximity to the citizens they serve. The first and most basic means of maintaining that close contact was the foot patrol. Officers were deployed by time of day (watches) and area (beats). Beats were kept geographically small to allow officers to respond to incidents in a timely manner. In larger rural jurisdictions, officers were deployed on horseback. Both foot and mounted patrols continue to be used throughout the world. Foot patrol is used in congested urban areas, in high-density housing complexes, and at special events; mounted patrol is also used for special events and for crowd control.

Foot and mounted patrols were followed by bicycle patrol, which spread throughout continental Europe at the end of the 19th century. Bicycle patrol made a comeback in the late 20th and early 21st centuries as a compromise between foot and car patrols. Bicycle patrol officers are specially trained and equipped with robust but lightweight urban bicycles. Bicycles are very useful for patrolling urban parks, housing complexes, school campuses, and locations where there are multiple large walkways not immediately accessible from the street.

The development of the automobile in the late 19th century dramatically transformed police work in the early 20th century. The city of Akron, Ohio, U.S., claims to have deployed the first automobile police patrol wagon in 1899. The vehicle was powered by an electric battery, however, which greatly limited its range over distances. A motorcycle patrol was instituted in New York City in 1905. By 1910 in France, 12 regional mobile brigades of police had become fully motorized; they used gasoline-powered automobiles manufactured by the De Dion-Bouton company to crisscross France. The motorization of police forces took place simultaneously in virtually all Western countries; by World War I, many urban police departments were using motorized patrols. Automobiles allowed police to expand patrol beats and reduced the time required for responding to incidents. However, the mobility and speed that police cruisers provided came at the expense of police visibility, as officers were increasingly encapsulated in their cars.

The police cruiser played a bigger role in the cities of the New World—Australia, Canada, New Zealand, and the United States—than elsewhere. New World cities generally were laid out in a gridlike pattern with large intersecting avenues that facilitated motorized police patrols. By contrast, European cities typically featured a maze of small, crowded streets that required foot patrols. The equipment carried by the standard police vehicle in these New World cities significantly evolved from the 1970s to the early 21st century. In the 1970s the police car was basically the same as the mass-produced vehicles owned by citizens. It was fitted with few accessories for enhancing comfort, such as air conditioning, and the specific police equipment that it carried consisted of a two-way radio with limited capacities and an external rotating light fitted on its roof; a metal screen between the front and the back seats was common but not standard. By the 21st century, the modern big-city patrol vehicle was routinely fitted with heavy-duty alternators to power numerous electronic devices and a powerful cooling system to handle engine heat while idling during hot weather. It also was equipped with an array of electronic devices, including radios, siren and light controls, a public-address system, a cellular telephone, a radar unit to measure motorists' speed, and, in many jurisdictions, a mobile digital terminal for access to police databases. Even the trunk was filled with equipment, such as first-aid and biohazard-response kits. Like the police vehicle itself, such equipment reflects the technologies produced by domestic industries. In countries whose industrial sectors are large and technologically advanced, such as the United States, Germany, and Japan, police cruisers tend to be very sophisticated instruments; elsewhere, they are more rudimentary.

The array of duties performed by police today requires a variety of different vehicles, ranging from minicars to buses and fully equipped mobile headquarters. For example, traffic-law enforcement is often conducted by patrol officers on motorcycles, but cars also are commonly used. In the United States, police often drive sport-utility vehicles (SUVs) for highway patrol. Police cruisers are generally smaller in Europe and Japan than in the United States and Canada, reflecting the standards of domestic auto industries. In Germany and Italy, police may use sophisticated sports cars, such as Porsches, BMWs, and even Ferraris, for high-speed chases.

Some police vehicles have been adapted from military vehicles. Police in South Africa use the Buffel, a vehicle derived from an armoured personnel carrier, and the Police Service of Northern Ireland (formerly the Royal Ulster Constabulary) uses military vehicles in its patrols. In the United States, some police departments have converted armoured scout vehicles to assist in high-risk operations. Vehicles built on large chassis can be used to transport a fully equipped command centre to a crime scene or disaster area.

The environment is another factor that determines the types of vehicles used by police forces. In many rural jurisdictions the typical four-door sedan has been replaced by SUVs and four-wheel-drive trucks. In areas where there are no paved roads (e.g., open country, beaches, and forests), the police use all-terrain vehicles and off-road motorcycles. Snowmobiles and tracked vehicles are used in areas where large snow accumulations are typical.

Police departments that patrol waterfronts employ small to midsize open-cockpit motorboats. Customs and border-surveillance agencies have access to some of the most complex and exotic watercraft to combat illicit drug-running and border incursions. In areas with large swamps, the police use airboats (flat-bottomed boat hulls with an aircraft engine and propeller for propulsion).

Various types of aircraft are used in police patrols as well. Helicopters, the most common type, are often equipped with a high-intensity spotlight that can provide overhead illumination for units on the ground. Another device used by aircraft, a passive infrared unit sometimes called forward-looking infrared (FLIR), provides night vision. FLIR units can measure the heat energy emitted by objects and living things, enabling ground units to be directed to a particular location. The police also employ fixed-wing aircraft for operations such as border patrols and drug surveillance, police-personnel transport over long distances, and highway traffic control. They range in size from single-seat planes to multiengine jet aircraft.

Communication

The vehicles discussed above would be nothing more than efficient conveyances if police officers were unable to communicate instantly with each other and the public. In the earliest police forces, communication was accomplished through oral or written orders in an administrative chain of command. As society progressed, the military was used less for domestic peacekeeping. Depending on whether a country evolved toward more or less centralization, systems of national or local control were established. In England the watch-and-ward system evolved to provide citizens with protection from crime. During times of duress, the men on watch would raise the hue and cry to summon assistance from the citizens of the community or, in the case of a larger community, from others already on watch. The watch standers were equipped with various signaling devices, including bells, ratchets, and rattles.

With the passage of the Metropolitan Police Act in 1829, the police in England were formalized into a full-time paid service, as they had been in France, Austria, and Prussia. The system was directed by a central command through face-to-face contact between supervisors and subordinates. As urban areas expanded and the police were deployed to more beats over larger geographic areas, this system of human communication became increasingly inefficient. Face-to-face contact gave way to the use of telegraphs in the mid-19th century, and in the late 1870s police departments began installing telephone systems. In urban jurisdictions call boxes, or street telephones, were placed on beats to enable patrol officers and citizens to alert the central command of disturbances. In 1937 the first emergency telephone system was established in London, where callers could dial 999 to speak to an operator.

Early systems of police dispatch involved a single operator who took calls from the public and dispatched officers via radio. In 1917 the police department of New York City began equipping patrol vehicles with a one-way radio receiver that enabled the central command to send emergency messages to officers. However, that and other early radio-communications systems were fraught with technical problems. In 1928, following several years of experimentation, the police department of Detroit improved the technology to allow regular contact between headquarters and patrol units; the system developed in Detroit was subsequently the basis of police communications systems used throughout the United States. Two-way radio receivers were first deployed in 1933 in Bayonne, N.J., and their use proliferated in the 1940s. Radios in patrol cars were eventually supplemented by portable radio transceivers carried by individual officers to allow uninterrupted radio contact between officers and the dispatch centre. Dispatch was improved in the United States in the late 1960s with the establishment of the 911 emergency telephone system. Similar systems have since been adopted in other countries throughout the world.

Police radio-communications systems benefited from the development of computers, which made possible the quick retrieval of information on stolen property, wanted persons, and other police intelligence. Computers were eventually placed in patrol cars. These mobile digital terminals (MDTs) enable officers to check licenses, wanted-persons lists, and warrants from the patrol vehicle without making an oral radio transmission. MDTs have been supplemented with a wide variety of digital pagers and cellular phones.

Computerization

The police were early adopters of computer database technology. In the United States the National Crime Information Center (NCIC) was established in 1967; police records were subsequently computerized and made available to police agencies throughout the country. The NCIC's database enables local police departments to apprehend offenders who might otherwise evade capture. The database contains fingerprints, a registry of sexual offenders, and mug shots, and it can be queried for detailed information on stolen vehicles and warrants for firearms violations; it can even search for phonetically similar names. Similar databases maintained by U.S. states provide police with access to misdemeanour warrants, driver-citation records, and vehicle-ownership information.

The European Union (EU) established a computerized information system—the Schengen Information System (SIS)—which allows the authorities of certain member states, plus some other European countries, to send or receive data about criminals, missing persons, stolen property, and other matters of interest to law enforcement officers. Each member of the EU, however, must devise its own computerized system to connect to the SIS. The European Police Office (Europol) also maintains a computerized database. In addition, Interpol manages databases of fingerprints, DNA profiles, and information on stolen property and other matters, which member countries can retrieve through a global police-communications system known as I-24/7.

Computer-assisted-dispatch (CAD) systems, such as the 911 system in the United States, are used not only to dispatch police quickly in an emergency but also to gather data on every person who has contact with the police. Information in the CAD database generally includes call volume, time of day, types of calls, response time, and the disposition of every call. The Enhanced 911 (E911) system, adopted in the United States, instantly identifies the number of the phone from which the call is made, as well as the name and physical address of the person who owns the phone. Data maintained in the E911 system sometimes include a history of calls to the police from the caller's location. When the CAD system is linked to a global positioning system (GPS), dispatchers can immediately identify the police cruiser nearest the scene of the emergency.

Although records are essential for effective police operations, police departments would be overwhelmed without a mechanism for filtering information and making sense of it. Police have long been able to gather information from related cases by using whatever records were available to them, but, until the advent of computerized databases, such cases could be found only through the recollection of experienced investigators. Computerized records systems can be extremely effective in drawing out relationships between past and present cases and suspects. The computer acts like a seasoned detective with an encyclopaedic memory. Systems known as Compstat, used by a variety of large cities, enable police departments to piece together information and to deploy personnel efficiently.

EQUIPMENT AND TACTICS

Police officers, whether plain-clothed or uniformed, carry a variety of equipment with them on service calls. Police in uniform carry much more equipment than those in plain clothes, and members of special operations teams, such as SWAT and crowd-control units, carry even more, sometimes including full body armour complete with helmet, leg pads, and shield.

The amount of equipment carried by uniformed officers has grown considerably since the 1950s, when it basically consisted of a handgun in a holster, handcuffs, and a nightstick. The holster was attached to a Sam Browne belt—a wide belt, usually made of leather, supported by a strap extending diagonally over the right shoulder. The belt was ill-adapted to changes in other police equipment, however, and its use declined in the late 20th century. Today, the belts worn by uniformed police officers in urban North America typically have a number of holsters or cases for carrying an automatic pistol, spare clips of ammunition, metal and plastic handcuffs, a portable radio, pepper spray, a collapsible baton, and a video microphone transmitter (if the officer's car contains a camera). A clipboard with spare report forms also is standard equipment. In addition, many police officers carry first-aid kits and other medical equipment, such as a defibrillator, in their patrol cars; they also may carry a portable breath analyzer for testing drivers who may be intoxicated. To this basic equipment many police officers add cell phones or pagers, flashlights, binoculars, tape recorders, portable scanners, plastic gloves, and extra weapons (e.g., a spare gun, a confiscated knife, a blackjack, or brass knuckles). The practice of bearing extra weapons, being of questionable legality, is mostly done surreptitiously, making it difficult to assess how extensive it is. However, it has been acknowledged by most police researchers. Finally, an essential piece of equipment is the bulletproof vest, which covers the torso of the officer and is worn either over or under the uniform shirt. Many such vests are made with the fibre Kevlar, which is capable of stopping most handgun projectiles and many types of knives. More robust vests, made of ceramic and fibre combinations that can withstand rifle fire, are used in bomb-disposal operations.

The quantity and diversity of equipment carried by police officers naturally depend on the financial resources allocated to police forces. North American police forces are generally better equipped than police forces in most other parts of the world; indeed, their equipment levels tend to be treated as benchmarks that other forces try to meet. Nevertheless, with the important exception of firearms, police equipment throughout the world is becoming increasingly standardized.

Arrest-and-control Technologies and Techniques

Nonlethal tactics and instruments

Police officers routinely arrest suspects in the course of their duties. Although most suspects surrender without incident, some resist being taken into custody. In most such cases, police are able to subdue the suspect by using unarmed techniques, some of which are drawn from various martial arts (e.g., judo and aikido) or are based on knowledge of nerve pressure points.

Nonlethal weapons include electronic devices, chemical agents, and a variety of different striking instruments, such as straight, side-handle, and collapsible batons and an array of saps, truncheons, and clubs. The nightstick carried by police officers was originally made of wood, but most now are made of composite materials.

The straight baton was developed in the mid-20th century. Known as a nightstick or billy club, it ranges in length from 12 to 36 inches (30 to 90 cm). Because it is smooth and can be held from either end, it tends to inflict few cuts or lacerations; it can be used for both striking and control tactics. Additional features of modified batons may include a built-in flashlight, an electric charge, or a syringe (e.g., for administering an antidote to nerve gas).

Electronic technologies include the stun gun, which delivers an electric charge that causes muscle spasms, pain, and incapacitation, and the TASER (a registered trademark), a type of electronic control device that fires two barbed projectiles which deliver an electric charge without requiring the officer to come within arm's reach of the suspect. Stun-gun technology is a good illustration of the globalization of police equipment. Most police forces that can afford nonlethal electric weaponry have invested in it—including those that resist the use of firearms.

Police firing tear gas at demonstrators during the 2001 Summit of the Americas, Quebec, Canada.(more) Tear gas is traditionally used to disperse large crowds. Early aerosol sprays were used only sparingly, because they vaporized quickly and could affect officers and others in close proximity to the suspect—particularly inside a squad car. Sprays containing capsicum oleoresin (*see* capsaicin), an irritant derived from pepper plants, proved to be more effective than other aerosols, and they possessed the additional advantage of being nonvaporizing.

For high-risk operations and crowd control, various irritating chemicals can be delivered by a handheld low-yield burst grenade, shotgun, or grenade launcher. The less-harmful PepperBall, which combines a compressed-air launcher and a projectile filled with capsicum oleoresin, was developed in the 1990s. Because the projectiles break upon impact, they usually do not cause permanent injury, even when fired at close range. The so-called "beanbag" projectile, which can be fired from shotguns and grenade launchers, contains a weighted flexible filler within a soft fabric pouch. Other nonlethal weapons include devices that use sound, light, or heat to cause confusion, pain, or temporary blindness.

Police dogs

Dogs were first trained for police work at the turn of the 20th century in Ghent, Belg., and the practice was soon adopted elsewhere. Although certain breeds with especially keen senses have been used for special purposes—such as detecting caches of illegal drugs and explosives and tracking fugitives and missing persons—the most widely trained dog for regular patrol work is the German shepherd, or Alsatian. Other breeds that are sometimes used include boxers, Doberman pinschers, Airedale terriers, rottweilers, schnauzers, and bloodhounds. For detection tasks, the size of the animal is less important than its olfactory sensitivity. Selected animals must meet specific criteria regarding physical characteristics and temperament, and their training is comprehensive and rigorous.

Firearms and explosives

Officer of the French National Police displaying his firearm.

Although police forces commonly authorize their officers to possess firearms and to use them when necessary, not all police carry these lethal weapons. There are four distinct cases in respect to the use of firearms by police.

First, there is the case of most police forces in the world: police officers carry firearms and are instructed to make minimal use of them. The number of police-caused fatalities varies greatly among such countries, the highest number being recorded in the United States.

Second, there are military police forces that are heavily armed with automatic rifles and submachine guns, such as the AK-47 used in countries in the Middle East, Asia, and other regions. Military police operate in most developing countries, where civilian police forces are typically underfunded and undertrained. Although many governments consider the use of heavy weapons by police to be justified by the threat to society posed by dangerous criminals, critics have claimed that heavily armed police tend to kill large numbers of people unnecessarily, sometimes in circumstances that amount to extrajudicial execution. In the Brazilian state of São Paulo, for example, military police shot and killed hundreds of people each year in the late 20th and early 21st centuries in what were officially reported as shoot-outs with criminals.

Third, there are some police forces that do not carry firearms in any circumstances. Such police operate in the cities of continental Europe under the local authority of a mayor. Unarmed, they perform various order-maintenance duties, such as the enforcement of local bylaws and traffic regulations.

Finally, a small number of police forces severely restrict the use of firearms by their personnel. Today police officers do not normally carry firearms in New Zealand, Norway, and the United Kingdom (except in Northern Ireland, where officers of the Police Service of Northern Ireland are armed). In New Zealand only the members of Armed Offenders Squads (AOS), which were established in 1964 after the fatal shooting of four police officers, are allowed to carry and use firearms. Each AOS is staffed with part-time police volunteers drawn from all branches of the police, and the squads operate only on a call-out basis. In Norway only a police chief can authorize the use of firearms by officers, and in the United Kingdom officers are allowed to use firearms only in specific circumstances. The Special Air Service, a paratrooper unit of the British military, administers special training in firearms to authorized police officers in the United Kingdom. In England and Wales, as in other countries, restrictions on the use of firearms by police have helped to minimize the number of unintended fatalities resulting from police operations. Nevertheless, after a series of terrorist bombings in the London public transportation system in 2005, there were calls in Britain for increasing the number of police officers authorized to use firearms.

Handguns, shotguns, and rifles

The first practical police firearm, the multishot revolver, was patented in 1835 by Samuel Colt. In the 1850s the British gun manufacturer Beaumont-Adams introduced the self-cocking double-action revolver. In contrast with the Colt, which needed to be cocked before firing, the double-action revolver could be fired by just a direct pull on the trigger. This allowed for quicker fire, at the expense of precisely aimed shots. In the United States and throughout the British Empire, the double-action revolver became, with few exceptions, the police sidearm of choice for more than a century.

Semiautomatic pistols were developed in Germany in the late 19th century by Peter Paul Mauser, whose Mauser rifle became a standard infantry weapon. In 1911 the .45-calibre single-action semiautomatic pistol developed by the American weapons designer John Browning was adopted by the U.S. military. Yet despite the advent of semiautomatics, double-action revolver pistols remained important police weapons not only for their capacity for quick firing; they also were perceived as more reliable than semiautomatics, whose firing mechanism tended to jam. In addition, double-action pistols were more secure than semiautomatics, as it took a significant amount of pressure on the trigger to fire them. Nevertheless, semiautomatics had more firing power and could be refilled with cartridges much more quickly through the use of magazines. In the 1970s, police departments in the United States began slowly to replace revolvers with semiautomatic pistols. The replacement of revolvers by semiautomatic firearms is now a worldwide police trend. Yet many plainclothes police officers all over the world still use a remodeled type of revolver with a very short barrel that makes it easier to carry.

In Western-style democracies, the standard police sidearm is strictly a defensive weapon. For offensive operations such as gunfights, more powerful firearms—e.g., shotguns and rifles—are necessary. Shotguns are capable of firing a variety of ammunition, including buckshot, slugs, tear gas, baton projectiles, and grenades. The pump-action shotgun, which was widely used in police departments from the early 20th century, began to be replaced by the semiautomatic shotgun in the late 20th and early 21st centuries.

The lever-action rifle accompanied the lawmen of the American West as they policed their jurisdictions in the 19th century. During the 20th century, police continued to use rifles of various descriptions and calibres. From the 1920s until World War II, some police departments in the United States adopted the Thompson submachine gun, or tommy gun, a weapon that was also embraced by the criminal underworld. The advent in the late 1960s of SWAT teams brought police countersniper units into service. Weapons used by such teams varied but typically included bolt-action high-calibre rifles fitted with telescopic sights.

Explosives

Explosives are used only sparingly by police, generally for breaching barricades and as distraction devices. Explosive "flash-bangs," which generate a loud explosion and a brilliant flash that disorient suspects, are usually tossed by hand or launched from firearms. One variation of the flash-bang, used particularly for riot suppression, discharges multiple small rubber balls or baton projectiles. Other explosives can be used to deliver tear gas or aerosolized capsicum. Police also use sophisticated automated devices to handle explosives planted by terrorists or other criminals.

Operated by police from a safe distance, the small tanklike vehicles with steel pincers can defuse or explode bombs after the public has been evacuated from the area.

Surveillance systems

Audio surveillance, or electronic eavesdropping, became practical for obtaining evidence and investigating leads after the development of magnetic recording in the early 20th century. Among the earliest automated surveillance systems were telephone pin registers, which recorded the phone numbers called from a certain surveillance location. Modern systems allow investigators to record the numbers of both incoming and outgoing calls, as well as any conversations. Other technologies enable audio surveillance through covert miniature microphones and radio transmitters and a variety of radio-receiving and voice-recording equipment. Self-contained wireless microphones are now so small that they can be secreted into virtually any object.

Police conduct visual surveillance with binoculars, telescopes, cameras with telephoto lenses, video recorders, and closed-circuit television (CCTV). Cameras fitted with telescopic and other specialty lenses have become a standard covert surveillance tool. Night-vision devices, or "starlight scopes," can be combined with telescopic lenses, both film and digital cameras, and video recorders. Similar to the forward-looking infrared units on aircraft, handheld passive thermal-imaging devices allow for covert observation in complete darkness. These instruments are particularly useful for searches inside unlit structures, for operations in which darkness must be maintained, and for locating lost persons in open areas. CCTV is widely used by both public law enforcement and private security providers. Cameras may be equipped with telephoto or variable-power lenses and motor drives. Low-light cameras can record images in almost complete darkness; those equipped with infrared emitters can record images in total darkness. In high-risk operations, CCTV cameras enable police to look under doors, through windows, or around corners. They also may be placed in waterproof housings attached to umbilical cables as long as 150 feet (45 metres) to conduct underwater search operations. A specialized application of CCTV cameras captures images of drivers committing specific traffic offenses (such as speeding) and automatically issues citations to them. In addition, CCTV cameras are often placed in patrol vehicles to record traffic stops and other events. The recorded images may be used as evidence in court to confirm or refute allegations of improper or illegal conduct by police officers.

CCTV technology is used extensively in the United Kingdom to monitor both public and private spaces, including underground train stations, urban commercial spaces, suburban shopping malls, parking structures and loading bays, bus stations, supermarket aisles and entrances, hospital entrances and exits, workplaces, schools, police precincts, and prisons. First implemented in the 1980s as a part of an initiative called Safer Cities, CCTV monitoring was eventually accepted by a majority of the British public despite initial objections from civil libertarians. Its popularity was boosted in 1993, when the taped abduction of a two-year old boy helped to identify and convict those responsible for kidnapping and murdering him, and in 2005, when the system helped to identify the terrorists behind the bombings of London's public transportation system.

Some other countries, however, have opposed the use of CCTV in public spaces because they consider such monitoring by the police without prior grounds for suspicion to be an unacceptable infringement of civil liberties. Nevertheless, CCTV is used to monitor private spaces in nearly all countries, and its use in various public spaces continues to increase.

Lie Detectors

Throughout history, those responsible for enforcing the law have attempted to develop lie detectors. One ancient interrogation method used in Asia was based on the principle that salivation decreases during nervous tension. The mouths of several suspects were filled with dry rice, and the suspect exhibiting the greatest difficulty in spitting out the rice was judged guilty. In India, suspects were sent into a dark room where a sacred ass was stabled and were directed to pull the animal's tail. They were warned that if the ass brayed it was a sign of guilt. The ass's tail had been dusted with black powder; those with a clear conscience pulled the tail, whereas the guilty person did not, and an examination of the hands of the suspects revealed the person with the guilty conscience.

Scientific advances led to the development of polygraphs in the 1920s. The polygraph is based on the premise that an individual who is lying will have subtle but measurable changes in specific physical indicators. Lie detectors utilize sensors placed on the test subject to record respiration, heart rate, blood pressure, and galvanic skin response or moisture in the fingertips. Taken together under highly controlled interview conditions and interpreted by an expert, the results of such measurements may indicate an attempt to deceive. Although the polygraph has proved an invaluable aid to police, its scientific validity has been questioned by some psychologists. Accordingly, the results of polygraph tests are not always admissible in judicial proceedings.

Voice-stress analyzers (VSAs), which became commercially available in the 1970s, rely on the detection of minute variations in the voice of the subject. Advocates of voice-stress analysis contend that inaudible vibrations in the voice, known as microtremors, speed up when a person is lying. During a VSA test, computer equipment measures the microtremors in a subject's voice and displays their patterns on a screen; certain patterns may indicate lies. Despite their initial promise, VSAs have not gained universal acceptance; critics argue that VSAs cannot distinguish between stress that results from lying and high stress in general. Other lie-detection techniques developed in the late 20th century relied on thermal images of facial-skin temperature and on measurements of brain-wave activity.

CRIMINAL IDENTIFICATION

Criminal identification based on various scientific methods has acquired a mythical dimension thanks to popular fictional accounts of police investigation. However, scientific methods of criminal identification are actually more useful for producing evidence to be used in court to secure the conviction of a suspect—typically identified through the traditional investigative method of questioning the witnesses of a crime—than they are for identifying who the perpetrator of a crime is, particularly if the perpetrator has no previous criminal record.

Scientific means of criminal identification can be classified in two categories. The oldest and most traditional means, such as photography and anthropometry, depend initially on the arrest of a suspect, who is then photographed and described physically. These photographs and anthropometric descriptions can be used at a future time to reidentify a criminal, but this person needs to have been caught in a first offense to trigger the system. Newer identification techniques have no such limitations. They do not consist of depictions of a whole individual; rather, they involve the scientific analysis of traces that a perpetrator may leave behind—e.g., fingerprints or blood (a source of DNA). The results of such analyses can be matched with the physical characteristics of a suspect who has never been arrested before and thus can result in a new positive identification.

Nevertheless, the few studies of criminal investigation that have been conducted stress the limited contribution of such scientific methods to the identification of unknown perpetrators. The most efficient identification technique—that is, the questioning of witnesses—is also the most time-honoured. The probability of solving a crime drops dramatically when there are no witnesses of any kind.

Photography

As early as the 1840s in Brussels, police used photographs to keep track of criminals. Such photographs, or mug shots, are an essential tool for police investigators. A variety of different formats have been used—including, most recently, digital images—and there is no single universal system employed throughout the world. Digital mug shots have the advantage of being instantly transmittable anywhere in the world via the Internet.

Anthropometry

The science of anthropometry was developed in the late 19th century by Alphonse Bertillon, chief of criminal identification for the Paris police. The Bertillon system, which gained almost immediate acceptance worldwide, used meticulous physical measurements of body parts, especially the head and face, to produce a detailed description, or *portrait parlé*. Initially, the system was used much less to identify unknown perpetrators than to allow investigators to determine whether the suspects they arrested had been involved in previous crimes. Known recidivists were believed to be more dangerous and were accordingly punished more severely.

Fingerprinting

Anthropometry was largely supplanted by modern fingerprinting, which developed during roughly the same period, though the origins of fingerprinting date from thousands of years ago. As noted above in the introduction to the section on police technology, the Babylonians pressed fingerprints into clay to identify the author of cuneiform writings and to protect against forgery. The Chinese also were using fingerprints in about 800 CE for purposes of identification. Following the pioneering work of Francis Galton, Britain adopted fingerprinting as a form of identification in 1894. In Argentina, police officer Juan Vucetich, inspired by Galton's work, developed the first workable system of classifying fingerprints—a system still widely used in many Spanish-speaking countries. In Britain, a system of classifying prints by patterns and shapes based on Galton's work and further developed by Sir Edward R. Henry was accepted by Scotland Yard in 1901; that system, or variants of it, soon became the standard fingerprint-classification method throughout the English-speaking world.

Fingerprint identification, or the science of dactyloscopy, relies on the analysis and classification of patterns observed in individual prints. Fingerprints are made of series of ridges and furrows on the surface of a finger; the loops, whorls, and arches formed by those ridges and furrows generally follow a number of distinct patterns. Fingerprints also contain individual characteristics called "minutiae," such as the number of ridges and their groupings, that are not perceptible to the naked eye. The fingerprints left by people on objects that they have touched can be either visible or latent. Visible prints may be left behind by substances that stick to the fingers—such as dirt or blood—or they may take the form of an impression made in a soft substance, such as clay. Latent fingerprints are traces of sweat, oil, or other natural secretions on the skin, and they are not ordinarily visible. Latent fingerprints can be made visible by dusting techniques when the surface is hard and by chemical techniques when the surface is porous.

Fingerprints provide police with extremely strong physical evidence tying suspects to evidence or crime scenes. Yet, until the computerization of fingerprint records, there was no practical way of identifying a suspect solely on the basis of latent fingerprints left at a crime scene, because police would not know which set of prints on file (if any) might match those left by the suspect. This changed in the 1980s when the Japanese National Police Agency established the first practical system for matching prints electronically. Today police in most countries use such systems, called automated fingerprint identification systems (AFIS), to search rapidly through millions of digitized fingerprint records. Fingerprints recognized by AFIS are examined by a fingerprint analyst before a positive identification or match is made.

DNA fingerprinting

The technique of DNA fingerprinting, which involves comparing samples of human DNA left at a crime scene with DNA obtained from a suspect, is now considered the most reliable form of identification by many investigators and scientists. Since its development in the 1980s, DNA fingerprinting has led to the conviction of numerous criminals and to the freeing from prison of many individuals who were wrongly convicted.

The Combined DNA Index System (CODIS), developed by the U.S. Department of Justice and the FBI, combines computer technology with forensics, enabling investigators to compare DNA samples against a database of DNA records of convicted offenders and others. CODIS is used worldwide for sharing and comparing DNA data; it is available for free to all police forensics laboratories. The first national DNA fingerprinting database (NDNAD) in the United Kingdom was established in 1995. Other countries, including France, Canada, and Japan, created DNA databases as well.

Although DNA fingerprinting cannot empirically produce a perfect positive identification, the probability of error—a false positive—can be decreased to a point that it seems nonexistent. When enough tests are performed, and when the DNA sample is suitable, DNA testing can show that a suspect cannot be excluded as the source of the sample. Sufficient testing also may exclude virtually every other individual in the world as the source of the sample. However, making scientific identification coincide exactly with legal proof will always remain problematic. As low as it may be, even a single suggestion of the possibility of error is sometimes enough to persuade a jury not to convict a suspect, as was shown spectacularly by the acquittal of O.J. Simpson, the American former gridiron football star, of murder charges in 1995. By contrast, DNA can exculpate a suspect with absolute certainty. If there is no DNA match between a sample taken from a crime scene and a sample provided by a suspect, then there is no possibility at all that the DNA-fingerprinted suspect may be guilty. Consequently, DNA fingerprinting is playing a crucial role in proving the innocence of persons wrongly convicted of violent crimes.

Biometrics

In criminal investigations biometric analysis, or biometrics, can be used to identify suspects by means of various unique biological markers. Biometric devices can map minutiae in a single fingerprint and then compare it with an exemplar on file, conduct a retinal or iris scan of the eye, measure and map an entire handprint, or create a digital map of the face. Biometric facial-mapping systems, or "facecams," when linked to offender databases and CCTV cameras in public places, can be used to identify offenders and alert police. Such facecam systems were implemented in London and other areas of Britain beginning in the 1990s and in several U.S. cities and airports in the early 21st century. Some advocates of biometric technology have proposed that biometric data be embedded into driver's licenses or passports to enable security officials to identify suspects quickly; such arguments were made more frequently after the September 11 attacks in 2001. However, critics of the technology contend that it unduly infringes upon the civil liberties of law-abiding citizens; they also point out that biometric systems such as facecams and thumbprint matching would not have identified most of the hijackers involved in the September 11 attacks—much less foiled their plot—because only 2 of the 19 hijackers were on the CIA's "watch list."

CRIME-SCENE INVESTIGATION AND FORENSIC SCIENCES

The first police crime laboratory was established in 1910 in Lyon, France, by Edmond Locard. According to Locard's "exchange principle," it is impossible for criminals to escape a crime scene without leaving behind trace evidence that can be used to identify them. That principle gave rise to the forensic sciences, which are the accumulated methods for developing and analyzing physical evidence from crime scenes. Crime-scene investigation, which is often performed by experts known as crime-scene investigators (CSIs), involves the careful gathering of such evidence, which is then analyzed at a crime laboratory. In some cases evidence gathered by CSIs and analyzed by forensic experts is the only incontrovertible evidence presented at trial.

Evidence Collection

Because there is rarely more than one opportunity to obtain evidence from a crime scene, the investigation by the CSIs must be methodical and complete. In keeping with Locard's exchange principle, CSIs collect evidence from the crime scene that may have been touched or microscopically "contaminated" by the suspect or suspects. They also take samples of fibres, dirt, and dust. After a preliminary search, the crime scene is photographed; some police departments also make a videotape of the scene. CSIs take careful measurements, make detailed notes, and draw sketches. Evidence is collected and carefully catalogued. Scientific and technological advances have resulted in the development of laser and alternative-light sources that can reveal latent fingerprints, stains, hairs, fibres, and other trace evidence.

For example, luminol, a substance that fluoresces when in contact with blood, is capable of detecting blood traces that have been diluted up to 10,000 times, making it useful for searching crime scenes that were cleaned in order to conceal evidence. In addition, the patterns of blood stains often indicate many of the dynamics of the crime; investigators trained in blood-pattern analysis, for example, can determine whether a victim was standing still, walking, or running at the time of death. Although some larger police departments have specialists to take photographs and fingerprints and to collect trace evidence, most CSIs are generalists who are trained to perform all these tasks.

Forensic Analysis

Hairs and fibres

Although a single hair or fibre cannot place a suspect at a crime scene, collections of hair or fibre can be used to establish with a high degree of probability that the suspect is connected to the crime. Hairs possess class characteristics (patterns that naturally occur in specific percentages of the population) that indicate some general features of the individual from whom they are obtained, such as what diseases he may have and sometimes what race he belongs to. If the hair has any follicular material or blood on it, a DNA test can determine with a certain degree of probability whether the sample came from a particular individual.

Toxicology

Toxicology was first systematized by the Spanish physician Matthieu Orfila (1787–1853). Toxicologists examine blood and tissues to ascertain the presence and quantity of drugs or poisons in a person's body. Toxicological reports can assist investigators by showing whether the drug ingested was fatal and the approximate time the drug was introduced into the body.

Serology

Serology is the study of serums such as blood and other human fluids. In 1901 Karl Landsteiner, a researcher at the University of Vienna, published his discovery that human blood could be grouped into distinct types, which became known as the ABO blood group system. In 1915 the Italian scientist Leone Lattes developed a simple method for determining the blood type of a dried bloodstain. The Rh blood group system, which classifies blood according to the presence or absence of the Rh antigen, was developed in 1939–40. Since that time more than 100 different blood factors have been discovered. Because those factors appear unevenly in the population, they can be used to identify the particular groups to which potential suspects belong. As various blood factors are defined in a sample, the percentage of people who have that combination of factors is narrowed, and the sample becomes more individualized. The introduction into forensics of DNA analysis has enabled investigators to detect identifying characteristics of body fluids and cells with unprecedented precision, making them better able to implicate or eliminate potential suspects.

Examining documents

The work of the "questioned document" examiner concerns such problems as identifying handwriting and typewriting, determining the age of a document, and determining the sequence of events involved in a document's preparation, handling, or alteration. Document examiners employ a variety of technologies and techniques. Handwriting analysis, for example, is based on the premise that, by the time people become adults, their writing has acquired peculiarities that may be used to identify them. A forged signature presents other problems. Simulated signatures based upon recollection contain a combination of the forger's own writing habits and his recollection of the victim's habits.

In many cases such simulations can be identified. When the perpetrator makes a careful drawing of the victim's signature or traces an authentic signature, however, the forgery can be exposed but cannot be identified with the handwriting of the perpetrator. Two individuals making careful tracings of the same signature can produce virtually identical drawings.

In the era before computers, investigators would sometimes examine typewriters to determine the make and model used to prepare a document. Ink comparisons provided evidence that was frequently of value. Chemical tests of various kinds are used for ink comparisons. Papers can be differentiated on the basis of fibre, filler, and sizing constituents. Fibres can be identified by differential staining and microscopic examination. Fillers can be distinguished by X-ray diffraction because they are crystalline substances. Chemical tests are used for the identification of sizing constituents. Through chemical analysis it is even possible to identify paper by batches.

Firearms and tool marks

Firearms identification was developed in the 1920s by American ballistics expert Calvin Goddard, who first applied his new technique to help solve the St. Valentine's Day Massacre in Chicago in 1929. Each firearm leaves individual markings on a bullet and case when it is fired. Such markings can be used to determine whether evidentiary bullets were fired from a suspect weapon. Similar techniques are applied to marks left behind at crime scenes by pry bars, screwdrivers, and other tools.

Organic and inorganic analysis

Police use organic and inorganic analysis to examine the chemical composition of trace evidence found at a crime scene, which may then be matched to substances associated with a suspect. Organic analysis, which is performed on substances containing carbon atoms, involves various techniques, including chromatography, spectrophotometry, and mass spectrometry. Inorganic analysis, which is performed on all substances that do not contain carbon, employs spectrophotometry, neutron-activation analysis (a technique involving chemical analysis by radioactivity), and X-ray diffraction, among other techniques.

Supplemental forensic sciences

Various other life and physical sciences are used to assist police investigations. Specialists approach the problem from different scientific perspectives, and the results of their investigations can provide police with a wealth of information about a case.

Forensic pathology is a specialty within the field of medical pathology. Forensic pathologists conduct an autopsy in cases of violent, unexplained, or unattended deaths, closely examining the decedent's wounds, blood, and tissue to ascertain how he died. Often said to be "speaking for the dead," forensic pathologists can establish a cause and a rough time of death and can often provide clues regarding the physical characteristics of the person or persons responsible for the crime.

Forensic anthropology is primarily concerned with the identification of human skeletal remains. Forensic anthropologists can differentiate animal remains from those of humans and, given the proper bones, can determine the gender and in some cases the race of the victim. In the 1970s American forensic anthropologist William Bass established the first human-decay research facility, known as the "body farm," at the University of Tennessee, Knoxville. The centre's studies of the physical changes that decomposing corpses undergo over time have helped to establish an empirical basis for estimating time of death.

Facial reconstruction combines both art and science. A skull can be used as a foundation and the face reconstructed with clay. By using charts of specific points of skin and tissue thickness, scientists can produce a relatively unique face that can then be used to help identify the decedent.

Forensic entomology is another field that assists police in determining time of death. Insects infest a corpse at a very predictable rate. Certain insects immediately invade the body to feed or to lay eggs, while others will not approach the body until it has reached a more advanced stage of decomposition. Thus, the types of insects or eggs present in a corpse indicate how long the victim has been dead. A forensic entomologist also can assist in determining where packages or cargo originated if insects or eggs are found in the shipment.

Forensic odontologists examine teeth and bite marks. They can compare the teeth of an unidentified body with an individual's antemortem dental X-rays or dental molds. They also may tie a suspect to a crime by comparing a bite mark taken from the crime scene with dental casts taken from the suspect.

Forensic botanists examine plants and plant matter to determine their species and origin. In some cases suspects may leave behind plant parts, spores, or seeds that had adhered to their clothing. If the plant species in question is found only in limited areas, its presence at the crime scene may indicate where suspects have been or where they live. Forensic botanists also can be essential in locating clandestine gardens or greenhouses used to cultivate such illegal plants as marijuana.

Forensic engineers perform accident reconstructions and failure analyses of vehicles and structures. The science of forensic engineering was instrumental in understanding the physical dynamics of the Oklahoma City bombing in 1995 and in explaining the collapse of the twin towers of the World Trade Center in the September 11 attacks of 2001. Forensic engineering also is useful in police investigations of motor-vehicle accidents. Forensic art or illustration is used for reconstructing crime or accident scenes. Artists can produce sketches of suspects from the recollections of victims or witnesses; they also can produce illustrations to assist prosecutors in court. An increasingly used technique involves illustrating the step-by-step development of accidents or crimes by means of computer-generated animations.

As the use of computers and the Internet in all types of activities grew rapidly in the late 20th century, forensic computing became an important field for investigating cybercrimes, including crimes involving computer hacking (the illegal entry into and use of a computer network) and the programming and distribution of malicious computer viruses. In many cases personal computers are confiscated at crime scenes or pursuant to warrants. Police may require the assistance of a computer expert to break any password protections or to unlock encrypted files to reveal evidence of criminal activity. Some police departments have assigned officers to pose as minors in Internet "chat rooms," where pedophiles sometimes attempt to discover the physical locations of teenagers and children or to arrange illicit rendezvous with them. Identifying pedophiles or cyberstalkers (people who engage in stalking by means of computers) sometimes requires police to seek the cooperation of Internet service providers, which maintain records (such as Internet protocol addresses) that may indicate the particular computer network used by the suspect.

Criminal Profiling

Criminal or offender profiling, also known as criminal investigative analysis, rests on the assumption that characteristics of an offender can be deduced by a systematic examination of characteristics of the offense. Criminal profiling is most effective in investigations of serial crimes, such as serial murder, because details may be gathered from more than one case. Many law enforcement agencies now use computerized systems to aid them in such investigations; the FBI's Violent Criminal Apprehension Program (ViCAP), for example, is a database that contains information on violent crimes committed across the United States. The system compares all new cases with all previously entered cases; when two cases are similar enough to have been committed by the same offender, the system alerts the appropriate law enforcement agency. Other countries have developed systems similar to ViCAP; one of the most elaborate is the Violent Crime Linkage Analysis System (ViCLAS), which is managed by the Royal Canadian Mounted Police. ViCLAS collects extensive data on all homicides and attempted homicides, sexual assaults, missing persons, unidentified bodies of persons known or thought to be homicide victims, and nonparental abductions and attempted abductions. A number of countries, including Australia, Austria, Belgium, The Netherlands, and the United Kingdom, as well as some U.S. states, have adopted ViCLAS. However, although such systems have become an important part of police technology worldwide, their effectiveness has not been independently assessed.

INNOVATIVE – POLICE TECHNOLOGY

Technology is transforming police work in the 21st century — introducing new tools to fight crime and new categories of crime to fight. For example, while more and more police departments across the country are deploying drones as eyes in the sky, the FBI reports they are also being used for criminal activities.

When this post was first written in 2016, these technologies were just rolling out across agencies. Now, with the rapid pace of technological developments, agencies are finding new and innovative ways to leverage these tools to enhance public safety, catch criminals and save lives.

Eyes on Innovation – Police Technology

Digital Forensic Software

This type of software is used to find, recover and preserve digital evidence that's often associated with electronic crimes, such as credit card fraud or child pornography. But many non-electronic crimes also include digital evidence, such as bank account information, phone numbers, emails, text messages and social media posts.

Digital forensic software has special capabilities, such as identifying and recovering hidden (or deleted files), performing complicated searches and determining the contents of a file beyond the file extension (.doc, .pdf, etc.).

Information Sharing Technology

Communication among law enforcement agencies has always been a challenge, but certain types of technology are helping to bridge the gap so that everyone is on the same page. One of the goals of the Department of Homeland Security Science and Technology Directorate is to "fund projects that help state and local response agencies share timely information about emergencies with each other and the public." A few of these include the Next-Generation Incident Command System and Wireless Emergency Alerts.

Another example: OpenFox® information sharing products and programs. In particular, the Message Switch System "provides access to a wide variety of city, county, state and federal criminal justice agency information and allows criminal justice integration efforts between probation and parole officers, the U.S. Department of Homeland Security and other law enforcement entities around the world."

Virtual Reality Training

Virtual reality (VR) training for law enforcement provides a safe, immersive experience that simulates real-life behavior and scenarios as much as possible. It also demonstrates to potential officers that a department or agency is serious about the latest innovations and educational tools, which can help with recruiting.

VR training is now being used for new recruits in the Pulaski County Sheriff's Office in Arkansas. The flexibility of the system allows officers to vary scenarios and settings to include shopping malls, neighborhoods and schools. At the Tequesta Police Department in Florida, officers use VR tools to practice responding to hostage and active shooter situations and help individuals in mental distress.

eCitations and Mobile Printers

Advances in technology now make it possible for law enforcement officers to issue citations without spending precious minutes filling out paperwork by hand.

Here's how the process works: The officer uses a device to scan the barcode on the driver's license. The information populates a citation, which the officer prints using a mobile printer. The officer can also send the citation to the courthouse digitally, all of which saves time, increases efficiency and reduces errors.

In one successful example, the police department in Olathe, Kansas switched to this technology, decreasing the time it takes to issue a citation from 15–20 minutes to 2–3 minutes.

Facial Recognition Software

One of the more controversial emerging police technologies involves the use of facial recognition software. When this tool first made its way into law enforcement repertoires, many were concerned that it would be used unethically. Thankfully, that has not been the case, and facial recognition is proving to be an effective investigative tool.

The goal of facial recognition software is that it will help improve safety and security in a number of instances. NYPD officers were able to find and arrest a rape suspect within 24 hours of the attack using facial recognition software. And, because facial recognition is so promising, the U.S. Department of Homeland Security predicts that it will be used on 97 percent of travelers by 2023.

Biometrics

Police have been using fingerprints to identify people for more than a century. Now, in addition to facial recognition and DNA, there is an ever-expanding array of biometric (and behavioral) characteristics being utilized by law enforcement and the intelligence community. These include voice recognition, palmprints, wrist veins, iris recognition, gait analysis and even heartbeats.

The FBI has developed a database called the Next Generation Identification (NGI) system, "which provides the criminal justice community with the world's largest and most efficient electronic repository of biometric and criminal history information."

With comprehensive electronic databases now in place to more effectively use DNA and other biometric data in law enforcement, even the use of fingerprints to identify suspects has gone high-tech. For example, a CNBC report explains how police in London can now use a mobile INK (Identity Not Known) biometrics device to scan a suspect's fingerprints and in many cases reveal their identity within 60 seconds.

Voice Technology

An officer's patrol car is like a mobile command center, meaning there are numerous computers and tools that an officer can use while on the road. But because there are so many different features, safely multitasking can be difficult. One of the latest innovations being incorporated into police cars is a new voice command technology that empowers officers to control many functions in their vehicle while driving and performing other patrol duties.

The capabilities of these voice systems vary from vehicle to vehicle, but most can handle commands to run a license plate or turn on a siren. The more advanced and most promising capability of voice command technology in police cars will make filing reports much easier — officers can dictate their notes which are then logged directly into their agency's RMS system.

Robots

Many law enforcement agencies are now using next-generation robotic cameras to deliver visual and audio surveillance of potential crime scenes that may be too dangerous or too hard for officers to reach.

Some of these devices are even "throwable" (up to 120 feet and capable of withstanding repeated 30-foot drops) — powered by an electric motor and equipped with high-tech wheels that enable them to move, climb and explore even the most challenging spaces while being operated wirelessly by a trained officer.

Automaker Ford has filed a patent for a self-driving police car equipped with artificial intelligence. These high-tech cruisers are designed to catch violators of traffic laws or impaired drivers by transmitting information to human officers or carrying an optional passenger officer who could make arrests.

Additional applications for using robots in police work, now and on the near horizon, include:

- Ever-expanding capabilities for robots to gather surveillance information, take police reports and provide communications in settings where human officers' safety would be compromised
- China's ongoing development of an "AnBot" robot to patrol banks, airports and schools
- Patrolling tourist attractions with a touchscreen-equipped robot officer, as is now on duty in Dubai

Video Doorbells

Video doorbells have been installed by thousands of homeowners as a way to enhance home security and give them peace of mind. It turns out, though, that these surveillance systems are also helping law enforcement when it comes to criminal investigations. In 2020 alone, law enforcement agencies across the U.S. made more than 20,000 requests last year for footage captured by Ring video doorbells and other home-security cameras. Amazon — which owns Ring — has entered into more than 2,000 cooperative agreements with law enforcement agencies, which allows them to automatically ask camera owners for their security footage if they live near a crime scene.

ShotSpotter

"Shots fired!" is not an uncommon dispatch from witnesses or officers on patrol, but pinpointing the exact location of the gunfire takes up precious time when every moment counts. Today, more and more cities are implementing ShotSpotter technology that uses sensors to detect gunfire and analysts to track the data and instantly relay it to police, enabling them to arrive on the scene more quickly than ever before. Named for the leading provider of this technology — California-based ShotSpotter — the service can cost $40,000 to $60,000 per square mile per year for cities to cover high-crime areas. The company claims it can "detect 90%+ of gunfire incidents with a precise location in less than 60 seconds to significantly improve response times." A dramatic example of ShotSpotter in action took place in 2017 in

Fresno, Calif., where police used it to apprehend a criminal on a killing spree. The technology enabled police to trace the killer's movements and apprehend him in 4 minutes and 13 seconds.

Thermal Imaging

Thermal imaging has become an important police technology tool that is especially helpful in dark conditions. Thermal image cameras, some available as small hand-held units, utilize infrared imaging to detect heat emitted by such objects as humans and animals, and to deliver a "heat picture" or "heat map" of the environment in question. As seen on any number of TV crime shows, it can be used to track the motion of suspects in a darkened building. Such technology has life-saving applications — from firefighting to search and rescue missions (for example, finding a lost child or senior citizen in a blinding snowstorm).

Artificial Intelligence

The ongoing expansion of the Internet of Things (IoT) means more data is being generated, collected and analyzed than ever before — much of which can be incredibly valuable in a law enforcement context.

But the process of deriving actionable insights from immense amounts of data is so incredibly time-consuming that it is not remotely cost-effective when performed by humans. That's where artificial intelligence (AI) and its subcategory machine learning come in. AI is used to support many other police technologies, including some of those mentioned above like ShotSpotter, facial recognition and biometrics. It can also be used for crime mapping: crunching data that can be used to far more effectively pinpoint high-crime areas, so police can monitor them more closely and deploy additional resources. Artificial intelligence is also being used for "crime forecasting." Utilizing so-called "deep learning" algorithms, programmers can train computers to analyze data from a vast array of sources and categories to actually predict when and where crimes are likely to occur. This allows agencies to properly allocate resources and increases the likelihood that officers will be in the right place at the right time.

Smarter Cruisers

Police cruisers have come a long way since the first police car hit the streets of Akron, Ohio, in 1899 (with a gong for a siren and a cell in the back for prisoners).

Innovation in modern police cruisers (and those of the future) has brought about such upgrades as fingertip access to Wi-Fi connected laptops, tablets, and in-dash computers, giving officers the benefit of instant access to vital information, communication systems, and more.

Enhanced dashcam capabilities are highly useful for surveillance and information gathering, as well as for evidentiary and accountability purposes. Next-generation officer safety features (for example, armor-piercing bulletproof doors) are also being incorporated into some police vehicles, and semi-autonomous operational capabilities are not far down the road.

Automatic License Plate Recognition (ALPR)

The same technology that enables toll collectors to automatically scan and collect the registration numbers and letters on your license plate to charge you a fee is now being used by police for a variety of law enforcement purposes, from identifying stolen cars to catching up with people who have active warrants or monitoring "Amber Alerts." However, the technology law enforcement uses for ALPR has taken another innovative step forward.

The latest in ALPR technology combines optical recognition technology with AI, allowing law enforcement to reliably and consistently identify license plates. Before the enhanced AI capability, some ALPR cameras provided low-resolution and blurry images, making proper identification difficult. With AI, ALPR cameras can identify "the make, model and color of cars even in low light and poor weather, distinguish individual characters on license plates, learn new plates as they appear and expand its database to include updated and unfamiliar designs."

The reality that multiple cameras could be capturing images of the same license plate potentially gives police the ability to track a vehicle's movements over time, revealing details about an operator's whereabouts, which could obviously be helpful in catching criminals.

However, privacy advocates like the ACLU — asserting that drivers are not voluntarily offering up detailed information on their comings and goings — warn that such powerful technology should be subject to restrictions and close monitoring to ensure it is not being abused. Many states and law enforcement agencies have put in place limitations to how this valuable technology is deployed.

Enhanced Body-Worn Cameras

Video of police officers doing their jobs in challenging situations used to be rare; today it is ubiquitous, as seen in a number of high-profile incidents that have drawn intense public and media scrutiny.

As more cities and communities choose to equip police departments with body-worn cameras, the ability of law enforcement supervisors, as well as the public, to gain a street-level view of on-duty police work has expanded dramatically — setting in motion an ongoing debate around the importance and the impact of this technology.

In addition to being smaller, less cumbersome, and more durable, some body-worn cameras are designed to better integrate with in-car systems to provide synchronized video of an event from multiple points of view. Other advancements include higher resolution, clearer audio, wider fields of vision, and heightened resistance to environmental conditions such as extreme cold.

Related technology now includes smart holsters that are designed to activate the body camera anytime the officer draws his or her firearm. At least one manufacturer of body-worn police technology makes a camera capable of issuing an alert when an officer is down. On the horizon: body-worn police cameras equipped with facial recognition capabilities.

Drones

Also called unmanned aerial vehicles (UAVs), drones are increasingly being used by police to gain aerial vantage points for crime scene work, search and rescue efforts, accident reconstruction, crowd monitoring and more. Some of the more sophisticated models can be equipped with thermal imaging or 3D mapping software to offer GPS-enhanced precision to the areas being surveyed.

Many police drones and UAVs are also equipped with zoom cameras, making them incredibly valuable for delivering actionable, real-time intel in high-risk, "armed and dangerous" situations.

Mastering the Use and Implications of Police Technology

As police technology continues to evolve, law enforcement leaders have a powerful stake in staying well-informed about these advanced capabilities — both their positive impact on the safety of officers and the public, and the ethical questions involving rights to privacy. Police chiefs and agency executives will need to understand the pros and cons to make informed recommendations on what technologies their departments and communities should be investing in. Retired California police chief Jim Davis explains that, when he started his career, "if we were 10 to 20 years behind in technology it really didn't matter that much. But now, if you are 10 to 20 days behind in your technology the bad guys are getting way ahead of you." Chief Davis, a faculty member of the online Master's in Law Enforcement and Public Safety Leadership program offered by University of San Diego, emphasizes the importance of lifelong learning for any law enforcement leader wishing to stay abreast of the accelerated pace of police technology development. "It is clear that our profession has become much more complicated. Now more than ever, continuing education is a critical component of your ability to lead your organization and serve your communities."

Police Technology Jobs

Technology jobs are booming in practically every industry, and law enforcement is no exception.

Technology jobs in policing include drone pilots, electronic surveillance officers, digital forensic investigators, real-time crime analysts, social media researchers and accident reconstructionists — among many others.

In fact, a search for technology jobs in law enforcement on LinkedIn and Indeed revealed hundreds of results with titles such as:

- Data analyst
- Computer forensic instructor
- Intelligence analyst
- Research analyst
- Police business systems analyst
- Computer scientist
- Laboratory technician
- Law enforcement technology project manager
- Police systems administrator
- Law enforcement data science program manager
- Law enforcement content developer
- Senior cybersecurity incident investigator
- Cybercrime analyst/investigator

These types of positions are available not only at sheriff's departments, police departments and government agencies such as the Federal Bureau of Investigation, but also cities, states and companies like Lexipol that create training solutions for law enforcement.

REFERENCES

1. https://onlinedegrees.sandiego.edu/10-innovative-police-technologies/#:~:text=Technology%20is%20transforming%20police%20work,being%20used%20for%20criminal%20activities.
2. https://www.britannica.com/topic/police/Equipment-and-tactics
3. Manning, P. K. (2008). *The Technology of Policing: Crime Mapping, Information Technology, and the Rationality of Crime Control*. NYU Press.
4. Chan, J. (2001). *The Technological Game: How Information Technology Is Transforming Policing*. Federation Press.
5. Wilson, J. Q., & Kelling, G. L. (1982). *Broken Windows: The Police and Neighborhood Safety*. Atlantic Monthly Press.
6. Brayne, S. (2017). *Big Data Surveillance: The Case of Policing*. American Sociological Review, 82(5), 977-1008.
7. Lum, C., & Koper, C. S. (2017). *Evidence-Based Policing: Translating Research into Practice*. Oxford University Press.
8. Garicano, L., & Heaton, P. (2010). *Information Technology, Organization, and Productivity in the Public Sector: Evidence from Police Departments*. Journal of Labor Economics, 28(1), 167-201.

5 POLICE TECHNOLOGY: FACT-CHECKING THE CRITICISMS

INTRODUCTION

Police tech could transform the way law enforcement operates, reducing crime and saving lives. Policymakers should focus on advancing adoption while enacting regulations to maximize the benefits and minimize the risks of police tech. Emerging technologies such as AI, robotics, drones, augmented and virtual reality (AR/VR), and the Internet of Things are transforming and improving many sectors. Therefore, it should come as no surprise that these technologies are poised to do the same for policing. Since at least the 1920s, the United States has seen law enforcement adopt new technologies, such as fingerprinting, two-way radios, and databases, to improve their productivity and effectiveness. But technological adoption has often been slow. The President's Crime Commission in 1967 noted, "The police, with crime laboratories and radio networks, made early use of technology, but more policy departments could have been equipped 30 or 40 years ago as well as they are today." Today a suite of existing and upcoming technologies can allow law enforcement to do their jobs more safely, efficiently, and effectively. Widespread adoption of these technologies at all levels of law enforcement would result in more crimes solved (and possibly prevented), more lives saved, greater safety for officers, and taxpayer dollars put to better use.

However, there are many obstacles to greater adoption of technology by law enforcement. In response to a series of highly publicized instances of police killings of Black Americans—including George Floyd, Philando Castile, and Breonna Taylor—a nationwide movement to increase police oversight and accountability has gained steam. Some in this movement have issued calls to defund or even abolish police forces. Others have called for targeted reforms such as restrictions on use of force, creating a duty to intervene in instances of police misconduct, improving misconduct reporting, and ending qualified immunity to reduce police violence and reduce structural discrimination against people of color within the U.S. criminal justice system. Some digital rights and civil libertarian organizations, which have a long history of opposing police's use of technology, have tapped into this new wave of public anger with law enforcement to launch new campaigns against law enforcement's use of technology, or "police tech." Common criticisms highlight the potential for surveillance, misuse or abuse, and racial or other bias. They also point out the cyber security concerns, lack of transparency, and a need to evaluate police tech's effectiveness. While some of these concerns are legitimate, some are born more out of "worst-case scenario" arguments and slippery-slope fallacies and are a smokescreen for police tech bans. This is why many police tech critics conflate legitimate concerns with worst-cases speculation and offer little in the way of solutions to address these concerns other than banning law enforcement from using certain technologies that have the potential to cause harm. But banning this promising set of technologies would cut law enforcement and the general public off from the many substantial benefits of police tech. Moreover, it would eliminate opportunities to use technology to address police violence, bias, and accountability civil rights groups have been working toward. Rather, the Department of Justice (DOJ), state lawmakers, and police departments should accelerate the testing and deployment of police tech while at the same time creating rules, regulations, and best practices for police tech that would protect the public, curtail misuse and abuse, eliminate bias, and ensure transparency and effectiveness.

This report first explains the different types of police technologies and how law enforcement currently uses them or may use them in the future. Then it outlines and responds to the common criticisms of police tech. Finally, it recommends solutions for advancing adoption and addressing the legitimate criticisms of police tech to maximize benefits and minimize risk, including:

- DOJ should conduct independent testing of police tech that may display bias to guide police procurement.
- DOJ should tie federal funding for police tech to baseline minimum cybersecurity requirements.
- DOJ should establish a police tech grant challenge.
- DOJ's Bureau of Justice Statistics (BJS) should conduct more research on the effectiveness police tech.
- Congress should increase technology budgets for federal law enforcement agencies.
- State lawmakers should regulate police data collection.
- State lawmakers should pass transparency requirements for police departments.
- More police departments should establish voluntary programs that allow residents to share doorbell camera footage.
- Police departments should require officers to complete training programs before using new police tech.
- Police departments should require officers to only use police tech as intended by its developers.
- Police departments should mandate basic cyber hygiene training for all officers.
- Police departments should conduct pilot studies on new police tech to ensure its effectiveness in the field.

THE OPPORTUNITIES

There are a variety of technologies police departments have used or may use in the future for every aspect of their jobs that are not limited to preventing, responding to, and solving crime. There are also technological applications for keeping officers safe, streamlining back and front office processes, improving officer training, and maintaining public oversight and accountability.

These applications rely on AI and machine learning, robotics, biometrics, sensors, cameras, and other technologies, often in combination. Law enforcement and police tech entrepreneurs are only just beginning to tap into the potential of these technologies, such as AI algorithms that can predict where crime is likely to occur, robots that can wade into hostage situations without risking human life, facial recognition algorithms that can help find missing children and identify known criminals, gunshot detection that can drastically reduce the time it takes police to respond to an incident, and body-worn cameras that can help ensure police accountability.

Some technologies, such as DNA identification and traffic enforcement cameras, have been in use for decades, with established rules and best practices for their use. Others, such as predictive policing algorithms and facial recognition, are more recent and potentially controversial additions to the law enforcement tool kit. Law enforcement, government, civil rights advocates, and other stakeholders are still working out the rules and best practices for these emerging technologies.

Preventing Crime

Effective law enforcement helps reduce crime rates. As such, technologies designed to help law enforcement prevent crime rely on AI and machine learning to predict when and where crimes are likely to occur. These technologies build on old techniques law enforcement used before the development and deployment of AI.

Law enforcement has used crime mapping, a technique that aims to predict where crime is likely to occur based on where it has occurred in the past, for hundreds of years to study the relationship between crime and various geographic or demographic characteristics and to help police departments decide where to concentrate their resources. Early crime mapping involved physical maps officers marked with pins to represent recent crimes. With the advent of computers, police could do the same using a virtual map, and in the 1990s began using a tool specifically developed for crime mapping known as a geographic information system (GIS).

A GIS is more interactive than earlier crime maps. When officers add a pin to a physical map to represent where a crime took place, the only information that pin displays is the location of the crime. When officers add a point to a digital map, they can also add information about the exact time and date the crime took place along with other details of the crime that may be useful for analysis.

A GIS also contains data layers officers can use to organize data, with each layer containing a different type of data. For example, one layer may display the roads that run through an area, and a layer on top of that may display the bus routes that run on those roads, and a layer on top of that may display the bus stops along those routes. These layers could be viewed independently or together, stacked on top of each other.

With all the data contained in a GIS, police departments can analyze trends in criminal activity, but the software only contains historical data and cannot make predictions. In the past decade, advances in technology have allowed law enforcement to more accurately predict crime, a technique known as "crime forecasting," which builds on crime mapping.

Crime forecasting, or predictive policing algorithms, uses historical crime and demographic data and data collected by police patrols and stakeouts, from social media, and by other police technologies such as drones, facial recognition cameras, license plate recognition, and body cameras. The algorithms then identify patterns in criminal activity and predict crime with greater accuracy than human analysis can. These predictions give law enforcement the opportunity to deploy their resources more effectively.

Several studies have evaluated the accuracy and effectiveness of machine learning algorithms at forecasting crime. A review of the available literature conducted in 2019 by researchers from Utrecht University finds mixed results, with some studies showing that predictive algorithms are effective and some showing no statistically significant results. Positive outcomes are mostly associated with algorithms that predict where crime is likely to occur, as opposed to who was likely to commit crime. Predictive policing can thus be useful for helping police departments determine where to allocate resources, such as more officers or street cameras.

Due to concerns surrounding efficacy, public opinion, and budget, some early adopters of predictive policing have since shelved their programs, including the Los Angeles Police Department (LAPD) and Chicago Police Department. The New York Police Department (NYPD) has been using its own in-house predictive policing software since 2013.

Responding to Crime

Law enforcement also has technologies, including gunshot detection, drones, and thermal imaging, to more quickly, safely, and effectively respond to crime. Gunshot detection relies on sensors equipped with microphones placed around an area. The sensors constantly record audio and monitor for the sound of gunshots. When at least three sensors detect a possible gunshot, they transmit the audio to humans who review the audio and alert the local police.

ShotSpotter, a popular vendor for gunshot detection, provides its services to more than 120 cities and claims a 97 percent accuracy rate. The company places between 15 and 20 sensors per square mile, at least 20 feet above the ground to minimize ambient noise. The goal is to reduce the amount of time it takes to dispatch officers to the scene of a shooting and hopefully, in the long term, reduce gun violence.

In California, ShotSpotter alerted the Oakland Police Department (OPD) to more than 6,000 gunshots in 2020, 91 percent of which were not called in to the police, meaning the OPD may not have been able to respond, especially not in a timely manner. These numbers include 22 homicides and 101 shooting victims. The OPD was able to provide emergency medical response to the 101 surviving victims quicker than if ShotSpotter hadn't alerted the police to the incidents. In some cases, police and medical response took less than two minutes.

A GIS can also be used for similar purposes, with the goal to increase officer productivity, particularly the amount of time it takes them to respond to a crime in progress. The Lincoln Police Department (LPD) in Nebraska tested a GIS app that identifies the locations of persons of interest—including parolees, sex offenders, gang members, and others—in real time. All 75 police officers who tested the app reported that they would recommend the app to others, and a cost-benefit analysis suggests that the app could save the LPD around $800 per officer every five years due to increased productivity.

Police can also use unmanned aerial vehicles (UAVs), colloquially known as "drones," to respond to crime. In many instances, drones can save law enforcement time and money when responding to crime; they are faster than sending officers on the ground and significantly cheaper than helicopters. They are typically equipped with cameras that can capture images and record or livestream video, and may also be equipped with other technologies such as thermal imaging.

The most common law enforcement's use of drones, according to a 2020 survey by the Police Executive Research Forum (PERF), is for search and rescue operations, such as searching for missing persons. Drones can cover a lot of ground and livestream footage back to central command, allowing police to conduct searches remotely.

In the wake of Hurricane Ian in September 2022, several drone teams, featuring members from local sheriff's offices and fire departments and the Florida Department of Law Enforcement, assisted in search and rescue operations. The teams flew drones over areas impacted by the hurricane to provide on-the-ground search and rescue teams with information that helped them allocate resources and coordinate their efforts more effectively.

Another common application area is crime scene photography and reconstruction, including traffic collision reconstruction. Drones take photos of all angles of a crime scene or collision, which officers can later use when they attempt to reconstruct what occurred at the scene.

Drones may be equipped with thermal imaging capabilities, or police may use thermal imagers on the ground. Thermal imagers convert infrared radiation—part of the electromagnetic spectrum that is invisible to the human eye and shows the heat that objects or living things emit—into a visible format. Thermal imagers can "see" past smoke, dust, and chemical agents—situations when normal visibility would be reduced.

The Weber County Sherriff's Office Search and Rescue Team in Utah uses drones with thermal imaging capabilities for their missions. In one instance, a drone found a stranded snowboarder and shined a spotlight on him to direct the team to his location. This also helped the snowboarder, who knew even before the team arrived that help was on their way. Once rescuers found the snowboarder, the drone showed them the safest path off the mountain. Because of the drone, the rescue took half the time it otherwise would have.

Law enforcement uses thermal imaging to search for fugitives or missing persons by seeing their body heat. Additionally, objects will sometimes retain a trace of a suspect's body heat, aiding officers in evidence retrieval. According to a 2001 Supreme Court ruling, law enforcement needs to obtain search warrants to use thermal imaging to search a suspect's home in the same way they would need to obtain a search warrant to conduct a traditional search. But they rightly do not need permission to use thermal Imaging In public locations.

Solving Crime

There are a variety of technologies law enforcement can use, has used, or may be able to use in the near future to solve crime. These include cameras, biometrics, location-based services, and photo editing software.

Law enforcement can use cameras and photographs to solve crime, either by capturing an image or video of someone committing a crime, a suspect or victim, or evidence that leads the police to a suspect or victim. Often the cameras that capture this footage are paired with technology that allows for greater analysis.

Law enforcement has used traffic enforcement cameras to enforce traffic laws for decades. Arizona was the first state to begin using speed cameras in 1987, and New York was the first to employ red-light cameras in 1992. Speed cameras use detectors built into either the cameras themselves or the road to measure a vehicle's speed and issue a citation to the owner or driver if their speed exceeds the posted limit by a predetermined amount. Red-light cameras take a photo before a vehicle enters an intersection and while the vehicle is in the intersection and issues a citation if the traffic light was red in both photos.

Some states have laws prohibiting the use of traffic enforcement cameras, while others have rules for their use. Existing evidence suggests that traffic enforcement cameras can be effective at reducing collisions and related casualties if implemented correctly. However, some drivers object to being caught by an automated system as opposed to a human officer—or to being caught in general—and opponents have raised concerns about municipalities using traffic enforcement cameras as a source of revenue, possibly unfairly. These concerns have led to bans in some jurisdictions.

Some modern traffic cameras can automatically capture all the license plate numbers that come into their view. These systems use what is known as automatic license plate recognition (ALPR). In addition to capturing images of license plate numbers, these systems also typically record the precise date, time, and location the image was captured.

ALPR does not capture images of drivers or passengers, only license plates. The International Association of Chiefs of Police (IACP) has issued guidance to police departments on responsible use of ALPR, including maintaining audit logs for every an time officer accesses ALPR data and their justification for doing so in order to prevent misuse or abuse. According to IACP, ALPR data should only be accessed to locate stolen vehicles, suspects, witnesses or victims of violent crimes, or missing persons; to protect critical infrastructure; and for situational awareness during special events.

These days, an increasing number of homes have doorbell cameras equipped with motion detectors that automatically record video of anyone who approaches. Typically, these cameras allow residents to see who is at their door or capture evidence of package theft. But in addition, doorbell cameras sometimes capture footage law enforcement can use to solve other crimes. In the vast majority of cases, residents voluntarily decide whether to share the footage with police, although occasionally law enforcement may obtain the video directly from the technology company via a subpoena or emergency order. Some police departments offer doorbell cameras to local residents for free or a reduced price in exchange for permission to view the cameras' footage, while others set up networks with current camera owners the police can call or email to request access to their footage in the event of a crime in the area. In Rutherford County, Tennessee, as of 2019, the Sherriff's Office had used security footage from doorbell cameras in two homicide cases and several property crime cases thanks to homeowners agreeing to share their cameras' footage with the police. As of 2021, nearly 1 in 10 U.S. police departments had partnered with Ring, a doorbell and security camera company owned by Amazon, to request video footage from customers (who can opt out of the program if they so choose).

This practice of residents sharing doorbell camera footage builds on existing law enforcement practices using footage from publicly owned cameras or requesting footage from private establishments to solve crime. Retail stores have been using closed-circuit television (CCTV) systems since the 1970s for theft prevention, and the United Kingdom pioneered the use of public CCTV systems for crime prevention in the 1990s—a strategy some American cities later adopted. Multiple police departments have voluntary sharing programs for privately owned security cameras, similar to programs for doorbell cameras, and some even offer incentives to private businesses in high-crime areas to install them.

In addition to cameras, law enforcement often uses biometrics to solve crime. A biometric is a unique physical or behavioral characteristic, something that no two people share. When law enforcement can obtain biometrics (e.g., DNA or fingerprint evidence from a crime scene), it can use these characteristics to narrow down a pool of suspects or, when a suspect has already been identified, as evidence that the suspect committed a crime.

Law enforcement's use of biometrics to solve crime dates back to the early 20th century. The first criminal trial in the United States that used fingerprints as evidence concluded in 1911, and police still use many of the same techniques to evaluate fingerprints as they did then. Fingerprints are highly unique; not even identical twins share the same fingerprints. There are some limitations when police use latent prints, which are fingerprints left behind on surfaces at the scene of a crime. Latent prints can result in false positives or false negatives, but can still be a useful tool for narrowing a list of suspects or building a case against a suspect.

Many decades later, police added another powerful tool to their crime-solving tool kit: DNA evidence. The first conviction based on DNA evidence in the United States occurred in 1987. As with fingerprints, there are limitations to DNA evidence. A full DNA profile will only match with one person, but police can often only obtain partial DNA profiles, which could match with several people. A partial DNA profile can rule out suspects but not definitively confirm the identity of a perpetrator. Additionally, police finding an individual's DNA at the scene of a crime does not always mean that person committed the crime, which law enforcement and the courts often have to take into account.

Police have also begun using a technique known as "genetic genealogy" to identify criminals. In cases where police cannot match a DNA profile found at the scene of a crime to an individual in any police DNA database, they can request genetic data from companies that offer at-home DNA testing to consumers. These at-home tests provide consumers with information about their ethnic background, ancestry, and predisposition to certain diseases. If police can find a relative of the perpetrator in one of these companies' databases, they can use this information to help identify a suspect. Notably, police used this technique in 2018 to identify the Golden State Killer, a serial murderer who operated in California in the 1970s. The suspect they identified, Joseph DeAngelo, ultimately pleaded guilty in 2020.

More recently, law enforcement has been using another biometric tool: facial recognition. Facial recognition compares images of faces in order to estimate their similarities and verify or determine a person's identity. The technology has many law enforcement applications, such as locating missing children, detecting fraudulent activity, solving cold cases, and identifying criminals.

For example, the International Center for Missing and Exploited Children (ICMEC) developed its Global Missing Children Network Engine (GMNgine) that uses facial recognition to search the Internet and dark web for photos matching missing children.50 Of course, the effectiveness of this technology is directly related to the number of cameras in place and the ability to use facial recognition on the images to identify the children.

Additionally, the New York State Department of Motor Vehicles (DMV) uses its Facial Recognition Technology Program to identify people with more than one driver's license, including those who've stolen another's identity and tried to obtain a driver's license in that other person's name. As of 2017, the program had led to the arrest of 4,000 people.

In 2014, the Federal Bureau of Investigation (FBI) used facial recognition to find a fugitive who'd been on the run for 14 years after facing charges of child sex abuse. A special agent ran FBI wanted posters through facial recognition software that contained images of U.S. visa and passport photos and found a match, leading to the fugitive's arrest in Nepal.

There are many other biometrics, including voice recognition, iris recognition, retina scans, gait analysis, and signature recognition. As technologies continue to develop, law enforcement could use a wide variety of biometrics to solve crimes that, in the past, may have been unsolvable.

There are multiple federal fingerprint and DNA databases law enforcement can access to compare fingerprints or DNA found at a crime scene to those of convicted offenders, arrestees, or detainees. The FBI oversees the Combined DNA Index System (CODIS), a collection of DNA databases that includes the National DNA System (NDIS), deployed in 1998, which contains DNA profiles submitted by federal, state, and local forensic laboratories.

States have differing laws on the collection of arrestee DNA. Some states do not allow police to collect DNA from people who have been arrested but not convicted of a crime. Others allow the practice but have certain restrictions, such as excluding juvenile arrestees or requiring police to expunge the records either automatically or upon request. Most states that allow the collection of arrestee DNA only allow it for felony arrests (not misdemeanors), and several states further restrict the collection to certain felonies. Restrictions on the collection of arrestee DNA protect the privacy of individuals who may have been wrongfully arrested or arrested without enough evidence for a conviction. The FBI also maintains the Integrated Automated Fingerprint Identification System (IAFIS), deployed in

1999, which contains digital fingerprint data from criminals, detainees, persons of national security interest, federal applicants and employees, immigrants, and the military. In 2011, the FBA deployed its Next Generation Identification (NGI) system to expand on the IAFIS with improved and bolstered capabilities, including a facial recognition search, palm prints, and an iris image repository.

Another controversial technique law enforcement frequently employs to solve crime is location-based services. Geofencing technology uses GPS, RFID, Wi-Fi, and cellular data to set up a virtual boundary within the physical world, called a "geofence." A geofence warrant enables police to ask a tech company for an anonymous list of all the active devices within a geofenced area both during a certain time when and where a crime took place. Police narrow down the list to devices they believe could be connected to the crime and ask the tech company for those users' personal data.

Geofence warrants are a controversial approach, though one law enforcement frequently uses. Google had a 1,500 percent increase in geofence warrant requests from 2017 to 2018 and a 500 percent increase from 2018 to 2019. Concerned over the number of overly broad requests it received—such as warrants requesting data that would identify all users within a certain geographical area and time frame—Google began objecting to any warrant that did not first request de-identified data and then narrow down that data to likely suspects before requesting the users' identities.

Finally, law enforcement can sometimes use photo editing software to solve cases. The National Center for Missing and Exploited Children (NCMEC) has partnered with Adobe since 2007 and uses its software for tasks such as aging up photos of missing children to show what they might look like in the present, helping find over 3,000 children between 2014 and 2018. NCMEC has also used Adobe software to create facial reconstructions of deceased children from scans of their skulls, helping identify over 150 deceased children as of 2020. Finally, NCMEC has used photo editing software to enhance images in order to search for evidence that may lead to the child's location or identify a suspect behind the abuse.

Keeping Officers Safe

Existing and emerging technologies designed to keep officers safe rely on robotics and unmanned or autonomous capabilities. Drones and robots add a layer of separation between human police officers and potential danger, such as a bomb or an armed criminal.

Just as it can use drones to help solve crime, law enforcement can also use drones to help keep officers safe. According to PERF, "investigating armed and dangerous suspects" is the third most common law enforcement use case for drones, tied with disaster response. As an example, during an active shooter incident, drones can livestream aerial footage to law enforcement so officers have intel on the shooter's precise location and the locations of possible casualties.

Active shooter incidents are a real risk to officer safety. From January to September 2022, the FBI reported that 49 law enforcement officers were intentionally killed. Firearms were used in over 80 percent of those deaths. Fifteen of the officers were confirmed to have been wearing body armor when they were killed. Similarly, law enforcement can use robots to reduce the risk posed to human officers. Law enforcement and the military have used remote-controlled "robots" for bomb disposal for over 40 years. These robots examine and disable unexploded bombs, landmines, and munitions up close while their human operators remain at a safe distance.

Perhaps the most famous modern example of a law enforcement robot is Boston Dynamics' "Spot," a robot dog used in manufacturing and construction as well as by police. The company describes Spot as an "agile mobile robot," with four legs and the ability to navigate spaces and climb stairs. The NYPD acquired its own Spot, dubbed "Digidog," in 2020, but terminated its lease of the robot in 2021 after it became the target of opposition from activists during the "defund the police" movement who claimed Digidog was a representation of overfunded police departments and over-policing in minority communities.

In that time, the NYPD used Digidog six times, including during multiple hostage situations. In February 2021, Digidog was sent into a building in the Bronx to investigate a hostage situation. In October 2020, it was sent into a basement in Brooklyn where witnesses of a shooting said the gunman was hiding. It also delivered food to hostages in a home invasion in Queens.

Back Office/Front Office

At the end of the day, law enforcement agencies are customer service organizations, with many of the same challenges as other government agencies. Through this lens, too, technology provides law enforcement with opportunities to both improve the customer experience and citizen engagement (front office), as well as streamline case management and internal operations (back office).

Case management software—broadly defined as the digital tools that allow an organization to manage its cases—can be transformative for certain administrative-intensive activities in law enforcement, such as chain of custody, which refers to the chronological "paper trail" involving the collection and tracking of evidence. As it includes both electronic and physical evidence, chain of custody is vital in the criminal justice system. Case management software easily accommodates inventory management and digital filing, reducing human error across the various documentation handoffs to ensure evidence is appropriately tracked and chain of custody is maintained.

Modern case management software is frequently cloud-based, offering improved security for sensitive data and greater flexibility for staff and officers to access the software across multiple platforms (e.g., desktop, laptop, mobile, etc.). This is particularly helpful for organizations with field staff, but also improves resilience during emergency situations that disrupt normal operations, as was the case with the COVID-19 pandemic.

Additionally, most case management systems come "out of the box" with data analytics and visualization features that offer organizations insight into their caseload and workflow performance, as well as reporting functions for police departments to easily compile and share statistics or compliance requirements to other local, state, and federal agencies.

Some law enforcement agencies, such as the NYPD, have already rolled out or plan to roll out modern case management systems, but many others continue to rely on manual paper processes or outdated legacy software that is error-prone and inefficient.

On the customer side, mobile technology offers citizens a different access point for police services—one many people are familiar with in their day-to-day lives. A mobile app could allow citizens to easily report a crime on their own behalf or on behalf of others, including level of severity, type of crime, location, and other pertinent details.

Many law enforcement agencies receive an overwhelming number of calls from citizens, most of which are noncriminal or nonurgent. Mobile app messaging services—and even chatbots—offer customers a familiar, accessible method to interact with law enforcement, while also helping to reduce the substantial workload of police dispatch and telecommunicators.

Furthermore, case management software can be integrated with data feeds from citizen-facing mobile apps (as well as existing telephony infrastructure). The case management system generates tasks and initiates workflows based on the citizen request or crime reported, allowing law enforcement officers and staff to prioritize and organize caseloads more efficiently and quickly.

Lastly, the integration of front-office mobile apps and back-office case management technology contributes to fuller communication and improved relationships between citizens and law enforcement agencies. Citizens experience increased transparency through real-time case status and documentation updates fed from the case management software. Likewise, mobile app push notifications allow law enforcement agencies to disseminate critical information to particular areas or communities, such as all-points bulletins and "be on the lookouts" that would be worth sharing with the public about fugitives, missing persons, active shooters, or terrorists—similar to how police issue Amber alerts for missing or abducted children.

Improving Officer Training

Police departments across the country have implemented VR tools to optimize officer training. Police departments have continuously struggled with undertraining, particularly with nonlethal equipment such as tasers. For example, according to a 2010 study funded by the National Institute of Justice (NIJ), police officers receive an average of eight hours of taser training, with fewer than a quarter of law enforcement agencies exceeding the minimum training standards required or recommended by manufacturers. This lack of training is largely the result of financial, logistical, and knowledge issues, as police departments often do not see training as a priority in terms of funding, which means it is often underfunded. Additionally, training usually requires access to an appropriate venue to conduct these simulations and the presence of a knowledgeable trainer on-site. While a large, urban police department may accommodate these conditions, smaller departments in rural areas often struggle to do so.

The use of VR in officer training allows for a portable, more cost-effective option for police departments, as training can be done anywhere using a VR headset, requiring only the presence of a trained evaluator. Current training offerings allow officers to train with on-demand content online and even use exact, weight-accurate replicas of the actual tools. The immersive content and accurate replicas allow officers to train their muscle memory to make last-second decisions in a high-stress environment in the real world. These online, portable, and on-demand tools allow officers to schedule training in downtime without the need for any special room accommodations and without having to wait for an equipment specialist to be present. This makes it cheaper, more accessible, and more effective than in-person training.

VR training has also shown tremendous promise in empathy and perspective-based training. This type of training could help aid police departments' training in various fields, such as interactions with hard-of-hearing individuals, mental health crisis responses, and racial-sensitivity training. Immersive learning has resulted in a higher empathic response in trainees, allowing them to simulate scenarios that depict the difficulties these communities endure. In these simulations, police officers go through the experience of interacting with the police from the civilian's perspective. For example, in the case of hard-of-hearing simulations, the audio in the simulation is muffled to accurately reflect the difficulties these individuals experience during these scenarios. In cases of domestic violence training, the officer embodies a domestic violence victim trying to interact with the police while in a state of shock, reflected by visual and auditive cues such as a ringing sound.

Exposing police officers to the difficulties these individuals face in their day to day believably and realistically using immersive technology allows officers to understand the particular challenges and experiences these individuals face. Having a better understanding of these challenges might provide police officers with better tools to respond to situations involving members of these communities.

Maintaining Public Oversight and Accountability

There are a number of technologies used to increase police accountability, including cameras worn on police uniforms. These body-worn cameras document officers' actions and serve additional purposes on top of increasing accountability, such as documenting crimes, arrests, accidents, and other incidents and providing video evidence for investigation and prosecution.

The NYPD has the largest body-worn camera program in the United States, with 24,000 officers equipped with these cameras in a three-phased rollout that started in 2017 and concluded in 2019. The purpose of the cameras is to provide an "objective record" of police encounters, and officers are required to record certain events, such as arrests, uses of force, and searches. The NYPD retains video recordings for 18 months.

BJS published a report in 2018 on law enforcement's use of body-worn cameras in the United States. The report finds that by 2016, 47 percent of law enforcement agencies had acquired body-worn cameras; that number increased to 80 percent for large law enforcement agencies. BJS's cost-benefit analysis of body-worn cameras indicates that their benefits to society outweigh the financial costs associated with their use. According to NIJ's CrimeSolutions program, which rates criminal justice practices to evaluate what works, out of seven body-worn camera programs, five had statistically significant benefits, though none had statistically significant benefits in all categories, including use of force, citizen complaints, citizen injury, officer injury, citizen resistance, officer-initiated contact, citations, and arrests. The evidence on their use for other objectives thus far has shown mixed results. A 2019 meta-analysis of 70 studies of body-worn cameras published by researchers from George Mason University finds that body-worn cameras do not have consistent, statistically significant effects on officer behavior. Some studies show a decrease in uses of force, but other studies show no difference in uses of force between officers wearing cameras and officers not wearing cameras.

THE CRITICISMS

Each of the technologies law enforcement can use has potential benefits for keeping the public safe and bringing criminals to justice. However, many also have potential drawbacks, especially if deployed without appropriate limits and rules. These potential drawbacks have given rise to attacks on the technology from privacy and civil justice advocates and other stakeholders over the potential for police surveillance, as well as legitimate concerns over misuse or abuse of police tech, bias, lack of transparency, cybersecurity, and overall effectiveness.

Some of these concerns are based on real-life examples of misconduct or harm. Others are based more on "slippery slope" arguments and anti-technology sentiment, ignoring the myriad benefits of police technology, if utilized correctly.

Every technology has pros and cons, and when it comes to police technology, the key for maximizing the pros and minimizing the cons will be finding ways to address the top concerns associated with the technologies at law enforcement's disposal through rules and best practices for their procurement and use.

It is important to note that many civil liberties groups that prioritize individual rights over public safety oppose such increases in police technology. Others believe that the U.S. criminal justice system is an inherently racist system, and any increase in police capabilities will lead to the further oppression of racial minorities. Therefore, it is futile to attempt to find a compromise with groups that fundamentally oppose any increase in the technological capabilities of law enforcement.

Surveillance Concerns

One of the most common arguments against police's use of technology is a concern that the use of new and emerging technologies amounts to a form of surveillance. Critics express concern over the erosion of privacy post-9/11 and draw connections to both China's use of mass surveillance to control its population and science fiction dystopias such as the one depicted in *Minority Report*.85 These critics postulate a world in which Americans would have no privacy in public or potentially even private spaces and law enforcement agencies would track their movements and activities and trample on their constitutional rights.

Surveillance concerns are at the heart of opponents' arguments against ALPR, gunshot detection, facial recognition, geofencing, and drones. These opponents point out that police could use facial recognition and ALPR to track individuals' movements. Because gunshot detection sensors are constantly recording audio, critics are concerned that police could use the sensors for general audio surveillance. Finally, overly broad geofence warrants could mean that "anyone whose commute takes them by the scene of a crime might suddenly become vulnerable to suspicion, surveillance, and harassment by police," according to the Electronic Frontier Foundation (EFF).

There are legitimate concerns attached to law enforcement's use of technologies such as facial recognition, including concerns over how and how long police retain facial recognition data. But these concerns can be addressed through policy, such as setting data retention policies for biometric data. And there are also many benefits attached to these technologies. Surveys show that the majority of Americans support beneficial uses of facial recognition, including by law enforcement.

Banning law enforcement's use of new technologies is not the answer, and lawmakers should not fall for the opposition's arguments. If lawmakers can instead create rules that would limit the risks involved, law enforcement could still get the benefits of these technologies without violating valued civil liberties.

In the case of geofencing, future court cases will likely determine whether law enforcement's current broad use of geofence search warrants is permissible under the Fourth Amendment and potentially establish more concrete guidelines. Notably, in 2022, a U.S. District Judge in Richmond, Virginia, denied a geofence warrant and raised concerns over its constitutionality with police having first established probable cause (as law enforcement must do for all other types of warrants). State and local governments may regulate the use of certain other technologies, as a number of cities have done by banning facial recognition.

Singling out specific risks attached to technologies is legitimate—and there should be rules in place to mitigate those risks. But arguments that rely on hypothetical risks, especially sensational claims that law enforcement's use of certain technologies will "end privacy," leading to bans that will cut law enforcement and the public off from the benefits of technology. In fact, that is the reason certain privacy groups make these claims.

These types of extreme claims are far too common. According to Privacy International, "[T]he radical introduction of [facial recognition technology] will inevitably result in the normalization of surveillance across all societal levels." The American Civil Liberties Union (ACLU) claims, "Automatic license plate readers have the potential to create permanent records of virtually everywhere any of us has driven." Finally, the Electronic Privacy Information Center has argued, "Surveillance from the skies threatens to end privacy in public." It would be more beneficial for civil liberties and public safety if these groups focused their efforts on helping craft appropriate rules that allow widespread use of police technologies with appropriate safeguards.

In addition to fears of broad, widespread surveillance, critics also express concern over the potential for more-targeted surveillance, such as surveillance of protestors, journalists, minority communities, or critics of the police or the government. There are many examples of these types of abuses in nondemocratic countries. However, the United States has strong political rights and civil liberties, guaranteeing Americans free press and the freedom to protest and criticize the government that stand in the way of the United States becoming like China. To the extent law enforcement engages in activities that violate Americans' rights, the practice should be subject to legislative oversight and judicial review so that these practices do not continue.

Ultimately, the fear that police tech will lead the United States down the path toward dystopia is a slippery-slope argument based more on worst-case scenarios than facts. If critics believe that the only thing standing between democracy in the

United States and a totalitarian surveillance state is technology, that indicates a problem with society, not with technology. The U.S. court system should and will continue to uphold Americans' constitutional rights regardless of the technology law enforcement uses.

Misuse and Abuse of Tech

A related concern is individual law enforcement officers or entire police departments might misuse or abuse the technology at their disposal, either intentionally (e.g., an officer using police tech to stalk a domestic partner) or unintentionally (e.g., an agency failing to provide its officers with proper training, resulting in misuse). But this is true for any technology, including guns, vehicles, and cameras.

Unlike many surveillance concerns, concerns over potential misuse or abuse of police tech are not merely hypothetical. There is a history of individual police officers violating policy or even the law, and sometimes using police resources to do so. The Associated Press found that officers from state law enforcement agencies and major police departments were fired, suspended, or resigned at least 325 times between 2013 and 2015 for misusing confidential databases. An additional 250 instances of abuse resulted in reprimands, counseling, or other discipline.

Motivated by personal reasons and acting outside their police duties, officers can dig up information on a variety of individuals, such as current or former romantic partners, romantic interests, or journalists who publish negative stories about the officers or their departments. For example, in Massachusetts, an officer who worked for the Lanesborough Police Department was fired in 2021 for using a police database to stalk and harass women.

In the same way officers sometimes misuse or abuse police databases, they could also misuse or abuse other police technology, some of which may collect potentially sensitive personal information about individuals.

Officers may also unintentionally misuse technology if they have not received adequate training on how to use police tech. For example, Washington County police ran police sketches, rather than photos, through Amazon's facial recognition software Rekognition, which is not an appropriate use of the technology and would certainly increase error rates and false positives. Washington County's use of police sketches was only an experiment, but actual use of facial recognition in this way has resulted in false arrests, though it has also resulted in legitimate arrests.

This is not the only example of police misusing facial recognition. A report published by Georgetown Law's Center on Privacy and Technology in 2019 finds that at least half a dozen police departments in the United States permitted officers to run facial recognition searches on police sketches. It also shows examples of police using celebrity look-alikes to run facial recognition searches and editing photos of suspects in ways that could change the results of a facial recognition search, such as replacing an open mouth with a closed mouth or closed eyes with open eyes.

These and other examples of misuse or abuse of police tech and police databases demonstrate that the concern over potential misuse and abuse is legitimate. The potential for misuse or abuse necessitates oversight, over both individual officers' actions and police departments as a whole to ensure that officers receive adequate training and are not using police tech for their own personal benefit outside the line of duty.

Bias

Another popular argument against police tech is a concern that either the technology itself or law enforcements' use of it will result in increased bias, potentially exacerbating existing problems of racial profiling and over-policing of minority communities. Critics frequently cite this argument when it comes to technologies powered by AI or machine learning, claiming that the algorithms that power certain law enforcement technologies are likely to be biased against certain racial, ethnic, or other minority groups.

Ideally, an AI system would be 100 percent accurate and provide purely objective results. But humans create and test AI systems, and thus there is always the possibility of human error and human bias. A significant potential source of bias in an AI system is the data it is trained on. Biased data has a much higher risk of producing biased results. Another potential source of bias comes when humans interpret—or potentially misinterpret—an algorithm's outputs.

In 2018, the ACLU used Amazon's facial recognition software, Rekognition—a technology some police departments also use—to compare photos of members of Congress against a database of mugshots. The ACLU claimed Rekognition made 28 false matches, a disproportionate number of which were for people of color.106 However, when the ACLU ran this test, it used a confidence threshold of 80 percent. Amazon recommends using a 99 percent threshold. Rather than proving that modern facial recognition technology is inherently biased, the ACLU's test proves that facial recognition technology is more likely to give biased results if used incorrectly.

AI bias isn't only a concern in police tech. Bias in AI systems is a topic of discussion, research, and debate across all AI applications: in healthcare, hiring, housing, education, and more. Notably, the concern about bias in facial recognition has resulted in multiple cities banning government use of facial recognition. Indeed, many of the organizations that criticize law enforcement's use of facial recognition technology, such as the ACLU and EFF, support bans.

In police tech, the concern over AI bias is heightened due to existing racial bias in the U.S. criminal justice system. Studies show that Black people are more likely to be arrested for drug violations than white people despite comparable drug use rates; Black and Hispanic drivers are more likely to have their cars searched; Black drivers are more likely to be arrested during a traffic stop; and Black men are more than twice as likely than white men to be killed by police. And Black and Hispanic people are more likely to receive heavier sentences for similar crimes.

Bias in police tech is a legitimate concern, but not an unsolvable one. Depending on the data an AI or machine learning algorithm is trained on, the quality of the algorithm itself, and the way it's used, AI has the potential to either exacerbate or reduce bias in policing. A report by the National Institute of Standards and Technology (NIST) assessing facial recognition algorithms reveals that the most accurate algorithms display "undetectable" bias and have low rates of false positives and false negatives.

These highly accurate, higher quality algorithms are significantly less biased than humans. It is the less accurate, lower quality algorithms that display significant bias and could lead to biased policing outcomes. Police departments should procure more accurate AI systems and avoid less accurate systems. This would lead to a decrease in biased policing by shifting some of the decision-making from biased humans to unbiased algorithms.

Over-Policing

A related concern to police tech exacerbating bias is police tech exacerbating the problem of over-policing. Over-policing refers to police maintaining an excessive presence, using excessive force, and responding aggressively to minor offenses in certain communities. In the United States, this problem primarily affects poor communities, especially poor communities of color.

For example, critics of gunshot detection argue that the technology may exacerbate over-policing of communities of color. In Chicago, police districts with ShotSpotter had a higher Black and Latino population, whereas districts without ShotSpotter had a relatively higher non-Hispanic white population. As a result, a disproportionate number of Chicago police dispatches related to ShotSpotter were in police districts with a higher Black and Latino population.

Critics of predictive policing make a similar argument. As EFF has pointed out, if police have historically concentrated their efforts on marginalized communities, then the historical data that predictive policing relies on will identify those areas as criminal hotspots and predict that more crime will occur there. Police will respond to the algorithm's predictions by concentrating resources in those communities, which will result in police responding to more crime in those areas, which will perpetuate the cycle.

Police tech can exacerbate over-policing in the same way it can exacerbate bias: through bad data. The predictions of an algorithm are only as good as the data the algorithm has. If a police department has been over-policing communities of color for decades, then the historical data from that police department will be biased toward predicting more crime in those communities. And if cities such as Chicago only use ShotSpotter in police districts with higher Black and Latino populations, then more police will be dispatched to those districts. In other words, over-policing leads to more over-policing.

However, it is also important to consider the need for more police resources in areas with more crime, especially violent crime. In addition to problems of over-policing, many poor communities also face problems of under-policing: lack of adequate police presence or police response to violent crime impacting members of the community. This indicates that a significant part of the problem of over-policing is not simply that there is too large of a police presence in certain communities, but that police focus a disproportionate amount of their energy and resources on responding to minor infractions and perhaps not enough energy and resources on major crime. This is not a problem of police's use of technology, but rather of police training and priorities.

Over-policing is a legitimate concern, but the solution isn't for police to stop using data-driven technologies, but rather take a closer look at how they use data. For example, a police department that has reoriented its strategy away from aggressively pursuing low-level offenses may decide not to use data about certain misdemeanors and instead focus on using data about violent crime.

Lack of Transparency

A concern that touches on every aspect of law enforcement's use of technology is a lack of transparency. Without transparency requirements, individuals would have no way of knowing how police departments are using technology and what they are doing with the data they collect. This makes holding law enforcement accountable for potential abuse or misuse of technology far more difficult, and degrades public trust in law enforcement institutions. Data-driven technologies, which require police to collect data from the public in order to gain useful insights, are of particular interest to critics of police tech. Examples include facial recognition, predictive policing, gunshot detection, and automated license plate recognition. All these technologies collect some form of data from the public, which may include sensitive personal data (e.g., face scans, in the case of facial recognition, or location data, in the case of ALPR) or more generalized data (e.g., historic crime crates in an area, in the case of predictive policing).

Critics of police tech aren't the only people concerned about a lack of transparency. Transparency concerns have been a major theme in the wider backlash against technology—or "techlash"—that has particularly targeted large tech companies. For example, AI systems, such as those used to moderate content on social media, are often compared to a "black box" because users and researchers have little to no insight into how these algorithms make decisions (although there is also often little insight into how human moderators make decisions). On social media, the worst that can happen to an individual is their account gets banned. But when it comes to law enforcement's use of technology, misuse or abuse could lead to wrongful imprisonment or even death. This makes transparency in law enforcement even more important than in other spheres.

Concerns over a lack of transparency in law enforcement's use of technology are legitimate. Transparency is necessary to ensure adequate public oversight over law enforcement's activities. However, some concerns over police tech have been seemingly counterproductive when it comes to transparency and accountability. For example, digital and civil rights groups have opposed police's use of body-worn cameras out of concern police will use them as a surveillance tool, despite body-worn cameras being an important oversight tool for police behavior.

There are a number of areas where greater transparency is needed. When it comes to body-worn cameras, civilians should know when they're being recorded, and the public should have access to certain body-worn camera footage, such as footage depicting police's use of force. When using technologies that collect data on individuals, departments should share information on what data they collect, why they collect it, how it is stored, and how long it is stored. Departments should also continue to share information on their police tech budgets so taxpayers know where their money is being allocated.

Cybersecurity Concerns

A perpetual concern for any organization's use of technology is bad actors could hack the technology and access, alter, or erase important data. This concern is even more relevant for organizations that collect a lot of sensitive information. For law enforcement, this may include suspects', victims', or witnesses' personal information, evidence against a suspect, or information about an ongoing case.

Cybersecurity should always be top of mind for any organization that uses Internet-connected technology. While robust cybersecurity programs come with costs, these up-front costs are worth it to avoid suffering a significant data breach. According to a 2022 IBM report, the average public sector data breach costs over $2 million. On top of that, organizations often suffer reputational damage after a significant data breach, and individuals whose data has been compromised suffer as well.

In an extreme example of the potential risks of a law enforcement data breach, the Shanghai National Police was the victim of an alleged leak containing police records—including names, addresses, national ID numbers, phone numbers, ages, birthplaces, and incident reports—of one billion Chinese citizens. The data was left unsecured for over a year via a backdoor link that didn't even require a password, and officials didn't become aware of the leak until an anonymous user offered the data for sale in a hacker forum in June 2022. Just two months later, another Chinese government database leaked, this one containing over 800 million records, including photos of faces and license plates.

Closer to home, the Metropolitan Police Department of Washington, D.C., suffered a data breach in 2021, which experts claimed to be the worst known ransomware attack on a U.S. police department. The data breach was the result of a ransomware attack by a Russian-speaking cybercrime syndicate; when D.C. police refused to pay the ransom, the gang released thousands of sensitive documents, including disciplinary files and intelligence reports.

One approach the federal government has taken to cybersecurity, specifically regarding drones, is country-of-origin restrictions. DOJ's Office of Justice Programs (OJP) revised its drone purchasing policy in 2020 to prohibit the use of OJP funds to purchase drones manufactured by certain foreign companies. The Defense and Interior Departments have similar policies that incentivize the procurement and use of U.S.-manufactured drones.

While intended to address the threat of foreign security risks, country-of-origin requirements are a misguided solution. The security of drones—or any other technology—does not depend on where they were manufactured but rather the security controls in place.

Still, cybersecurity is a legitimate concern, as many police technologies collect data that could put officers' or civilians' privacy at risk or even hinder an investigation if it were leaked or tampered with. The location data collected by ALPR and GIS, traditional biometrics such as DNA and fingerprints, suspects' personal phone data obtained via a geofence warrant, body-worn camera footage depicting officers and civilians, and all the other forms of data law enforcement may collect to more effectively keep people safe would be dangerous in the wrong hands.

Effectiveness

The final common argument against law enforcement's use of technology is that, in practice, it may not work as intended and even be less effective than existing methods. Not only would a lack of effectiveness potentially impact law enforcement's ability to solve crimes, it would also be a waste of taxpayer money during a time when many American police departments have already drawn criticism for being overfunded or funds being improperly allocated. This is also often an argument opponents of the technology make as a smokescreen for their real motivation: less-effective policing.

Many police departments have experimented with new and emerging technologies in recent decades and will continue to do so. Sometimes a new technology completely changes the way police do their jobs, as was the case with DNA profiling. Sometimes a new technology has a less revolutionary but nonetheless positive impact, making certain processes safer or more efficient or otherwise aiding officers in doing their jobs. Finally, sometimes police departments adopt a certain technology or implement new technology in a certain way that either fails to improve on existing methods or does not yield enough of a benefit to justify the cost of the technology.

To some extent, this is an unavoidable part of the process of experimenting with new technology. Police departments need to experiment with new technology in order to discover what is effective and determine how to use it in the most effective way. But the concern that certain technologies may be ineffective or a waste of taxpayer money is still a legitimate one, and there have been numerous examples of police departments discontinuing their use of certain technologies when they don't prove effective.

Both the LAPD and the Chicago Police Department ended predictive policing programs due to concerns regarding their effectiveness. In 2019, the LAPD's inspector general released an independent audit on two of the LAPD's predictive policing programs, LASER and PredPol, as well as a third "data-driven policing" program, ELUCD. LAPD deployed LASER in 2011 to identify crime hotspots and reduce violent crime, and deployed PredPol the same year to identify when and where vehicle-related crimes were likely to occur.

While the inspector general's audit did not prove that either of the LAPD's predictive policing programs were ineffective at reducing crime, it also didn't prove that they were effective, and the LAPD discontinued LASER to reassess the program's data. It later discontinued PredPol in 2020 due to budget constraints from the COVID-19 pandemic, although some departments had already stopped using the technology before that due to concerns over its effectiveness.

Meanwhile, the Chicago Police Department discontinued its program, the Crime and Victimization Risk Model (previously known as the Strategic Subject List) in 2020 after the RAND Corporation released a report finding that the program was ineffective at reducing homicides. The program was established in 2012 and aimed to create a list of people most likely to commit or be victimized by a shooting.

It is important to note that the LAPD and Chicago Police Department ending their predictive policing programs also came in the midst of fierce opposition to predictive policing by activist groups, which likely factored into both departments' decisions to stop using predictive policing.

Police departments may choose to discontinue police tech programs for a number of reasons. Budgets, priorities, and public opinion may change and influence what technology a given department uses. One police department may use a certain technology with great success while another department may be dissatisfied with its results from using that technology. Alternatively, a police department may discontinue its use of a certain technology over effectiveness concerns only to later discover how to get the most out of that technology and begin using it again.

For this reason, police departments need to be able to maintain some flexibility over the technologies they use and how they use them. Bans and other overly restrictive regulations fail to provide that flexibility. Rules that govern the use of technology, on the other hand, allow police departments to decide which technologies suit their needs and fit their budgets, while also safeguarding against known risks. Experimentation is a crucial part of the process of adopting new technology. Police tech will continue to improve in its capabilities over time, and police departments' use of police tech will become more effective as they experiment and learn what strategies work better than others.

Imagining the Future of Police Tech

Even the most well-equipped police departments are only scratching the surface of possibilities when it comes to deploying police tech. As technology continues to improve and costs continue to decline—and especially if the federal government takes the lead in deploying police tech and providing funding for state and local law enforcement—more police departments will take advantage of new and emerging technologies for a variety of applications that will make police more efficient and effective and keep officers and civilians safe.

- **Preventing Crime:** As AI becomes more sophisticated, predictive policing software will become more accurate and therefore even more useful to law enforcement as a crime prevention tool. With AI predicting where different types of crimes are likely to occur, police departments could more efficiently allocate their resources and decrease response times.
- **Responding to Crime:** With improvements in natural language processing, which allows AI to understand and replicate human language, automated dispatchers could answer 911 calls, thereby decreasing the burden on human 911 operators. Gunshot detection and other sensors will alert police to crime as soon as a disturbance takes place, and officers will receive these alerts via apps on their smart devices that will also tell them the location of their colleagues so the officers closest to the scene of the disturbance can respond.
- **Solving Crime:** The more cameras that exist in the world—cell phone cameras, security cameras in or outside homes and private businesses, and city-owned cameras in public spaces—the more likely a crime will be caught on camera. With facial recognition, police will be able to more easily identify suspects, victims, and witnesses from photos or videos, and advanced photo editing and reconstruction capabilities could aid in that process.
- **Keeping Officers Safe:** Police departments will procure robots to take over dangerous tasks and drones to enter dangerous situations ahead of human officers. In an active shooting scenario, police could send

a drone to give them an aerial view of the scene before engaging. In a hostage scenario, police could send a robot to provide food and supplies to hostages while hostage negotiators work to resolve the situation. In a scenario wherein police do not know if a suspect is armed and dangerous, they could send in a drone or robot first to assess the level of risk and better prepare officers before they engage.

- **Back Office/Front Office:** In the future, case management will be a fully digital process, streamlining back-office processes so officers spend less time filling out paperwork and more time out in the streets solving crime. Office automation will take even more work off human officers' hands and remove opportunities for human error. Fully digital systems not only save time but also allow for greater cooperation, which is key in law enforcement, as cases sometimes require collaboration between multiple police departments or levels of government.
- **Improving Officer Training:** More officer training will take place in AR and VR environments, allowing officers to train under realistic but safe conditions. Instead of gaining their first experience with dangerous or risky situations on the job, officers could first experience simulations of those situations—such as an active shooter or hostage situation—in a controlled environment. Simulations of police interactions from a civilian perspective could also help officers better understand how to interact with victims, suspects, and witnesses.
- **Maintaining Public Oversight and Accountability:** Cameras will not only be important in identifying persons of interest and creating a trail of evidence, they will also continue to serve as an important tool for public oversight. Officers required to use body-worn cameras will have an additional incentive to follow proper protocol, and evidence from body-worn cameras can hold officers accountable if they break the rules or use unnecessary force. Audit trails in digital systems will help hold officers accountable for how they use new technologies.

TECHNOLOGY ACQUISITION

Technology use among law enforcement can spark animated debates that ultimately relate to the role and power of the police in contemporary society. For example, technology such as LPRs has generated much debate about privacy, whereas BWCs have been heralded as a method of improving police–community relationships by promoting more civil interactions. The present study sought to better understand fundamental questions about the prevalence of various technologies in the nation's police departments, the key factors that encourage their acquisition, processes of implementation, and the perceived impact of technology on policing activities.

Generally speaking, the processes by which technology is acquired within LEAs are not well understood. However, the existing literature on organizational choice provides a useful starting point and an overarching theoretical framework because it describes four perspectives of understanding how organizations identify and achieve agency goals. The rational perspective suggests that organizations behave rationally by identifying official goals, designing strategies to accomplish those goals, and then implementing technology that supports and facilitates the strategies that they have designed. It is well understood, though, that rationality is limited; goals can be fuzzy, knowledge about the best way to accomplish them is often incomplete, and organizations are constrained by resources and human limitations. The contingency perspective emphasizes that each organization operates in a particular environment and its choices may depend on external factors and events. The institutional perspective argues that organizations have their own interests as well, including survival, status and prestige, maximizing resources, and protection from threats. One additional perspective depicts organizations more as anarchies than as welloiled machines, and notes that they often identify solutions (strategies, technology) before they have a specific problem demanding to be solved. Thus, organizational options (such as use of technology) are frequently just waiting for an opportunity to be adopted.

Another commonly invoked theoretical perspective for understanding technology acquisition within organizations is the diffusion of innovation model, which classifies adopters of technology as innovators, early adopters, early majority, late majority, and laggards. Although there is some intuitive appeal to this taxonomy, the diffusion-ofinnovation model is limited in its ability to accurately describe how technologies are acquired by police departments. For example, the bespoke categories are not mutually exclusive in practice. Police agencies do not easily fit into one subgroup when considering a specific type of technology, let alone across different types of technology. An agency could be considered both an early adopter and a laggard when it comes to GIS technology if mapping is done at an aggregate level but without incident-based geocoding. In addition, the same agency may be a clear laggard in regard to LPR usage, but may be an innovator when it comes to the use of BWCs. Thus, although the diffusion of innovation model may be a useful starting point, a more comprehensive conceptual framework is needed to define the process of technology acquisition in law enforcement.

Additional work is also needed to understand the key factors that influence agencies' decisions to acquire specific forms of technology. Although it would be logical to assume that departments make decisions regarding what technology to acquire based on what has been shown to be effective for achieving key policing goals (e.g., enhanced efficiency, higher arrest rates, fewer crimes), there is reason to believe this is not necessarily the case. Some studies suggest that LEAs select, implement, and integrate technology independent of existing empirical evidence or support for how these systems affect departmental operations, strategic decisions, or crime outcomes. In essence, it is argued that law enforcement adopts technology before adequately evaluating the potential impact. Further research is needed to understand the accuracy of this description, and the extent to which it applies to all or only select types of technological advancements.

Moreover, much remains to be known about agency characteristics and their potential impact on the acquisition of particular forms of technology. There is some evidence to suggest that the size of an agency and its geographic location can influence its likeliness of adopting select types of technology, although the mechanisms that explain why this is the case are not entirely understood. Some believe that organizational size is an indicator of other characteristics that would facilitate the adoption of new technologies. For instance, agencies that tend to be larger could reasonably be expected to have more slack resources with which to invest in new technologies. Additionally, larger organizations may have a greater diversity of job functions, indicated in prior research as a higher degree of specialization within the larger organization, that would presumably lead to more adoption, as specialized units (i.e. crime analysis units, investigations, auto theft units, etc.) require certain technologies to perform their function at the highest level. Associations between higher numbers of employees in technical positions and greater capabilities in computerization and information technology (IT) have also been identified. The idea that agencies with larger numbers of specialized units are positively associated with technological innovations is consistent with prior findings in innovation research.

The adoption of technology can be understood as a complex interaction between several factors, including characteristics of the technology, organizational culture, and features of the larger social-structural environment. Using data from multiple iterations of the Law Enforcement Management and Administrative Statistics (LEMAS), Schuck examined key factors that could explain why agencies adopt dash and mobile cameras, including characteristics of the technology (i.e., design, functionality, and congruency with agency goals), organizational traits (i.e., hierarchical structure, formalization, spatial differentiation), characteristics of the community (i.e., income and demographic composition), and features of the political environment in which the agency operates. Findings indicated that while the strongest predictor of mobile camera adoption in large agencies was the level of crime in the community, organizational size and spatial differentiation (sprawl) were positively associated with mobile camera adoption in smaller and medium-sized agencies. Additionally, agencies that were situated in communities with higher levels of poverty, inequality, and crime operated more in-car cameras.

Despite discussions within the criminal justice arena about policing models and their impact on law enforcement activities, it indicated that very little research has been conducted on associations between different views about common policing strategies and the acquisition or perceived impact of technology. There is reason to believe that associations exist between an agency's devotion to a particular policing model (e.g., community or problem oriented) and the types of technology they use and perceive to be effective for achieving certain outcomes. Namely, technology could make a new strategy possible, provide a new tool for an existing strategy, or allow for a combination of both scenarios. For instance, the 9-1-1 system has played a critical role in shaping and reinforcing reactive policing, whereas a different set of technological advancements has been associated with supporting community policing. In addition, it seems that offender-targeting, hot-spot, and other policing models would be largely impossible without recent technological advances that have allowed police to better collect, manage, and analyze data, including records management systems, GIS, and predictive analytics software.

Impact of Technology

Technological advances in recent years have changed the nature of policing so significantly that many methods and tools from just a decade ago have become antiquated and incompatible with current technology. Some of these advances include location-monitoring devices for the tracking of high-rate offenders, predictive analytics and crime mapping software for the deployment of officers into locations that cause or are likely to cause crime, crime scene technology that enhances the collection and processing of evidence, and interoperable Web-based and other communication devices that facilitate connections between police and the communities they serve. The technological improvements have increased police capabilities, but it is not certain that they have enabled law enforcement to do their jobs more effectively. For example, despite dramatic advances in DNA technology and computer databases for handling forensic data, clearance rates for violent and property crime have remained relatively stable since the mid-1990s.

In addition, improved efficiency does not always translate to effectiveness. Historically, police use of radios, 9-1-1 systems, computer-aided dispatch, and GIS has provided a way to deploy officers to the scenes of crimes quicker and have been hypothesized to clear more cases at the scene through arrest. Yet, the idea that 9-1-1 systems result in more arrests has been contradicted by empirical research. For example, a study indicated that reducing response times does not impact the number of arrests, primarily because there are often delays in the reporting of crimes. Furthermore, the burden of answering 9-1-1 calls, roughly half or more of which are not urgent but require rapid response times, puts pressure on limited resources and tends to leave police with less time to engage in proactive or community-oriented policing.

Prevalence, Determinants, Process, and Impact

The remainder of the literature review is focused on six types of technology that were prioritized in both the nationally representative survey and site visits. These are crime mapping, social media, data mining, car cameras, LPRs, and BWCs. For each technology, we provide an overview of available literature or research that provides a background for what is known relative to our key research questions.

Crime Mapping

Computerized crime mapping software via GIS is used by police agencies to map, visualize, and analyze quality of life complaints, crime patterns over space and time, and paths to crime displaying distances between events within an incident. Using GIS, departments can identify clusters of crime incidents or types (i.e., hot spots and habitats), generate graphic displays of crime incidents for officers or the community, and identify other patterns of local crime activity that may ultimately help inform the allocation and deployment of officers into the field. In some cases, census demographics or land-use data are merged with GIS crime-incident data to better understand the contextual characteristics within which crime incidents are embedded.

Although little research has evaluated the effectiveness of computerized crime mapping across agencies or in experimental settings with pre- and postmeasurement of select outcomes (e.g., arrest clearances) within agencies, some research has demonstrated the effectiveness of specific reactive and proactive activities that depend heavily upon GIS techniques. For example, hot-spot policing, a largely reactive strategy, can reduce the number of reported criminal incidents, calls-for-service, and instances of observed physical and social disorder, whereas risk terrain modeling can be useful in making future deployment decisions. The use of GIS in a reactive policing framework is fairly well documented in research compared with literature on GIS-informed proactive policing, which is still largely underway.

Considerable variation in the techniques used, sophistication of methods, and frequency of use makes it difficult to establish estimates of the number of LEAs that use GIS or other forms of computerized crime mapping technology. Whereas some agencies use crime mapping primarily to generate visual displays of local crimes, others conduct more complex modes of spatial analysis to understand the relationship between crime types or incidents and select features of the physical or social environment. Spatial analysis techniques can also vary widely depending on whether an agency is adopting a proactive rather than reactive geographic policing strategy. Likewise, the degree of penetration varies across agencies: In some departments, crime analysts have sole responsibility for crime-mapping tasks, whereas in others, it is available to personnel throughout the chain of command, often via intranet-based dashboards.

Nonetheless, a handful of studies have attempted to identify the prevalence of crime mapping in U.S. police departments. In 1995, the International Association of Chiefs of Police (IACP) conducted a poll of 280 police agencies, of which 30% reported using crimemapping software on a regular basis. However, participating agencies represented many of the more-active users of computer technology in the U.S. at that time and, therefore, the estimate is likely inflated compared with what it would have been for a nationally representative sample. A survey of 2,004 agencies conducted by the National Institute of Justice's Crime Mapping Research Center indicated that about 13% had used computerized crime-mapping software to produce automated pin maps and to map various types of law enforcement data (e.g., offense, calls-for-service, and vehicle recovery data). Of those that had not used it, 20% planned to purchase it within the next year. A survey administered in 2003 by the Bureau of Justice Statistics indicated that nearly 18% of U.S. LEAs used computers for crime mapping, an increase of 3.5% compared with results from the same survey administered 3 years before.

Social Media

As noted by Social Media the Internet and Law Enforcement (SMILE), social media use in law enforcement is in the very early stages. Thus, although there is a lot of national discourse about its use in law enforcement, there have been few rigorous or systematic studies that have examined prevalence and determinants of use, challenges of implementation, or impact of social media on policing or community outcomes. A 2014 survey by the IACP is one of few attempts to establish the extent to which the nation's LEAs use social media in any capacity. Results from a sample of 600 agencies indicated that 96% of departments use social media, although it is not clear whether their sample was representative of U.S. police agencies more generally. Among the 4% of agencies who did not report using social media at the time of the survey, more than half were considering it as an option.

Much of the available literature, although mostly informal or journalistic, has suggested that social media has tremendous potential in modern-day law enforcement. Many have highlighted the importance of social media for building trusting relationships between police and the local community, because social media can establish a forum for open communication. With a vested interest in community outreach, departments can use social media to post crime prevention tips, community-related news, issues related to pedestrian and motorist safety, and information about weather or traffic-related emergencies. Likewise, citizens from the community also have the opportunity to communicate with the police via social media, which can deliver valuable feedback and raise the department's awareness of community perceptions of local law enforcement. Recent high-profile events have underscored the potential for police departments' use of social media to promote public safety in times of unrest, and the potential for active social media use to humanize the local police force by showing that officers are also members of the community they serve has also been voiced.

Notwithstanding widespread conjecture about how social media is used by law enforcement, there have been few attempts to address this issue systematically. A 2014 survey of law enforcement officials by LexisNexis investigated the extent to which police personnel use social media for various policing activities. About 34% of the sample reported that they used social media to notify the public of emergencies, crimes, and criminal suspects, and 29% solicited crime tips from the community. Another 30% used social media to promote positive relationships with the community, and about half of the sample monitored social media for criminal activity. The most commonly used social media Web sites were Facebook (93%), YouTube (67%), and Twitter (50%). There is some anecdotal evidence indicating that some agencies also use Pinterest to "pin" photos of stolen property or to spotlight individuals with a warrant out for their arrest, or Next-door to alert neighborhoods of a nearby robbery or break-in.

Similarly, little is known about the perceived value of social media for specific law enforcement activities. In a survey of agencies by the IACP in 2013, 80% of the sample reported that social media was a valuable investigative tool because it had helped them to solve crimes, and nearly three-quarters of the sample reported that using social media facilitated more cooperative relationships with the community. Similar estimates were found in the 2014 IACP survey. The 2014 survey by LexisNexis revealed that the majority of respondents (67%) perceived social-media monitoring to be an effective investigative tool and approach to anticipating future crimes, and 73% believed social media helped them to solve cases quicker.

Not much is known about the unique challenges associated with the implementation of social media within police departments. However, despite a lack of rigorous studies investigating these issues, there are several available resources online that make recommendations about how to successfully implement social media technology into the law enforcement business model. These recommendations include posting frequently, but only posting content that has real-world value; mitigating the limitations of individual platforms by using multiple types of social media; designating a team responsible for managing social media accounts; establishing metrics to measure the impact of various platforms; and becoming knowledgeable about available social media platforms and how to use them correctly. There has also been considerable discussion about to the need for formal social media policies that protect against potential legal risks associated with using the technology. The 2014 IACP survey of law enforcement social media use found that about 72% of agencies that use social media also have a formal policy about the use of the technology, and about 12% were crafting a policy.

Data Mining

Since the 9/11 terrorist attacks, federal and local LEAs in the United States have been under pressure to become more data driven in their daily operations. However, despite a generalized shift in policing philosophy toward better resource management and an emphasis on data-driven policing, police departments face the challenge of managing and using an ever-growing amount of data. Moreover, these data can take numerous forms; for example, they may derive from the agency's RMS, census databases, mobile resources (e.g., smartphones), automated LPRs, or social media.

Data mining technology was designed to address needs related to handling large quantities of data from diverse sources. Specialized mining software allows departments to analyze massive amounts of data in a fraction of the time it would take using manual methods and, thus, are speculated to save time and personnel-related resources. Crime analysts may use specialized data mining software to mine text data, visualize crime networks, identify possible suspects, or recognize crime patterns and characteristics associated with them to guide the deployment of officers. Crime data can also be merged with other forms of external data, such as traffic or weather information, and analyzed to identify complex relationships between multiple variables. Most software packages also allow for the creation of automated reports and dashboards, prediction maps, and crime trends.

Data mining is often discussed in tandem with predictive policing, a strategy based on the logic that future crimes can be better anticipated, responded to, or prevented using intelligence collected and analyzed from a variety of data sources. In one example, as a result of frequent random gunfire on New Year's Eve, the Richmond Police Department in Virginia examined data collected from previous years and was able to anticipate when and where future incidents might occur on New Year's Eve in 2003. Officers were strategically deployed based on the data analyzed and, as a result, the department witnessed a 47% decrease in random gunfire and a 246% increase in weapons seized, while at the same time saving $15,000 in personnel costs. The potential for data mining software to uncover underlying causes of crime trends and patterns that can then inform the allocation of police resources as a crime prevention strategy is also viewed as consistent with the basic premise of predictive policing. In Arlington, Texas, the police department studied residential burglary data to identify associated hot spots and compared these locations to areas with code violations. The analysis revealed a direct relationship between neighborhood levels of physical decay and the likelihood of residential burglaries. Based on this analysis, the department developed a Formula to identify what they termed "fragile neighborhoods" and worked with other city agencies to help prevent crime in them.

Car Cameras

Efforts to implement video recording systems in officer patrol cars date back to the 1960s; however, it was not until the early 2000s that dashboard-mounted cameras became prevalent. The diffusion of dash cameras throughout American law enforcement was a consequence of several historical factors that include increased attention on drinking and driving in the 1980s, the war on drugs, allegations of racial profiling against the police, and demands from within law enforcement for greater officer safety. Recognizing the potential for in-car cameras to document the circumstances of arrests or other officer–citizen encounters and to deter assaults against police officers, the Department of Justice's COPS initiated the In-Car Camera Incentive Program in the late 1990s to provide funding to state and highway patrol agencies to get and use in-car camera systems. The program dramatically increased the number of agencies with dash cameras in the next few years. Before disbursement of financial aid in 2000, only 11% of state and highway patrol agencies had in-car camera systems; by 2004, nearly three-quarters had such systems. Other studies have demonstrated that in-car cameras systems have also become common among local agencies.

In 2002, the IACP conducted a study of in-car camera systems and their use among the 47 state police agencies that had received COPS grant funding under the In-Car Camera Incentive Program. The study included a survey of agencies, on-site interviews, and a series of focus groups to inform process and impact evaluations of the technology. Results indicated that officers perceived numerous benefits of in-car camera systems, including increased agency accountability, improved community perceptions, and enhanced officerrelated behaviors (i.e., professionalism).

Footage retrieved from cameras was also perceived to facilitate criminal prosecutions in court and to provide a valuable resource for new recruit and in-service training. Interviews with patrol officers suggested that in-car cameras also augmented officer safety because the presence of a camera has the potential to de-escalate confrontational situations when citizens are informed of being recorded.

The 2002 IACP study also documented several challenges common to the use of in-car cameras. For instance, many agencies were described as narrow sighted in their implementation plan, designing systems that were incapable of accommodating significant demands related to storing, filing, and retrieving video evidence. Other agencies believed they had not spent enough time researching the technology and issues that should be considered when implementing in-car camera technology, such as different technology formats (e.g., analog or digital) and costs required for equipment maintenance. Respondents also reported several technical difficulties, such as poor quality and the restricted range of the cameras' audio transmitters. Some patrol officers believed they had not received adequate training for using the technology, and some worried that camera footage was being used by command staff as a way to monitor officer behavior and performance.

Although the IACP study offers considerable value for detailing the process, challenges, and perceived impact of in-car camera use, it is limited to state police and highway patrol agencies and, therefore, says little about municipal and county police departments or sheriff's offices that make up the majority of LEAs in the United States. In addition, because all agencies in their sample had received funding to implement in-car cameras, it does not attempt to unveil key factors that differentiate those agencies that do and do not use such systems.

License Plate Readers

Automatic LPRs are high-speed cameras paired with character recognition software that can read and document thousands of license plates per minute while also recording the date, time, and location of every scan. LPRs can be mobile (i.e., mounted on police cars) or stationary (i.e., mounted on structural objects such as overpasses), and information obtained can be compared with existing hotlists of license plates compiled by agencies and relevant matches can be used to send alerts to active officers on patrol. This technology has attracted controversy in recent years because license plate information collected from LPRs can be retained by law enforcement and even merged into regional information-sharing systems. Accordingly, the American Civil Liberties Union has raised concerns related to citizens' rights to privacy and the need for tighter regulations for LPR technology. Some states have moved to limit the use of LPR based on privacy concerns. For instance, in June 2015, Louisiana Governor Bobby Jindal vetoed legislation that would have allowed law enforcement to use LPRs to apprehend uninsured drivers.

A handful of studies have estimated the prevalence of LPRs within U.S. law enforcement, although there are pronounced differences in these assessments, which are likely due to sample differences. Data analyzed from the 2013 LEMAS survey suggest that about 16% of local police departments used LPRs in the past year. Other studies indicate that the prevalence among large agencies is closer to one-third and that many more departments plan to obtain the technology in the future.

Body-Worn Cameras

BWCs have received increased public attention in the wake of recent high-profile police incidents, such as those in Ferguson, Missouri; North Charleston, South Carolina; New York City; and Cincinnati, Ohio. Recent estimates suggest that about one-third of local police departments use BWCs, although these numbers are expected to increase substantially in the future. In December 2014, President Obama proposed reimbursing communities half the cost of purchasing cameras and storing data. However, it is important to note that there are mixed views from the field about the potential impact of BWCs on community relations.

A 2014 PERF study, conducted with support from the COPS Office, found that although police leaders who have deployed BWCs state that they have many benefits (e.g., documentation of evidence, preventing and resolving complaints brought by the public, and bolstering police accountability and transparency), others raise concerns about privacy and trust. Some have expressed concern that the constant use of BWCs may erode community relationships and hinder their community policing efforts. For example, witnesses and informants might be reluctant to pass information on to police officers if the interaction is being recorded, especially in high-crime areas where they may fear retaliation if the footage is released into the public.

Research into BWCs to date has focused on the impact on citizen complaints and on use of force. Both issues can severely undermine any community policing or problem-oriented policing strategy. In terms of the effectiveness of BWCs, the Rialto Police Department in California found that shifts on which BWCs were not deployed had more than twice as many use-of-force incidents than shifts that used them, and complaints against the police had decreased from 24 complaints filed during the 12 months before the trial to three during the trial. A 2013 study of the Mesa Police Department in Arizona found that camera users experienced decreases in both departmental complaints and use-of-force complaints. It also found that when policy shifted from making activation mandatory to a policy of officer discretion, there was a 42% decrease in the rate of use, with volunteer officers substantially more likely to use the BWC than officers assigned to the study. In a 2015 study in Arizona of the Phoenix Police Department's use of cameras, arrests increased by 17% among officers using BWCs compared with 9% in the comparison group. Complaints also dropped sharply among the BWC group, with a 23% reduction compared with a 10.6% increase in the comparison group and a 45.1% increase among officers in other precincts that were not part of the study.

REFERENCES

1. Webster, J. A. (1970). Police task and time study. *The Journal of Criminal Law, Criminology and Police Science, 61*(1), 94–100.
2. White, M. D., & Fradella, H. F. (2016). Stop and frisk: The use and abuse of a controversial policing tactic. New York University Press.
3. Wilson, J. (1968). Varieties of police behavior: The management of law and order in eight communities. Harvard University Press.
4. Wu, X., & Lum, C. (2017). Measuring the spatial and temporal patterns of police proactivity. Journal of Quantitative Criminology, 33(4), 915–934.
5. Wu, X., & Lum, C. (2020). The practice of proactive traffic stops. Policing: An International Journal, 43(2), 229–246.

6 CRIME PREVENTION AND COMMUNITY POLICING

INTRODUCTION

Community policing is generally defined as a law enforcement philosophy that allows officers to continuously operate in the same area in order to create a stronger bond with the citizens living and working in that area. This allows public safety officers to engage with local residents and prevent crime from happening instead of responding to incidents after they occur.

These are integral components of modern law enforcement strategies aimed at reducing crime and enhancing public safety. Crime prevention involves a proactive approach to deterring criminal activities before they occur, employing measures that address the root causes of crime and mitigate potential risks. It encompasses a range of strategies, including environmental design, social programs, and community engagement. By focusing on improving the socio-economic conditions, education, and employment opportunities within a community, crime prevention aims to create an environment less conducive to criminal behavior. This holistic approach recognizes that reducing crime requires more than just law enforcement but also involves addressing underlying social issues such as poverty, lack of education, and inadequate housing.

Community policing, on the other hand, is a philosophy and strategy of law enforcement that emphasizes building strong relationships between police officers and the communities they serve. It seeks to foster trust, cooperation, and mutual respect through regular, positive interactions and active engagement with community members. Community policing is based on the premise that police effectiveness is enhanced when officers are familiar with the community and its specific issues, allowing for tailored responses to local problems. This approach encourages officers to act as problem-solvers and facilitators rather than just enforcers of the law. By being visible and accessible, police officers can gather valuable information, identify potential problems early, and work collaboratively with residents to develop solutions. Both crime prevention and community policing underscore the importance of community involvement in ensuring public safety. Effective crime prevention strategies often involve partnerships between law enforcement agencies, local governments, businesses, schools, and community organizations. These partnerships enable a more coordinated and comprehensive approach to addressing crime and its causes. For instance, neighborhood watch programs, youth outreach initiatives, and crime prevention through environmental design (CPTED) are examples of collaborative efforts that can significantly impact crime reduction. By engaging community members in these efforts, a sense of shared responsibility and collective efficacy is fostered, empowering residents to take an active role in safeguarding their neighborhoods.

The integration of crime prevention and community policing also leads to more effective and sustainable outcomes. When police officers are viewed as allies and partners, community members are more likely to report crimes, cooperate in investigations, and participate in prevention programs. This collaborative dynamic not only helps in solving crimes but also in preventing them from occurring in the first place. Additionally, the trust and goodwill built through community policing can enhance the legitimacy of law enforcement agencies, leading to improved public confidence and reduced tensions between police and the communities they serve.

COMMUNITY POLICING

Community policing as a social construct conveys two components, community and policing. The policing component has received a great deal of attention, while the community component has not. Only recently has the idea of community reflected the expanded conceptualization of a "sense of community." Elements of a sense of community include membership, influence, reinforcement, and emotional connection. The development of a sense of community from the standpoint of facilitating informal social control should be the main goal of community policing. Crime prevention initiatives should identify conditions of the physical and social environment that facilitate criminal acts. Police agencies should recognize that a significant part of their mission is crime prevention and that a community orientation to crime prevention is desirable.

The growing trend within communities to participate in the fight against crime and disorder has paralleled a growing recognition by police that traditional crime-fighting tactics alone have a limited impact on controlling crime. Community policing is the synthesis of these two movements. The foundations of a successful community policing strategy are the close, mutually beneficial ties between police and community members. Community policing consists of two complementary core components, community partnership and problem solving. To develop community partnership, police must develop positive relationships with the community, must involve the community in the quest for better crime control and prevention, and must pool their resources with those of the community to address the most urgent concerns of community members. Problem solving is the process through which the specific concerns of communities are identified and through which the most appropriate remedies to abate these problems are found. Community policing does not imply that police are no longer in authority or that the primary duty of preserving law and order is subordinated. However, tapping into the expertise and resources that exist within communities will relieve police of some of their burdens. Local government officials, social agencies, schools, church groups, business people—all those who work and live in the community and have a stake in its development—will share responsibility for finding workable solutions to problems that detract from the safety and security of the community.

The Concept of Community

The goal of community policing is to reduce crime and disorder by carefully examining the characteristics of problems in neighbourhoods and then applying appropriate problem-solving remedies. The "community" for which a patrol officer is given responsibility should be a small, well-defined geographical area. Beats should be configured in a manner that preserves, as much as possible, the unique geographical and social characteristics of neighbourhoods while still allowing efficient service. Patrol officers are the primary providers of police services and have the most extensive contact with community members. In community policing efforts, they will provide the bulk of the daily policing needs of the community, and they will be assisted by immediate supervisors, other police units, and appropriate government and social agencies. Upper level managers and command staff will be responsible for ensuring that the entire organization backs the efforts of patrol officers. Effective community policing depends on optimizing positive contact between patrol officers and community members. Patrol cars are only one method of conveying police services. Police departments may supplement automobile patrols with foot, bicycle, scooter, and horseback patrols, as well as adding "mini-stations" to bring police closer to the community. Regular community meetings and forums will afford police and community members an opportunity to air concerns and find ways to address them. Officers working long-term assignments on the same shift and beat will become familiar figures to community members and will become aware of the day-to-day workings of the community. This increased police presence is an initial move in establishing trust and serves to reduce fear of crime among community members, which, in turn, helps create neighbourhood security. Fear must be reduced if community members are to participate actively in policing. People will not act if they feel that their actions will jeopardize their safety.

Although the delivery of police services is organized by geographic area, a community may encompass widely diverse cultures, values, and concerns, particularly in urban settings. A community consists of more than just the local government and the neighborhood residents. Churches, schools, hospitals, social groups, private and public agencies, and those who work in the area are also vital members of the community. In addition, those who visit for cultural or recreational purposes or provide services to the area are also concerned with the safety and security of the neighborhood. Including these "communities of interest" in efforts to address problems of crime and disorder can expand the resource base of the community. Concerns and priorities will vary within and among these communities of interest. Some communities of interest are long-lasting and were formed around racial, ethnic, occupational lines, or a common history, church, or school. Others form and reform as new problems are identified and addressed. Interest groups within communities can be in opposition to one another—sometimes in violent opposition. Intra-community disputes have been common in large urban centers, especially in times of changing demographics and population migrations. These multiple and sometimes conflicting interests require patrol officers to function not only as preservers of law and order, but also as skillful mediators. Demands on police from one community of interest can sometimes clash with the rights of another community of interest. For example, a community group may oppose certain police tactics used to crack down on gang activity, which the group believes may result in discriminatory arrest practices. The police must not only protect the rights of the protesting group, but must also work with all of the community members involved to find a way to preserve neighbourhood peace. For this process to be effective, community members must communicate their views and suggestions and back up the negotiating efforts of the police. In this way, the entire community participates in the mediation process and helps preserve order. The police must encourage a spirit of cooperation that balances the collective interests of all citizens with the personal rights of individuals.

The conflicts within communities are as important as the commonalities. Police must recognize the existence of both to build the cooperative bonds needed to maintain order, provide a sense of security, and control crime. Police must build lasting relationships that encompass all elements of the community and centre around the fundamental issues of public safety and quality of life. The key to managing this difficult task is trust.

Community Partnership

Establishing and maintaining mutual trust is the central goal of the first core component of community policing—community partnership. Police recognize the need for cooperation with the community. In the fight against serious crime, police have encouraged community members to come forth with relevant information. In addition, police have spoken to neighbourhood groups, participated in business and civic events, worked with social agencies, and taken part in educational and recreational programs for school children. Special units have provided a variety of crisis intervention services. So how then do the cooperative efforts of community policing differ from the actions that have taken place previously? The fundamental distinction is that, in community policing, the police become an integral part of the community culture, and the community assists in defining future priorities and in allocating resources. The difference is substantial and encompasses basic goals and commitments.

Community partnership means adopting a policing perspective that exceeds the standard law enforcement emphasis. This broadened outlook recognizes the value of activities that contribute to the orderliness and well-being of a neighbourhood. These activities could include: helping accident or crime victims, providing emergency medical services, helping resolve domestic and neighbourhood conflicts (e.g., family violence, landlord-tenant disputes, or racial harassment), working with residents and local businesses to improve neighbourhood conditions, controlling automobile and pedestrian traffic, providing emergency social services and referrals to those at risk (e.g., adolescent runaways, the homeless, the intoxicated, and the mentally ill), protecting the exercise of constitutional rights (e.g., guaranteeing a person's right to speak, protecting lawful assemblies from disruption), and providing a model of citizenship (helpfulness, respect for others, honesty, and fairness).

These services help develop trust between the police and the community. This trust will enable the police to gain greater access to valuable information from the community that could lead to the solution and prevention of crimes, will engender support for needed crime-control measures, and will provide an opportunity for officers to establish a working relationship with the community. The entire police organization must be involved in enlisting the cooperation of community members in promoting safety and security. Building trust will not happen overnight; it will require ongoing effort. But trust must be achieved before police can assess the needs of the community and construct the close ties that will engender community support. In turn, as Figure 1 illustrates, this cooperative relationship will deepen the bonds of trust.

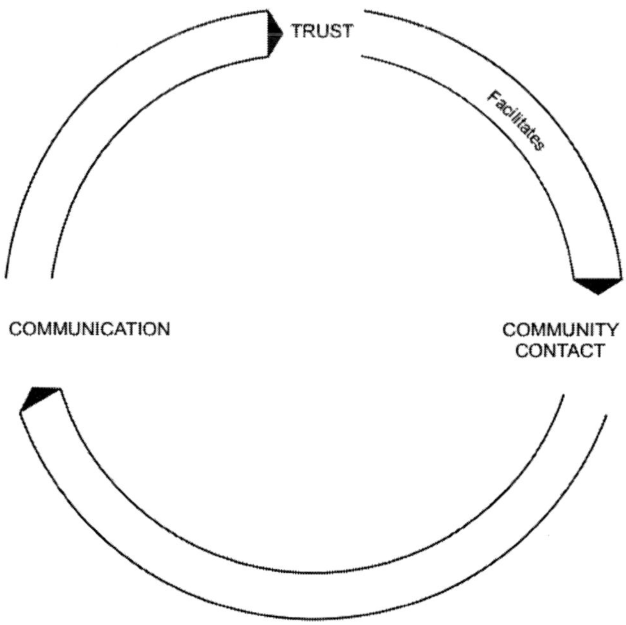

Figure 1. Community Partnership Process.

Source: https://www.ojp.gov/pdffiles/commp.pdf

To build this trust for an effective community partnership police must treat people with respect and sensitivity. The use of unnecessary force and arrogance, aloofness, or rudeness at any level of the agency will dampen the willingness of community members to ally themselves with the police. The effective mobilization of community support requires different approaches in different communities. Establishing trust and obtaining cooperation are often easier in middle-class and affluent communities than in poorer communities, where mistrust of police may have a long history. Building bonds in some neighbourhoods may involve supporting basic social institutions (e.g., families, churches, schools) that have been weakened by pervasive crime or disorder. The creation of viable communities is necessary if lasting alliances that nurture cooperative efforts are to be sustained. Under community policing, the police become both catalysts and facilitators in the development of these communities.

Community policing expands police efforts to prevent and control crime. The community is no longer viewed by police as a passive presence or a source of limited information, but as a partner in this effort. Community concerns with crime and disorder thus become the target of efforts by the police and the community working in tandem. The close alliance forged with the community should not be limited to an isolated incident or series of incidents, nor confined to a specific time frame. The partnership between the police and the community must be enduring and balanced. It must break down the old concepts of professional versus civilian, expert versus novice, and authority figure versus subordinate. The police and the community must be collaborators in the quest to encourage and preserve peace and prosperity. The more conspicuous police presence of the long-term patrol officer in itself may encourage community response. But it is not sufficient. The entire police organization must vigorously enlist the cooperation of community residents in pursuing the goals of deterring crime and preserving order. Police personnel on every level must join in building a broad rapport with community members.

For the patrol officer, police/community partnership entails talking to local business owners to help identify their problems and concerns, visiting residents in their homes to offer advice on security, and helping to organize and support neighborhood watch groups and regular community meetings. For example, the patrol officer will canvass the neighborhood for information about a string of burglaries and then revisit those residents to inform them when the burglar is caught. The chief police executive will explain and discuss controversial police tactics so that community members understand the necessity of these tactics for public and officer safety. The department management will consult community members about gang suppression tactics, and every level of the department will actively solicit the concerns and suggestions of community groups, residents, leaders, and local government officials. In this police/community partnership, providing critical social services will be acknowledged as being inextricably linked to deterring crime, and problem solving will become a cooperative effort.

Problem Solving

Two Problem solving is a broad term that implies more than simply the elimination and prevention of crimes. Problem solving is based on the assumption that "crime and disorder can be reduced in small geographic areas by carefully studying the characteristics of problems in the area, and then applying the appropriate resources." and on the assumption that "Individuals make choices based on the opportunities presented by the immediate physical and social characteristics of an area. By manipulating these factors, people will be less inclined to act in an offensive manner." The problem-solving process is explained further:

- The theory behind problem-oriented policing is simple. Underlying conditions create problems. These conditions might include the characteristics of the people involved (offenders, potential victims, and others), the social setting in which these people interact, the physical environments, and the way the public deals with these conditions.

- A problem created by these conditions may generate one or more incidents. These incidents, while stemming from a common source, may appear to be different. For example, social and physical conditions in a deteriorated apartment complex may generate burglaries, acts of vandalism, intimidation of pedestrians by rowdy teenagers, and other incidents. These incidents, some of which come to police attention, are symptoms of the problems. The incidents will continue so long as the problem that creates them persists.

As police recognize the effectiveness of the problem-solving approach, there is a growing awareness that community involvement is essential for its success. Determining the underlying causes of crime depends, to a great extent, on an in-depth knowledge of community. Therefore, community participation in identifying and setting priorities will contribute to effective problem-solving efforts by the community and the police. Cooperative problem solving also reinforces trust, facilitates the exchange of information, and leads to the identification of other areas that could benefit from the mutual attention of the police and the community. As Figure 2 illustrates, the problem-solving process, like community partnership, is self-renewing.

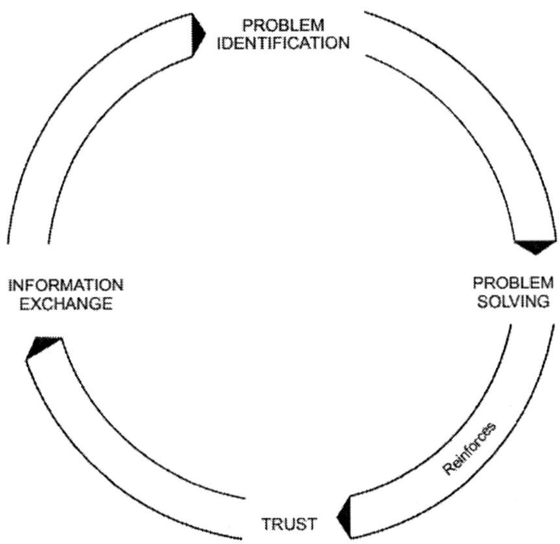

Figure 2. Problem-Solving Process.

Source: https://www.ojp.gov/pdffiles/commp.pdf

For this process to operate effectively the police need to devote attention to and recognize the validity of community concerns. Neighborhood groups and the police will not always agree on which specific problems deserve attention first. Police may regard robberies as the biggest problem in a particular community, while residents may find derelicts who sleep in doorways, break bottles on sidewalks, and pick through garbage cans to be the number one problem. Under community policing, the problem with derelicts should also receive early attention from the police with the assistance of other government agencies and community members. For example, one police captain reported the following:

What we found . . . was that maybe some things that we thought were important to them really weren't that important, and other things we didn't think were important at all, were very important . . . Like abandoned cars: in one of our areas, that was a very important thing. They were really bugged about all these abandoned cars, and they thought it was a bad police department that wouldn't take care of them. When we started removing the cars their opinion of us went up, even though because we'd changed priorities we were putting fewer drug addicts in jail

Therefore, in addition to the serious crime problems identified by police, community policing must also address the problems of significant concern to the community. Community policing in effect allows community members to bring problems of great concern to them to the attention of the police. Once informed of community concerns, the police must work with citizens to address them, while at the same time encouraging citizens to assist in solving the problems of concern to the police. The nature of community problems will vary widely and will often involve multiple incidents that are related by factors including geography, time, victim or perpetrator group, and environment. Problems can affect a small area of a community, an entire community, or many communities. Community problems might include the following:

- An unusually high number of burglaries in an apartment complex that are creating great anxiety and fear among residents.
- Panhandling that creates fear in a business district.
- Prostitutes in local parks or on heavily travelled streets.
- Disorderly youth who regularly assemble in the parking lot of a convenience store.
- An individual who persistently harasses and provokes community members.

In community policing, the problem-solving process is dependent on input from both the police and the community. Problem solving can involve:

- Eliminating the problem entirely. This type of solution is usually limited to disorder problems. Examples include eliminating traffic congestion by erecting traffic control signs, and destroying or rehabilitating abandoned buildings that can provide an atmosphere conducive to crime.
- Reducing the number of the occurrences of the problem. Drug-dealing and the accompanying problems of robbery and gang violence will be decreased if the police and community work together to set up drug counselling and rehabilitation centers. Longer range solutions might include intensifying drug education in schools, churches, and hospitals.
- Reducing the degree of injury per incident. For example, police can teach store clerks how to act during a robbery in order to avoid injury or death and can advise women in the community on ways to minimize the chances of being killed or seriously injured if attacked.
- Improving problem handling. Police should always make an effort to treat people humanely, (e.g., show sensitivity in dealing with rape victims

and seek ways to ease their trauma, or increase effectiveness in handling runaway juveniles, drug addicts, drunk drivers, etc., by working with other agencies more closely).

- Manipulating environmental factors to discourage criminal behaviour. This can include collaborative efforts to add better lighting, remove overgrown weeds and trim shrubbery, and seal off vacant apartment buildings.

There are as many solutions as there are problems. These solutions range from simple, inexpensive measures to complex, long-term answers that will require significant investment of staff and resources. Problem solving is limited only by the imagination, creativity, perseverance, and enthusiasm of those involved. Community policing allows solutions to be tailor-made to the specific concerns of each community. The best solutions are those that satisfy community members, improve safety, diminish anxiety, lead to increased order, strengthen the ties between the community and the police, and minimize coercive actions.

The following example describes such a solution:

A patrol officer faced with chronic night-time robberies of convenience stores discovered that a major contributing factor was that cash registers could not be seen from the street, either because of their location within the store or because of posters plastered on front windows. The officer did not identify the "root cause" or ultimate cause of crime, but instead identified an underlying condition that, once addressed, held promise of reducing the number of future convenience store robberies. To identify this underlying problem, the patrol officer talked with and solicited suggestions from convenience store owners and employees, other members of the business community, and community residents. The officer's identification of a contributing cause of the robberies is a high-leverage accomplishment in terms of its likely positive impact on the frequency of future robberies. Evidence of police concern and soliciting input from the community also reinforces cooperative ties.

Patrol officers serve as catalysts for joint police and community problem solving endeavours. They are involved with the community on a day-to-day basis, understand its unique physical and social characteristics, are aware of local problems, and when needed can help community members articulate their needs. Many problems within the community can be successfully handled by patrol officers or their immediate supervisors and members of the community—e.g., determining that better lighting would decrease the incidence of muggings at a local park. All levels of the police organization should contribute to problem solving, depending on the scope and seriousness of the problem. For example, crafting a solution to widespread incidents of spousal assault taking place in several communities in an agency's jurisdiction might involve multiple levels of police management. Patrol officers may have noticed a correlation between spousal assaults and excessive drinking by the perpetrators, especially at illegal after-hours clubs. The officers, their supervisors, and community members might explore ways to close down these clubs with the help of local zoning and city planning boards. Perpetrators with alcohol problems might be required to attend rehabilitation programs run by a city agency. Meanwhile, mid- and senior-level police managers and community leaders might confer with women's groups and other social agencies about providing temporary housing and counselling for victims and their families. In addition, members of the community might be able to repair an abandoned building to house the victims.

The problem-solving process relies on the expertise and assistance of an array of social and government agencies and community resources. At the senior command level, police managers might combine forces with a civil abatement agency to condemn and board up crack houses. One police officer seeking a system wide approach to the problem of spousal assault formed a team comprised of units from the police department and representatives from women's shelters, the YWCA, nearby military bases, the prosecutor's office, newspapers, hospitals, and social agencies. A tremendous amount of leverage can be attained through the collaboration and partnership of this type of far-ranging alliance. Community policing puts new emphasis on tackling the underlying causes of crime by addressing problems at the grassroots level. To maximize the time that the patrol officer can spend interacting with community members, community policing encourages the use of the 911 system only for true emergencies. Nonemergency calls should be handled through other means, including delays in responding and report handling by the police station or sheriff's office over the telephone or by mail. These alternative measures require a wide base of support within the community. To obtain this support, the police must instruct residents on the nature of an emergency and on alternative responses to non-emergencies. Alternative responses will need to be thoroughly explained before community members will accept them. The residents should be secure in the knowledge that the police response will be appropriate for the urgency of the demand for service, and that the reduction in the volume of 911 calls will allow officers to spend more time in the community and will maximize the use of the residents' tax dollars.

Implications for Management and the Organizational Structure

Effective community partnership and problem solving will require the mastery of new responsibilities and the adoption of a flexible style of management. Community policing emphasizes the value of the patrol function and the patrol officer as an individual. Patrol officers have traditionally been accorded low status despite the scope and sensitivity of the tasks they perform. Community policing requires the shifting of initiative, decision-making, and responsibility downward within the police organization. The neighbourhood officer or deputy sheriff becomes responsible for managing the delivery of services to a community, and "... everything of a policing nature [in that community] 'belongs' to that person."

With this responsibility comes wide-ranging discretionary and decision-making power. Under community policing, patrol officers are given broader freedom to decide what should be done and how it should be done in their communities—they assume managerial responsibility for the delivery of police services to their assigned area. Patrol officers are the most familiar with the needs and strengths of their communities and are thus in the best position to forge the close ties with the community that lead to effective solutions to local problems. The shift in status and duties of the patrol officer is critical to the community partnership and problem-solving components of community policing. Assignment stability of these neighbourhood officers is also essential if they are to develop close working relationships within their communities because ....they are expected to engage in activities other than simply reacting to calls for service. Having officers periodically rotate among the shifts impedes their ability to identify problems. It also discourages creative solutions to impact the problems, because the officers end up rotating away from the problems. Thus, a sense of responsibility to identify and resolve problems is lost. Likewise, management cannot hold the officers accountable to deal with problems if the officers are frequently rotated from one shift to another.

The enhanced role of the patrol officer has enormous organizational and managerial implications. The entire police organization must be structured, managed, and operated in a manner that supports the efforts of the patrol officer and that encourages a cooperative approach to solving problems. Under community policing, command is no longer centralized, and many decisions now come from the bottom up instead of from the top down. Greater decision-making power is given to those closest to the situation with the expectation that this change will improve the overall performance of the agency. This transformation in command structure is not only sound management, but is also crucial to the creation of meaningful and productive ties between the police and the community. To establish a partnership with the community,

........the police must move to empower two groups: the public itself and the street officers who serve it most closely and regularly. Only when the public has a real voice in setting police priorities will its needs be taken seriously; only when street officers have the operational latitude to take on the problems they encounter with active departmental backing will those needs really be addressed.

Community policing alters the contemporary functions of supervisors and managers. Under community policing, management serves to guide, rather than dominate, the actions of patrol officers and to ensure that officers have the necessary resources to solve the problems in their communities. Creativity and innovation must be fostered if satisfactory solutions to long-standing community problems are to be found. The transition to community policing requires recognizing that the new responsibilities and decision making power of the neighborhood patrol officers must be supported, guided, and encouraged by the entire organization. In addition, it requires establishing clearly stated values that provide both the police organization and the public with a clear sense of policing expanded focus and direction.

Values: The Guiding Principles

Community policing is ultimately about values—specifically, the change in values that is needed to adapt policing to these changing times. Values must be ingrained in the very culture of the organization and must be reflected in its objectives, in its policies, and in the actions of its personnel.

Values are the beliefs that guide an organization and the behaviour of its employees.......The most important beliefs are those that set forth the ultimate purposes of the organization. They provide the organization with its raison d'être for outsiders and insiders alike and justify the continuing investment in the organization's enterprise...... [They] influence substantive and administrative decisions facing the organization; they lend a coherence and predictability to top management's actions and the responses to the actions of employees. This helps employees make proper decisions and use their discretion with confidence that they are contributing to rather than detracting from organizational performance.

A clear statement of beliefs and goals gives direction to the organization and helps ensure that values are transformed into appropriate actions and behaviours. The entire agency must be committed to the values embodied by such a mission statement. This mission statement should be widely disseminated both inside and outside the police organization to garner public support and to facilitate accountability. In the move to community policing, where problem-solving efforts and accountability are shared by the police, the local government, and the community, explicitly defined values become critically important in assigning responsibility and attracting and mobilizing support and resources.

Community policing

........relies heavily on the articulation of policing values that incorporate citizen involvement in matters that directly affect the safety and quality of neighbourhood life. The culture of the police department therefore becomes one that not only recognizes the merits of community involvement but also seeks to organize and manage departmental affairs in ways that are consistent with such beliefs.

An organization's mission statement should be simple, direct, and unassuming. Values must be unequivocally communicated so that officers understand the influence on their actions:

Planners need to assess what specific behaviours by organizational members support or undermine the stated values. This assessment requires that the values be defined in operational terms such that an observer can know whether any particular employee action is on target or off target...............Planners must also think clearly about how management will know whether the desired changes are taking place; feedback and evaluative steps must be developed.

Community policing relies on the establishment of a clear, unambiguous link of values to behaviours. By creating a system of performance measurement, specific operational meaning can be given to seemingly abstract values. The guiding values central to community policing are trust, cooperation, communication, ingenuity, integrity, initiative, discretion, leadership, responsibility, respect, and a broadened commitment to public safety and security. A succinct mission statement that embodies these values and that is widely communicated to personnel, local government, and members of the community will form the basis of assessment systems that match actions and behaviours to the goals of community policing.

The Nature of Police Work

The myth of police as crime-fighters has been conveyed to the American people through television dramas, comic strips, and newspaper articles. It conjures up in one's mind an image of a police officer doing a dangerous job that requires him or her to outshoot, outpunch, and outwit dangerous criminals. For most American police, there is little correspondence between this image and reality. In a major metropolitan area (where crime rates are the highest), half of the officers in the local department will not make a felony arrest during a given year. The total annual rate of weapon discharges per hundred police officers is in the range of two to six. Even though we refer to the police as law enforcement officers, the enforcement of criminal law (in other words, investigating crime and apprehending criminals) is only one of several functions that the police perform. The functions of the American police include providing basic social services, maintaining order, and controlling crime.

- In the area of social service, the police help people who need emergency assistance, whether it is giving first aid or finding lost children. Typically, over 50 percent of the telephone calls to the police requesting assistance involve social service as compared with less than 20 percent relating to crime.
- Among the order-maintenance activities are traffic control, crowd control, resolving domestic disputes, and moving prostitutes from the streets. The focus of order maintenance is on handling situations to preserve the peace rather than enforcing the letter of the law. The appropriate order-maintenance solution may be making an arrest (for example, in case of domestic violence), but it often consists of some less formal action (for example, getting an illegal panhandler to move on).
- In the area of crime control, the police engage in a range of activities, such as patrol and criminal investigation.

The American Bar Association's *Standards Relating to the Urban Police Function* lists these 11 responsibilities:

- To identify criminal offenders and criminal activity and, when appropriate, to apprehend offenders and participate in later court proceedings.
- To reduce the opportunities for the commission of some crimes through preventive patrol and other measures.
- To aid individuals who are in danger of physical harm.
- To protect constitutional guarantees.
- To facilitate the movement of people and vehicles.
- To assist those who cannot care for themselves.
- To resolve conflict.
- To identify problems those are potentially serious law enforcement or government problems.
- To create and maintain a feeling of security in the community.
- To promote and preserve civil order.
- To provide other services on an emergency basis.

Several factors shape what the police do. Twenty-four hour availability broadens police contacts with the public. People call the police because there is no other agency available. A disadvantage is that such availability gives police a heavy workload. The authority to use force stamps police work with a uniqueness that sets it apart from other lines of work. Force includes the right to use deadly force, to arrest people, and to use physical force. Whatever aspect of the police mission is emphasized—whether it involves checking on suspicious persons who appear to be out of place or responding to reports of crime—the police have to be willing, in the last analysis, to threaten force and to back up the threat with action. Discretion leaves an imprint on all areas of policing. Police are often free to choose among alternative courses of action or inaction. They routinely rely on their own experience, training, common sense, and judgment to make decisions involving the life and liberty of citizens. Examples of discretionary decision making include decisions involving arrests, traffic tickets, deadly force, and domestic abuse. In each of these situations, officers determine whether or not to invoke the power of the law.

The seriousness of the crime and the strength of the evidence affect an officer's decision to arrest. The more serious the crime and the stronger the evidence, the more likely an officer is to make an arrest. A suspect's demeanor also makes a difference. The more disrespectful and the less deferent a suspect acts toward an officer, the more likely that officer is to use force.

How is community policing different from traditional policing?

- Intended to prevent crime before it happens rather than responding to crime after it occurs
- Focuses on creating a safe social environment
- Engages residents to determine which criminal activities they are most affected by, creating an accurate law enforcement priority list shaped by the people who live in the area
- Encourages residents to participate with law enforcement in order to keep their own community safe

In its simplest form, community policing creates a partnership between law enforcement and residents. The more involved law enforcement is with the residents they are sworn to protect, the more residents can help law enforcement achieve their goals.

Benefits of an Effective Community Policing Structure

- Residents having a more favorable view of their local police department
- Improved trust between law enforcement and residents
- More accurate information from residents regarding criminal activity in their community
- Better understanding of the needs of citizens and their expectations of the police

Many public safety agencies are using technology to better engage their residents and boost their community policing initiatives. Systems like Everbridge Nixle use tools such as mass notification, 2-way communication, anonymous tipping, and social media integration to engage residents on the platforms and devices they use most.

Does Community Policing Prevent Crime?

A growing consensus within police circles is that community policing is the best strategy for fighting crime in residential neighborhoods. This strategy is based on police-community reciprocity—the police and public cooperate to prevent and to solve crimes.

An important premise of this approach is that police should fight crime *locally* rather than follow dictates from Washington, D.C. Community policing often features decentralization of command through substations to increase police-citizen interaction. It also involves foot patrol so police can walk and talk with citizens. New York City and other metropolitan areas incorporate into community policing a zero tolerance attitude toward minor crimes and disorder to enhance feelings of community safety.

Community policing does prevent crime

To prove the effectiveness of community policing, proponents point to testimonials from police chiefs and mayors from various communities.

- Many chiefs of police and mayors credit community policing with lowering crime rates. They claim that community policing has restored order in neighborhoods where once open-air drug markets thrived and gangs hung out. New York City is a prime example. The zero tolerance policy, which has been given a showcase in New York City, holds that no crime—not the breaking of a window, not the jumping of a turnstile, not drinking in public—is too insignificant to capture the swift, decisive attention of the police.
- Arrest more petty offenders and make more arrests for petty offenses today, goes the reasoning, and you will have fewer hard-core criminals tomorrow. Under Mayor Rudolph Giuliani, the NYPD returned to a policy of proactive policing, frisking more than 45,000 suspects for guns and other weapons in 1997 and 1998. According to police officials, New Yorkers are getting results that range from fewer panhandlers to fewer shootings and murders.

Community policing does not prevent crime. Critics of community policing attack this approach to crime-fighting from different angles.

- No one knows what community policing is, according to criminal justice professor Carl Klockars. Even though a majority of police departments in America claim to be doing community policing, the differences between the actual operations may be significant. Community policing as it is organized in New York is different from its practice in Chicago, Washington, and Philadelphia. The lack of precision in defining community policing makes it impossible to say with any certainty that community policing is causing crime rates to decrease.
- The evidence from particular communities used to demonstrate that community policing reduces crime is suspect. By appealing to anecdotal evidence to support the claim that community policing reduces crime, proponents make a hasty generalization on the basis of a very few and possibly unrepresentative cases.
- The correlation between falling crime rates and the establishment of community policing may be coincidental. The fact is that over the past few years crime has been declining and has done so in communities where there is no community policing.
- Police brutality can be an unintended outgrowth of aggressive policing. There is a thin line between law enforcement that is aptly forceful and law enforcement that is unduly brutal or abusive. The New York police stepped over the line in the 1997 sodomizing torture of Haitian immigrant Abner Louima in a Brooklyn station house and in the 1999 killing of Amadou Diallo, an unarmed African immigrant, in a fusillade of police fire in the Bronx. Underlying this problem is the recurring tension between public safety and civil liberties. If the police become more aggressive, the streets may become safer, but innocent people's rights may be compromised as a result.

ASSESSING THE PROGRESS OF COMMUNITY POLICING

A critical aspect of implementation is the assessment of community policing efforts, both in terms of achieving necessary change within the organization itself and accomplishing external goals (such as, establishing working relationships with the community and reducing levels of crime, fear, and disorder). Ongoing assessment meets a number of fundamental needs. Every government and public agency, including the police, should be able to give an accurate account of its current activities to policymakers and taxpayers. Thus, ongoing assessment of policy and performance should be a primary function of any policing organization. Assessment becomes even more vital when an organization is undergoing the comprehensive changes that a shift to community policing will entail. Constant assessment of the process of change is needed for managers to determine how to keep the implementation process on track. The most effective strategies also need to be identified so managers can make informed choices about where to allocate limited resources.

Ongoing assessment helps give the organization a clear sense of direction and allows management to focus efforts on the most productive and efficient practices. Therefore, assessment is indispensable in determining which elements of community policing should be maintained, altered, or eliminated, and offers key decisionmakers in the jurisdiction a way to gauge the impact and cost-effectiveness of community policing efforts. Assessment will help determine whether necessary changes in the support systems are taking place and whether appropriate efforts are being made to accomplish the stated goals. Assessment also can help communicate agency expectations to employees. Giving community members a way to measure the success of community policing efforts is critical to maintaining strong ties, ensuring continued participation, and documenting the progress made. Conversely, evaluations of the community policing strategy from government and community leaders will affect how future cooperative efforts are constructed. Thorough assessment helps make police more responsive to the community's needs, which should strengthen the trust and partnership on which community policing is based.

Developing a sound assessment program should begin with a strategic plan that outlines the goals, methods, objectives, and timetables, and assigns personnel for internal and external changes. These goals and responsibilities will form the basis of performance assessment and will allow police leadership to detect failures and roadblocks, as well as to chart progress and document accomplishments.

Community Policing Engagement

Community policing is a proactive, collaborative approach to help prevent crime. It focuses on increasing community involvement, forming bonds between a community and law enforcement, and establishing an effective law enforcement presence in a community.

In defining what community policing is, it's important to understand the three major elements of community policing.

- **Partnerships between law enforcement and the community.** Creating partnerships between law enforcement and community stakeholders is key to community policing. When implementing community policing strategies, law enforcement agencies partner with schools, human services agencies, community residents, volunteer groups, and similar constituents to work together to address community issues.

- **Proactively solving problems in a community.** Through this component of community policing, law enforcement strives to identify and resolve the conditions that result in crime, rather than taking a reactive approach and responding to crime after it has occurred.
- **Organizational change.** Successful community policing also rests on law enforcement agencies being willing to modify their structures and management approaches. For example, this could mean a law enforcement agency provides greater transparency about its activities, adjusts the way it trains law enforcement officers, or changes how it deploys law enforcement officers across a city.

Law enforcement agencies at multiple levels—including local, state, and Native American tribal—have implemented an extensive range of community policing strategies. These range from broad based (such as increasing law enforcement foot patrols to improve their visibility in a community) or more narrow in scope (such as placing resource officers in schools).

Benefits of Community Policing

People who are pursuing criminal justice careers can benefit from learning about the potential advantages community policing offers. The examples below highlight some of those benefits.

Strengthening Trust between Law Enforcement and Community Members: Trust in law enforcement is critical, and increasing their interactions with, for example, community groups and marginalized individuals can help law enforcement agencies build strong relationships of trust. Establishing trust can encourage more citizens to report crime and initiate a greater level of communication between law enforcement and members of a community. Community policing programs have the potential to improve the public's perceptions of law enforcement and reduce mistrust.

Improving Public Safety: Community policing can improve public safety in a range of ways. For example, it can provide community members with information on steps they can take to help prevent crime. Community policing can also provide law enforcement with specific information that can directly relate to strengthening public safety. For example, community policing efforts can identify specific types of training that law enforcement officers need. Programs in community policing that focus on youth can help deter young citizens from committing crimes by educating them about the consequences of engaging in criminal activity.

Expanding the Cultural Competency of Law Enforcement: Through community policing programs, law enforcement officers have the opportunity to learn about the culture of the communities in which they work. For example, they can form an understanding of how community members communicate with one another and how they support each other. They also can learn from history, and how previous interactions between citizens and law enforcement officers have affected the relationships between law enforcement and a community. Improving cultural competency can enhance interaction between officers and the members of a community and inform the training of new officers.

Opening the Door to Innovation: Community policing is not limited to a specified set of programs. Innovation is crucial in community policing. Implementing creative community policing strategies enables law enforcement to take fresh approaches to address long-term problems. For example, rather than taking traditional approaches to policing, law enforcement can implement strategies that are tailored to specific situations, such as preventing crimes related to homelessness or addiction.

Community Policing in Action

Reviewing specific examples that demonstrate what community policing is can help in developing an understanding of its effectiveness. The following describes some community policing programs that have been adopted, and helps show the extensive range of community policing ideas and strategies.

- **Addressing citizens' mental health challenges.** The state of New Jersey has created a program to send mental health professionals on police calls when citizens are experiencing mental health distress. The Alternative Responses to Reduce Instances of Violence and Escalation (ARRIVE) Together program has resulted in reductions in both the use of force in these cases and in arrests. The program also has resulted in an increase in the use of social services to address citizens' mental health needs.
- **Engaging community youth.** Through its Youth Police Advisory Council, the Houston Police Department gives high school students from across the city the opportunity to communicate with police and city leaders and express their concerns. This council has improved young people's perception of law enforcement and enhanced law enforcement's understanding of the concerns of young people.
- **Reducing recidivism.** In Washington D.C., the Court Services Offender Supervision Agency and the Metropolitan Police Department have partnered to conduct joint visits at the homes of individuals who are on parole or probation. This collaboration gives law enforcement officers the opportunity to speak directly with these individuals and learn about their needs and concerns. Ultimately, the goal of the program is to keep offenders from committing more crimes and show them another path they can take.

Assessing Internal Changes

Large gaps can exist between policy and actions, therefore, management must take nothing for granted in the implementation of community policing policies and procedures. The chief executive should constantly ask, "How is the implementation going? Is it on track? What problems are occurring? What help is needed?" In smaller organizations, these questions can be answered through a process called "management by walking around" in which the chief visits key managers and implementation groups to get on-the-spot reports on implementation efforts. The chief should also consult patrol officers to obtain their views on the implementation process. In every organization, the chief executive should hold regular meetings with the personnel responsible for overseeing community policing implementation and should ask for reports on efforts with the goal of both reinforcing accountability and allowing for immediate discussion of problems. Regular reports on progress and problems relating to specific community policing objectives and timetables should be supplied by members of the implementation team.

Assessment of the more intangible internal changes, for example, the decentralization of management, can be complex. The chief executive and the head of the implementation team could meet regularly with groups of managers and supervisors to discuss changes in decision-making authority. Periodic personnel surveys can also help determine what modifications have occurred in management style, which obstacles stand in the way of change, and how agency leadership can facilitate the necessary adjustments in the roles of managers, supervisors, and patrol officers.

Criteria for Assessment

Evaluating the impact of community policing is critical for many reasons. Key decision makers must be able to judge the strategy's impact and cost effectiveness, and the police organization must be able to measure the success or failure of its policies and activities. As with implementation methods, assessment measures will vary depending on the size of the organization and the nature of its current policies. Ongoing monitoring will expedite the implementation process, attract support, and problem solving, and reveal new opportunities for productive partnerships with the community.

In the past, police efforts usually have been evaluated on a traditional and narrow set of criteria (e.g., crime statistics, the number of 911 calls, the length of police response, the number of arrests and citations, etc.). These assessments were often taken only at times of serious crime increases. Many of the traditional methods of assessment remain valid, but can measure only the effectiveness of crime-fighting tactics and cannot gauge the effect of crime-prevention efforts. Changes in the scope of policing necessitate a revised system for evaluating the performance of individuals, as well as agencies. As police take a proactive role in deterring crime, a broader set of assessment criteria, which incorporate traditional measures of crime-fighting activities with those that encompass community partnership and problemsolving activities, will be needed.

Traditional crime-control activities should become only one of the ways in which the community policing strategy and individual officers are assessed. Many indications of the success of community policing efforts are intangible (e.g., absence of fear, quality of interaction with community members, etc.); therefore, assessing a community policing strategy is a qualitative as well as a quantitative process. The values that the department promotes will form the basis of sound qualitative measures of effectiveness. Assessment should reward organizational and individual behavior that assists in deterring crime and solving other neighborhood problems. Creativity, initiative, and ingenuity should be emphasized in the evaluation of individual officers. Three major criteria—effectiveness, efficiency, and equity—can be used to provide the quantitative and qualitative measures needed to assess the success of a community policing strategy.

Effectiveness

An effective community policing strategy will reduce neighbourhood crime, decrease citizens' fear of crime, and enhance the quality of life in the community. An important goal of community policing is to provide higher quality service to neighbourhoods; therefore, customer satisfaction becomes an important measure of effectiveness. The perception of progress among community members and ongoing feedback from all elements of the community are essential parts of the assessment process. Randomly and routinely conducted surveys will inform the agency of the public view of police performance, the level of fear and concern, and will make the agency aware of the extent to which community members feel as if they are participants in the community policing effort.

One of the core components of community policing is community partnership. Therefore, an early measure of effectiveness will be the number and type of community partnerships that have been formed. The cooperation and participation of community members is necessary to deter crime and reduce the fear of crime in the neighbourhood. Assessing the effectiveness of community policing efforts includes determining whether problems have been solved and judging how well the managers and patrol officers have applied the community partnership and problem-solving components of community policing.

Assessment should measure whether a problem was solved and how this was accomplished. As stated earlier, the number of arrests made is only one possible measure of effective problem solving; solving problems often does not involve arrest and, in many cases, does not guarantee that a problem will disappear completely. For example, the officer, who determined that one of the underlying causes of an increase in convenience store robberies was that cash registers could not be seen by passersby, did not eradicate the burglary. However, his efforts did provide valuable information that could help deter future robberies. Satisfactory assessment measures for community policing must give proper credit to officers like this who successfully abate a problem through means other than arrest. The officer's contribution to solving the problem and his consultations with members of the community showed the concern and effectiveness of police officers and created the goodwill for the department that is crucial to the success of community policing.

The number and type of problems solved and the creativity and scope of the solutions will provide a way to measure community policing's effectiveness. Not all of the problems will involve criminal activity, and many will not even be considered a priority by the police agency. However, where serious crime is not involved, the concerns and fears of community members should order the priorities of the agency. In community policing, officers may act as facilitators to mobilize community support. They may also function as mediators in disputes between individuals or organizations, or take responsibility for referring a problem to the appropriate social or government agency. The effective use of government and community agencies in problem solving is an indication that community policing policies are working. Thus, the mobilization and intelligent use of community resources in solving problems and the sensitive handling of dissension become important factors in assessing the performance of officers and the success of the program. Increased levels of community participation in crime reduction and prevention efforts are another indication of program success. Community members will not act if they are afraid or suspicious. Community members should become more willing to work with the police in a variety of ways, ranging from converting abandoned buildings to community assets to involving police actively in neighbourhood watch groups. They might also be more comfortable providing information on criminal activity in the area. In fact, calls to report crime may increase considerably during the early phases of community policing implementation, as community confidence in police capability rises and community trust increases. However, the number of 911 calls will likely decrease over time, which will provide a quantitative measure of the strategy's effect. For instance, emergency calls in the pioneering Flint, Michigan, foot patrol district dropped 43 percent over the course of the experiment.

A concrete indication of community policing success is the commitment of an increased level of community resources devoted to crime reduction efforts. Active consultation and financial participation by public and private agencies, schools, and the business community will demonstrate that community partnership efforts are working. Communities also should begin to initiate and conduct projects with minimal guidance from the police. Renewed activity within the community also will demonstrate the effectiveness of community policing efforts, particularly in areas where citizens have been afraid to leave their homes. Reduction in fear can also result in the perception among residents that crime is on the wane, whether or not this is statistically accurate. An increased willingness of citizens to walk to schools and parks, patronize stores, and go to restaurants and movies will signal a general decrease in fear of crime. In turn, the very fact that community members are reclaiming their streets will help deter future criminal activity and create more vigorous neighbourhoods. Improved quality of life is difficult to measure but is an important goal of community policing and will be reflected in comments from community members. Ridding the streets of gangs, drunks, panhandlers, and prostitutes— perhaps with the help of public and private social agencies—will enhance the quality of life. Removing signs of neglect (e.g., abandoned cars, derelict buildings, and garbage and debris) will offer tangible evidence that community policing efforts are working to bring about increased order in the community. In community policing, the police function includes the provision of services that in the recent past have been regarded as outside policing purview. These services include aiding accident and crime victims, arbitrating neighbourhood and domestic disputes, and providing emergency medical and social services. An analysis of the nature of calls for police service (e.g., a lower percentage of calls reporting criminal activity in proportion to calls requesting social assistance) will provide a measure of how well the strategy is working.

Efficiency

Efficiency means getting the most results with available resources. To measure the efficiency of community policing, the resources of the police agency, local government and private agencies, citizen groups, the business community, and the neighbourhood must first be defined. The assessment must then determine whether these resources are being used to their fullest to solve any given problem.

Agencies that can successfully enhance and realign their resources by forming community partnerships will be able to make community policing more efficient and cost-effective. Two major shifts must occur within the police organization if community policing is to work efficiently. Staunch partnerships and collaborative efforts must first be established with the community. The command structure of the police organization must then be decentralized so that problem solving, decision-making, and accountability are spread to all levels of the organization. Such decentralization challenges personnel to be more creative and more effective because the decisions they make are timelier and influenced by firsthand knowledge of the facts. Decentralization also gives higher level managers more time to formulate strategies that will improve the organization's performance. In a decentralized policing organization, neighbourhood patrol officers are responsible for the daily policing needs of the community, with guidance and backing from supervisors. Their long-term shifts and neighbourhood patrol assignments give them the opportunity to function more efficiently and successfully.

Patrol officers who handle daily police functions can form stronger bonds with the community. This "pride of ownership" motivates both parties to solve the problems that affect the security and harmony of the neighbourhood. Patrol officers will experience greater job satisfaction as they accept higher levels of responsibility and accountability. Officers are often able to resolve issues quickly, allowing them to see the immediate results of their efforts. With high morale and greater job satisfaction, patrol officers will more effectively mobilize the community. If they are highly motivated, given the necessary support, and appropriately rewarded for their efforts, the job satisfaction they experience will help make the community policing strategy a success.

The roles and responsibilities of all personnel in the police organization are altered so that the leadership and ingenuity officers display will become important factors in determining the efficiency of the program. Assessment and reward procedures must therefore be revised accordingly. Community help will increase the efficiency of the program and relieve some of the strain of tight police budgets. Partnerships in the community can bring fresh resources to problems, even those traditionally considered "police-only" business. According to one sheriff, "There is virtually no limitation on how much more effective and efficient a sheriff's office can become, working collectively as a partner with community members while, at the same time, saving resources, dollars, and frustration on the part of constituents."

Decentralized decision-making and community partnership engenders new organizational and resource issues that must be addressed to operate the system efficiently. Budgets must reflect the goals of community policing by allocating money and resources in proportion to the results achieved. With decentralization police officers who have the greatest responsibility for the daily policing operations will have more direct input into budgetary decisions and greater accountability for financial decisions, actions taken, and results achieved. Efficiency must be built into each aspect of the community policing strategy—from the creation of community boundaries that cultivate productive alliances to the adoption of technologies that increase communication. Expanded and thorough training is paramount in an efficient shift to community policing. Intensive training, although initially costly in terms of dollars and time, will eventually make the process more efficient, as well-trained and experienced personnel share practical knowledge with colleagues.

Efficiency in larger agencies may be increased by redefining job functions at all management levels. For example, one large jurisdiction implementing community policing required sergeants to coordinate officer decision-making across beats as necessary and to confer with their lieutenants on decisions that involved a large or long-term commitment of resources. Lieutenants in turn apprised their respective captains about happenings on beats across their districts. Such amended roles for midlevel managers may promote efficiency through fewer levels of supervision. While an important supervisory role is to help maximize the amount of time neighbourhood officers can spend in their communities, community policing will require supervisors to coordinate problem-solving activities within and across communities, help secure resources, evaluate activities and decisions, and provide guidance and support to neighbourhood officers. Also central to achieving efficiency in time and dollars is controlling calls for service. Sophisticated technological advances can help prioritize calls and facilitate communication among community policing partners. Alternative response strategies for nonemergency calls include a delayed-officer response and officer response by appointment. Low-priority situations can be handled by telephone, walk-in, and mail-in reporting. "All indications are that these systems save an enormous amount of time, reduce officer frustration, and are equally satisfactory to the callers." Effectiveness and efficiency are important yardsticks by which to measure community policing achievements, but equity, the third major criterion for judging progress, has the greatest impact on the success of community policing.

Equity

Equity is grounded firmly in the Constitution of the United States, which all police officers are sworn to uphold. A foremost tenet of community policing is equity; that is, all citizens should have a say in how they are governed. Officers may relate better to citizens as individuals because they cooperate closely with and are recognized as an integral part of the community. Community policing can thus become a force for enhancing democratic principles. Community policing provides an opportunity to emphasize uncompromising integrity, unyielding standards of fairness, and unwavering equality because officers have to work closely with the community and will be increasingly confronted with ethical dilemmas. Equity, as understood in community policing activities, has three dimensions: equal access to police services by all citizens, equal treatment of all individuals under the U.S. Constitution, and equal distribution of police services and resources among communities.

Equal access to police services. All citizens, regardless of race, religion, personal characteristics, or group affiliation, must have equal access to police services for a full and productive partnership with a community. The paramount commitment of community policing should be respect for all citizens and sensitivity to their needs. Neighbourhood officers must not discriminate against any community members. Supervisors should help ensure that police services are readily available throughout the community. In addition, lines of communication must be kept open with all partners in the community policing effort. Favouritism of one group over another will severely hamper future cooperative efforts. Groups who are more vocal than others cannot be permitted to use community policing to serve their own purposes. Police must prevent such behaviour before it adversely affects the trust that has been established within and among communities.

Equal treatment under the constitution. Police must treat all individuals according to the constitutional rights that officers are sworn to protect and enforce. Careful attention to the constitutional rights of citizens, victims, or perpetrators will help to engender bonds of trust between the police and community. Police must treat all persons with respect and impartiality— including the homeless, the poor, and the mentally or physically handicapped. They must reject stereotypes; ignore skin colour, and use reason and persuasion rather than coercion wherever possible because inequitable or harsh treatment can lead to frustration, hostility, and even violence within a community. Such unethical behaviour will imperil the trust so necessary to community policing. Some contemporary community activists and leaders have experienced past confrontations with the police which may present serious challenges to implementing community policing and involving the community in policing efforts.

Equal distribution of police services and resources among communities. Because community policing customizes policing services to the needs of each community, services should be distributed equitably among poor and minority communities. Care must be taken, however, to ensure that this is the case. For equitable distribution of resources among communities, each community must articulate its needs and be willing to work with the police to ensure its share of police services. Each neighbourhood officer must listen to the community members, and be willing to work with the community members to meet those needs. Poor and minority neighbourhoods can present particular challenges for some patrol officers, who may have to bridge differences of race and class before a level of trust and cooperation can be established. Some neighbourhoods may appear unwilling to help police in their efforts to improve life in the community. Officers must realize that sometimes "the community seems so helpless because it feels abandoned and would discover new strengths if only the police could make an effective alliance with important community elements.. . . . . Departments that have taken early steps [into community policing] are full of stories of apparently lost neighbourhoods that flowered under new police attention."

One community must not be given preference over another; all communities must have equal access to police services. Equity, however, may not always mean equal distribution of police services and resources. Wealthier communities are often able to contribute more resources to the problem-solving process than can poorer communities. Crime rates will also be higher in some communities, requiring more police intervention and a larger share of police resources to decrease crime and transform neighbourhoods from places of fear into city or county assets.

Refining the Assessment Process

Assessment of community policing is an ongoing process that should include a re-evaluation of the assessment measures themselves. With more experience in community policing, a police agency will be able to develop measures that accurately chart successes and failures and indicate where changes need to be made. The values of the policing organization must guide the move to community policing, and shape every decision made and every action taken. Above all, police organizations must be responsive to community priorities and demands for service from the beginning of the community policing effort.

COMMUNITY POLICING AND CRIME REDUCTION

Community policing and crime reduction are closely intertwined concepts within the realm of law enforcement, focusing on building relationships and fostering collaboration between police officers and the communities they serve to create safer neighborhoods. Community policing is a philosophy that emphasizes proactive problem solving and community engagement, shifting the traditional model of policing from reactive responses to crimes towards a more preventative and interactive approach. This strategy is based on the belief that effective policing involves understanding and addressing the social dynamics and issues that contribute to crime. By forging strong, trust-based relationships with community members, police officers can gain insights into local concerns and work collaboratively to address them, thereby reducing crime rates and enhancing public safety.

The core principle of community policing is that law enforcement cannot achieve its objectives alone; it requires the active involvement of community members. This approach encourages police officers to engage with residents through regular meetings, community events, and collaborative projects, creating a platform for dialogue and mutual understanding. By being visible and accessible, police officers can build rapport and trust with community members, which is crucial for effective policing. This trust facilitates the flow of information, as residents are more likely to report crimes and provide valuable intelligence when they feel their concerns are heard and addressed. Moreover, community policing initiatives often involve partnerships with local organizations, businesses, and schools, which can provide additional resources and support for crime prevention efforts.

Crime reduction through community policing involves a variety of strategies tailored to the specific needs and characteristics of each community. One key aspect is the identification and analysis of local crime patterns and hotspots, enabling law enforcement to allocate resources more efficiently and implement targeted interventions. Problem-oriented policing, a component of community policing, involves analyzing specific crime issues and developing customized solutions to address them. For example, if a particular neighborhood experiences a high rate of burglaries, police might collaborate with residents to improve street lighting, encourage neighborhood watch programs, and increase patrols during peak hours. These localized strategies not only address immediate concerns but also contribute to long-term crime reduction by tackling the underlying factors that enable criminal activity.

Another important element of community policing is the emphasis on prevention and early intervention. Programs aimed at youth engagement, substance abuse prevention, and educational support can address some of the root causes of criminal behavior. By providing at-risk individuals with alternatives and support, these programs help divert them from the path of criminality. Additionally, community policing efforts often focus on improving the overall quality of life in neighborhoods, as safe, well-maintained environments discourage crime and promote community pride and cohesion.

Emphasizing the Community Policing

Community policing emphasizes working with neighborhood residents to co-produce public safety. Law enforcement agencies should, therefore, work with community residents to identify problems and collaborate on implementing solutions that produce meaningful results for the community. Specifically, law enforcement agencies should develop and adopt policies and strategies that reinforce the importance of community engagement in managing public safety. Law enforcement agencies should also engage in multidisciplinary, community team approaches for planning, implementing and responding to crisis situations with complex causal factors.

Examples of the ways the police department demonstrates best practices in community policing and crime reduction

- Officers are encouraged to visit with the public during their shifts by stopping at schools, daycares, businesses, neighborhoods and parks to get to know the community. Patrol officers are assigned districts annually to help strengthen these relationships and strengthen outcomes.
- Outreach groups and events are supported by the department, including National Night Out, Basketball in the Park, Coffee with a Cop, Fishing with a Cop, Skateapalooza, Cops 'n' Kids Holiday Shopping, IFTAR dinner, safety camp, Toys for Tots, Canadian Pacific Holiday Train, Backpacks for Kids, St. Louis Park Adult Options in Education and the New Americans Academy.
- A community engagement program at the police department that coordinates with the city.
- A committed partnership with our domestic abuse advocate partner, Cornerstone, to provide safety and services during a crisis, develop long-term strategies and access to numerous programs.
- Community relationships are fostered through programs like the department's Citizens' Police Academy, human rights commission (HRC), multicultural advisory committee (MAC), police advisory commission (PAC), St. Louis Park Adult Options in Education, neighborhood associations, retail business associations, new driver education and many more.
- Information management meetings are held on a weekly basis with department stakeholders and other departments to leverage opportunities, improve quality of life issues and identify crime trends and solutions.
- The department partners with other law enforcement agencies to prepare regional response strategies, solve crimes and deliver community outreach programs.
- The Community Emergency Response Team (CERT) is used to assist with critical incidents and planned city events.

- A public safety information specialist helps identify crime trends, crime patterns and target locations; aid in complex investigations; and develop crime prevention and public safety programs.
- The department regularly works with the Community Outreach for Psychiatric Emergencies (COPE) program and leverages a full-time clinician during critical incidents when appropriate.
- The department runs a chaplaincy program for both community and department members in need.
- Social media and other public awareness platforms are used to provide awareness and prevention tips on current crime trends and general safety.
- The department partners with Hennepin County to bring a licensed senior social worker into the police department to work directly with officers and supervisors, based on a short-term case management model, to identify individuals in need of services and help with mental illness. This pilot program, developed in collaboration with Hennepin County and other cities in the area, has resulted in almost 100 case reviews in 2020 for St. Louis Park.
- Youth are provided leadership skill development and community service opportunities through our Police Explorers program.
- Board membership on the Minnesota Organized Retail Crime Association (MNORCA).
- An internal system was developed that supports our participation in the Northstar Juvenile Diversion Program.

Community policing promotes organizational strategies supporting the use of partnerships and problem-solving techniques that proactively address immediate conditions that give rise to public safety issues. Through the past few decades, rates of both violent and property crime have dropped dramatically across the country. However, some communities and segments of the population have not benefited from the decrease as much as others, and some not at all.

Community policing combines a focus on intervention and prevention through problem solving by forming collaborative partnerships with schools, social services and other stakeholders. In this way, community policing not only improves public safety, but also enhances social connectivity and economic strength, which increases community resilience to crime. Law enforcement's obligation is to reduce crime fairly while protecting the rights of citizens. Any prevention strategy that unintentionally violates civil rights, compromises police legitimacy or undermines trust is counterproductive. It must also be stressed that the absence of crime is not the final goal of law enforcement. Rather, it is the promotion and protection of public safety while respecting the dignity and rights of all.

Building Trust between Police and Communities

Building trust between police and communities is a multifaceted process that necessitates transparent communication, consistent engagement, and mutual respect. At the heart of this trust-building is the establishment of open, honest dialogue between law enforcement agencies and the communities they serve. This dialogue must be ongoing and characterized by a genuine willingness to listen and respond to community concerns. Transparency in police operations, including the clear communication of policies and procedures, is crucial. This can be achieved through regular public reports, community meetings, and accessible complaint and feedback mechanisms. Moreover, transparency extends to accountability; when police misconduct occurs, it must be addressed swiftly and justly, with appropriate consequences for those involved.

Community policing is another pivotal element in building trust. This approach emphasizes police officers building relationships with community members through regular, non-enforcement interactions. These can include attending community events, participating in local meetings, and working with community leaders to identify and solve problems collaboratively. By being present and engaged in the community, officers become familiar faces, and residents feel more comfortable and secure in their presence.

Training is also essential. Police officers should receive comprehensive training not only in law enforcement tactics but also in areas such as de-escalation techniques, cultural competence, and implicit bias. Understanding and respecting the diverse backgrounds and experiences of community members can prevent misunderstandings and foster a more empathetic approach to policing. Additionally, involving community members in the training process can provide valuable insights and reinforce the commitment to a partnership-based model of policing.

Building trust also requires a commitment to addressing systemic issues that contribute to mistrust. This includes tackling issues such as racial profiling, excessive use of force, and the lack of diversity within police departments. Policies and practices must be reviewed and reformed to ensure they are fair, equitable, and just. Establishing civilian oversight bodies can provide an independent review of police actions and policies, adding an extra layer of accountability and reassurance for the community.

Furthermore, collaboration with other community institutions, such as schools, social services, and local businesses, is vital. These partnerships can help address the root causes of crime, such as poverty, lack of education, and inadequate mental health services, thereby reducing the need for law enforcement intervention and building a safer, more resilient community.

Lastly, trust-building is a two-way street. Communities also need to engage actively with law enforcement, participating in public safety initiatives and fostering an environment where mutual respect can thrive. Recognizing and celebrating positive examples of police-community collaboration can reinforce the progress made and encourage further cooperation.

Community Alienation

The experience of community alienation among police officers is closely tied to the experience of mastery, the state of mind in which an individual feels autonomous and experiences confidence in their ability, skill, and knowledge to control or influence external events. Community policing requires departments to flatten their organizational pyramid and place even more decision-making and discretion in the hands of line officers. Taylor and Fritsch say that as the level of community alienation or isolation that officers experience increases, there will be a corresponding decrease in officers' sense of mastery in carrying out their expanded discretionary role. Secondly, a strong sense of community integration for police officers would seem to be vital to the core community policing focus of proactive law enforcement, they say. Proactive enforcement is defined as the predisposition of police officers to be actively committed to crime prevention, community problem-solving, and a more open, dynamic quality-oriented law enforcement-community partnership.

A lack of community support resulted in an increased sense of alienation and a greater degree of apathy among police officers. This lack of community support along with working in a larger populated community was associated with an increased sense of alienation and a greater degree of inactivity among police officers. Alienation resulted in an increase of negative feelings and lethargy among police officers. Research has concluded that when police officers feel socially isolated from the community they serve, the more likely they were to withdraw and feel negatively towards their citizens.

Social media

Some positives that social media brings to law enforcement would include increasing trust in law enforcement, educating the public of safety issues, decrease crime, identifying the root cause of neighbourhood crime and the "good cop" frame. When talking about increasing trust in law enforcement, social media is regarded to improve agencies' capacities to engage with the community positively. Active social media use can humanize officers and eventually increase trust between the police and the community. Educating the public-on-public safety issues, departments with a stake in community outreach can utilize social media to disseminate details on suspects, crime prevention efforts, or other public safety concerns. Recent studies have found that social media is useful for both analyzing past crime and predicting those that will occur in the future, which is conductive to intelligence-driven and predictive police models. According to "good cop" frame or theory, police personnel are honorable, obedient, well-trained, and genuinely committed to preventing crime and safeguarding the public from harm.

Some negatives that social media brings to law enforcement would include the "bad cop" frame and rapid spreading. The "bad cop" frame or theory is where police officers are portrayed as ineffective, a little crooked, and most frequently incompetent within the evil cop frame. In contrast to reality, police personnel are portrayed in police shows as being more violent and aggressive. There are times when the media's misrepresentation of police and their work has blatantly detrimental effects on police. Rapid spreading happens when negative results of a situation are published online, it might be very difficult to remove them because, as the phrase goes, "Once on the Internet, always on the Internet."

Electronic Community-Oriented Policing (E-COP) or e-Community Policing is a methodical approach to police that integrates mass communication, individual behavior, and social behavior theories into everyday policing activities. It employs push, pull, and networking tactics to carry out community-focused policing online without making reference to particular geographic places. Social networking platforms, for example, have provided police departments of all sizes a great opportunity to engage with the people they protect and serve without using the traditional mainstream media. In this sense, having the police perform E-COP and verify authentic trustworthy information sources is a smart approach to assist citizens in defending themselves and aid the police to safeguard their reputation by communicating with the public in a true and official manner. Some strategies that E-COP use include digital technologies, crime mapping, Geographic Information System (GIS), fingerprints, DNA analysis, Integrated Automated Fingerprint Identification System (IAFIS), Combined DNA Index System (CODIS), hotspot policing, cameras, smartphones, body worn cameras, dash-mounted cameras, etc. When thinking about why departments should integrate E-COP into their departments, we remember that a key element of community policing is improved communication between the police and the public. A service like E-COP provides a novel opportunity for the department to inform the public while simultaneously giving residents a new way to engage with the department.

Just like E-COP, a key concept to community relations is improved communication, while a key element of community policing is improved communication between the police and the public. A service like this provides a novel opportunity for the department to inform the public while simultaneously giving residents a new way to engage with the department.

A new topic regarding social media is mass media and the mass media act. Mass media is evolving into ever-new forms and platforms. The best thing the police can do to keep and even increase public trust in them is to construct their own public image with tact and consideration for both professional standards and existing public expectations. The legitimacy of police can be strongly impacted by image management efforts, and the police frequently utilize image management to uphold and improve their validity. The mass media act regards the public's perception of facts about criminal attitudes is somewhat tainted by the mass media itself. It informs the public about crimes being perpetrated and the necessity for vigilance and self-protection, the mass media may, on the one hand encourage crime prevention. On the other side, the media may unnecessarily heighten public dread of crimes by fostering a moral panic, which is to say, by inciting a response among the populace based on incorrect perceptions of crime hazards resulting from media themes rather than real incidences of violent crimes.

Challenges and Barriers to Effective Community Policing

Community policing initiatives often face a range of challenges that can hinder their effectiveness. These challenges include limited resources, resistance from within police departments, and community apathy or distrust.

One of the primary challenges is limited resources. Community policing requires significant investment in terms of time, personnel, and funding. Police departments often struggle with budget constraints that limit their ability to allocate officers to community engagement activities instead of traditional law enforcement duties. This can lead to insufficient staffing for community policing efforts, inadequate training for officers, and a lack of necessary equipment or facilities to support these initiatives.

Resistance from within police departments is another significant obstacle. Traditional policing models are often deeply entrenched, and shifting to a community policing approach can be met with skepticism or outright opposition from officers and leadership. Some officers may view community policing as less critical or effective than more aggressive, enforcement-focused strategies. This resistance can stem from a lack of understanding of the benefits of community policing or from a cultural mindset that prioritizes immediate crime control over long-term relationship building. Overcoming this resistance requires strong leadership, ongoing education, and the demonstration of community policing successes.

Community apathy or distrust also poses a major challenge. In many communities, especially those with a history of negative interactions with law enforcement, there can be deep-seated mistrust and skepticism towards police initiatives. This distrust can result from past incidents of police misconduct, systemic discrimination, or perceived injustices. When communities are disengaged or hostile towards police efforts, it becomes difficult to foster the collaboration and cooperation essential for community policing. Rebuilding trust in these contexts requires persistent and genuine efforts to demonstrate change and accountability.

Another challenge is the inconsistency in the implementation of community policing strategies. The effectiveness of these initiatives can vary widely depending on the commitment and competence of local police departments. Inconsistent application of community policing principles can lead to uneven results and undermine the credibility of the approach. Establishing standardized practices and ensuring that all officers receive adequate training and support is crucial for the success of community policing.

Additionally, measuring the impact of community policing can be challenging. Traditional metrics of police performance, such as crime rates and arrest numbers, may not fully capture the benefits of community policing, which include improved public trust, enhanced community relations, and greater collaboration. Developing appropriate metrics and evaluation methods to assess the effectiveness of community policing initiatives is essential to demonstrate their value and justify continued investment.

Finally, community policing initiatives can be hindered by broader societal issues such as economic inequality, lack of social services, and systemic racism. These issues often contribute to the root causes of crime and can undermine efforts to build safe and cohesive communities. Addressing these broader issues requires a holistic approach that goes beyond the scope of traditional policing and involves collaboration with other sectors, including education, housing, healthcare, and social services.

REFERENCES

1. https://online.wilson.edu/resources/what-is-community-policing/
2. https://www.everbridge.com/blog/what-is-community-policing/
3. https://www.ojp.gov/pdffiles/commp.pdf
4. Allevato, S. Developing of a Law Enforcement Plan for California Cities Committed to Quality Service Through Community-Oriented Policing. Sacramento: California Commission on Peace Officer Standards and Training. 1989.
5. Banas, Dennis, and Robert C. Trojanowicz. Uniform Crime Reporting and Community Policing—An Historical Perspective. East Lansing, Mich.: National Neighborhood Foot Patrol Center, Michigan State University, School of Criminal Justice. 1985.

6. Belknap, J., Merry Morash, and Robert C. Trojanowicz. Implementing a Community Policing Model for Work With Juveniles—An Exploratory Study. East Lansing, Mich.: National Neighborhood Foot Patrol Center, Michigan State University, School of Criminal Justice. 1986.

7. Brann, Joseph E., and Suzanne Whalley. "COPPS: The Transformation of Police Organizations." Community Oriented Policing and Problem Solving. Sacramento: California Attorney General's Crime Prevention Center. 1992.

8. Brown, Lee P. Community Policing: A Practical Guide for Police Officials. Perspectives on Policing. Washington, D.C.: U.S. Department of Justice, Office of Justice Programs, National Institute of Justice; and John F. Kennedy School of Government, Harvard University. 1989.

7 COMMUNICATION AND REPORT WRITING

INTRODUCTION

Police communication is a multifaceted aspect of law enforcement that encompasses various methods and channels used to convey information effectively within the police force and between police officers and the public. Effective communication is essential for the successful execution of police duties, ensuring public safety, and fostering community trust.

Internally, police communication involves the exchange of information between officers, departments, and other law enforcement agencies. This internal communication can take various forms, including verbal briefings, written reports, electronic communications, and the use of centralized databases. Clear and concise communication among officers is critical during operations to coordinate efforts, share intelligence, and make informed decisions quickly. For example, during an ongoing investigation or a crisis situation, the ability to communicate effectively can be the difference between a successful resolution and a failure to control the situation. Additionally, internal communication is vital for administrative functions, such as scheduling, training, and policy dissemination.

Externally, police communication focuses on interactions with the community, victims, witnesses, and suspects. This includes both formal and informal communication channels. Formal communication often involves public announcements, press releases, and official statements delivered through media outlets. These communications are designed to inform the public about ongoing investigations, crime prevention strategies, and other public safety issues. The way police communicate with the public can significantly influence public perception and trust in law enforcement. Transparent and honest communication helps build credibility and trust, while poor communication can lead to misunderstandings, fear, and mistrust. Informal communication, such as community meetings, social media interactions, and one-on-one conversations, plays a crucial role in community policing. These interactions allow officers to engage with community members on a personal level, listen to their concerns, and address their needs. Social media has become an increasingly important tool for police communication, allowing departments to reach a broad audience quickly and efficiently. Through platforms like Twitter, Facebook, and Instagram, police can provide real-time updates, share safety tips, and engage in dialogue with the community. This level of engagement helps humanize the police force and creates a sense of partnership between law enforcement and the public.

Effective police communication also involves cultural competence and sensitivity. Officers must be able to communicate effectively with people from diverse backgrounds, taking into account cultural differences, language barriers, and varying levels of trust in law enforcement. Training in cultural competence and the use of translators or bilingual officers can enhance communication and ensure that all community members receive equitable and respectful treatment.

Moreover, crisis communication is a critical component of police communication. During emergencies, such as natural disasters, terrorist attacks, or active shooter situations, the ability to disseminate accurate information quickly and efficiently can save lives. Police departments must have established protocols for crisis communication to ensure that information flows smoothly and reaches all relevant parties, including the public, media, and other emergency services.

POLICE COMMUNICATION SKILLS

Police communication skills encompass a range of abilities essential for effective law enforcement. These skills include clear and concise verbal communication, active listening, and the ability to interpret and convey non-verbal cues. Officers must be adept at using radios and other communication devices to coordinate with colleagues and provide accurate information during emergencies. Effective communication is crucial in de-escalating tense situations, gaining the trust of community members, and ensuring clear, lawful instructions are given and understood. Written communication is equally important, as officers must produce detailed, accurate reports and documentation that can withstand legal scrutiny. Additionally, cultural sensitivity and empathy play vital roles, enabling officers to interact respectfully with diverse populations and understand different perspectives. Strong communication skills foster collaboration within the police force and between law enforcement and the community, enhancing overall public safety and trust. Mastery of these skills not only aids in conflict resolution and crisis management but also supports the broader goals of transparency and accountability in policing practices.

Perhaps today more than ever, communication matters. For police and law enforcement professionals, having the interpersonal skills necessary to effectively communicate with fellow officers, subordinates, higher-ups, community members, victims and their families, other departments and jurisdictions, and the court systems is critical to the mission of "protect and serve." Police communication skills — needed to investigate crimes; de-escalate situations; build trust with communities; and write memos, reports and grants — are crucial for everyone working in law enforcement, and especially for those with leadership aspirations. Many of the top officers and professionals in law enforcement have cited effective communication skills as a key ingredient to their success. That's because the most successful law enforcement leaders understand how to communicate with people from diverse backgrounds under varying and often unpredictable conditions. They use communication to build trust, create transparency and foster an atmosphere of mutual respect and empathy, be it in the office, on the streets or in the courtroom.

What Does Good Police Communication Look Like?

Using what are sometimes referred to as "tactical communication skills," many police officers are trained to use a set of strategies in the field that can help diffuse situations and identify the root cause before they escalate out of control. In order for officers to effectively communicate with their community, earn their trust and get citizens to cooperate with their instructions, some effective communication strategies that are deployed include:

- The "80-20 principle," which was originally used in sales, says that officers should spend 80% of their time listening and 20% talking, and then use what they hear to make a connection.
- Using body language to show the person that the officer is listening carefully.
- Asking many questions, and making simple requests, one at a time.
- Asking open-ended questions, especially questions that begin with "what" and "how."
- Understanding how "emotional contagion" can benefit or hurt you. A person with mental illness may not understand all of the words an officer says, but the person will sense their tone and attitude. If the officer is shouting orders and appears tense, that increases the tension. Speaking slowly and calmly can help de-escalate the situation and convey to the person that the officer is not in a rush that they have as much time as needed to converse and reach an understanding.

Breaking Down the Language Barrier for Better Communication

It can be hard enough to communicate with suspects and community members when they speak the same language, let alone when there is a language barrier involved.

As the diversity of citizens in the United States continues to grow, police departments are actively seeking officers and law enforcement professionals who possess second language skills – and many of these departments are willing to pay a premium for those skilled candidates. For example, police in San Diego, California, receive an additional 3.5% bonus for being bilingual, and the Salem, Oregon, police department offers a 5% pay incentive for bilingual speakers of Spanish, Russian, Asian dialects or American Sign Language.

Additionally, there are a number of language training programs geared specifically toward police officers, such as the free online language training courses offered through the National Institute of Justice.

Communication is Key in De-Escalation Strategies

Communication is also being heavily relied upon to help change police perceptions and improve community relations. In response to events that have taken place over the last few years and the high level of community–police tensions that currently exist in communities across the country, police departments are increasingly focused on de-escalation strategies when it comes to training officers, making arrests and interacting with community members. What many of the best chiefs and officers have long known is that communication, done right, works. "Sometimes when a person is in crisis, all they need is to be heard," said Craig Stowell, Crisis Intervention Officer and Staff Instructor, with the Stearns County (Minnesota) Sheriff's Office in an interview with the Crisis Prevention Institute.

De-escalation in policing is a technique that attempts to reverse the long taught and encouraged method of using force to control a situation. Instead, de-escalation attempts to diffuse a situation through peaceful means such as speaking calmly, showing empathy, and asking open-ended questions to engage people in a real dialogue rather than demanding answers and displaying power and authority.

The importance of de-escalation and educating officers about that skill is beginning to impact police departments around the country. Officer Stowell's department in Minnesota now includes in-depth crisis prevention training in their classroom sessions, and Minnesota has begun awarding six hours of continuing education credit for licensed officers who complete these programs. The Chicago Police Department has also updated its de-escalation protocols and emphasized their commitment to finding non-violent and non-lethal outcomes during incidents. The department mandates annual de-escalation and use of force training for officers. But learning how to communicate with diverse populations ranging from criminal suspects to victims, social service agencies, witnesses and other community members –some of who may be dealing with trauma, addiction, mental illness, poverty or any number of afflictions — is not easy. Communication techniques and skills, especially as they apply to modern police work, must be learned and practiced in order to be effective. That's why professional training and experience combined with higher education can be so effective.

Law Enforcement Communication

In addition to practicing active listening, asking questions when needed and using the right body language, there are other steps law enforcement agencies and departments can take to improve and strengthen communication.

- Talk less and listen more. As Lexipol Co-Founder Gordon Graham explains, "In law enforcement, the ability to communicate is one of our most important tools," emphasizing that both talking *and* listening are essential to being an effective law enforcement officer. "Take a few minutes to listen compassionately, emphatically to what they're saying. And who knows — you might even hear some valuable information."
- Be aware of potential language barriers. English is a second language for many in the United States, which is why it's important for law enforcement officers to keep this mind and seek out a translator, if needed.
- Ask open-ended questions. While "yes or no" questions are important, consider adding in questions that begin with "what" or "how," which may help you draw out more details or a more elaborate answer.
- Be mindful of body language and non-verbal cues such as body position, tone of voice, facial expression, eye contact, hand gestures and physical distance.

- Do not take any insults or any verbal attacks personally. Law enforcement officers are often faced with stressful situations, but they need to remain calm and poised — which is not to say they cannot show any signs of emotion.
- Be compassionate and empathetic. An effective law enforcement leader must be able to try and understand how someone else is feeling. It is also important to treat everyone with compassion and respect, regardless of whether they are fellow officers, victims, witnesses or community members.
- Understand the limits of verbal de-escalation. While verbal communication is typically the first step, it is important to understand when physical intervention is necessary, such as when immediate action is needed to prevent death or injury.
- Develop effective, consistent communication. It's crucial to have protocols in place, regardless of the situation. This includes everything from figuring out the process for public alerts and internal communication to deciding when, and if, officers are allowed to speak with the media. Agencies and departments also need to consider through which channels — and how often — information is communicated.
- Prepare for crisis communication, which includes identifying a crisis team and a spokesperson ahead of time. This is especially important when it comes to fast-paced situations in which a variety of stakeholders and individuals need to be quickly contacted or alerted.
- Be proactive. Law enforcement agencies should continually examine policies and procedures and update them if necessary. It's also important to communicate any updates to the appropriate parties (internal personnel, the public, etc.) This type of transparency and initiative will also help build trust with the community.
- Participate in specialized communication programs. One such example is the Crisis and Emergency Risk Communication (CERC) training from the Centers for Disease Control and Prevention. Both webinars and in-person training options are available.
- Engage in continuing trends and information. For example, the CERC Corner includes specifics on messaging and audience, crisis communication plans, community engagement and the role of social media, media and cell phone communication.

COMMUNICATION COMPETENCY

To understand the role of effective communication skills for police officers ask yourself this: how does a police officer develop the skills to communicate to a mother, her son has just died in a motor vehicle accident? How does a police officer deescalate a life threatening situation without the use of force or any party being injured? Communication skills are considered fundamental tools for policing. For police educators, the intrinsic unpredictable nature of policing with no two police/public interactions being identical requires preparing the new officer with a tool box of communication strategies which may be adapted to meet the myriad of situations confronted by the officer in their professional practice. Two of the most significant roles for communication in policing are providing information (i.e. traffic directions, court hearings, instructions for offenders and victims,) and receiving/seeking information (i.e. recording witness statements, collaborating with community agencies, encouraging cooperation from offenders, victims,) the manner and degree of effectiveness with which an officer carries out this communication has the capacity to have a life altering impact on the other parties involved. This chapter explores the essential components of communication, the societal and human influences which create barriers to effective communication for police officers and the guidelines for developing best practice as a communicator in the complex, often volatile world of policing.

Communication, irrespective of the medium used to communicate can be divided into two categories/forms. Intrapersonal communication and interpersonal communication. The intrapersonal communication as that which a person has with themselves, the dialogue they have in their head for example, weighing up the pros and cons when decision making, rehearsing messages to deliver to others. In the process of intrapersonal communication a person learns about themselves, they judge themselves, they reflect on the effectiveness of their communication with others what may be done differently in a similar situation in the future. Interpersonal communication is the communication between a person and one or more people. This interpersonal communication may be face to face, on the telephone/teleconference, video conference, email, electronic text message or printed document (letter, report). Intrapersonal communication and interpersonal communication are co dependant and influential. The key to being an effective, ethical and influential communicator lies in recognising, understanding and managing the various components of interpersonal and intrapersonal communication, in essence developing identify as communication competence. As the focus of this chapter is to provide a hands on guideline for developing best practice communication skills in the policing environment the essential concepts will be explained to the degree that will achieve this aim. However, there are a plethora of excellent communication books available which explore the key communication concepts in more depth.

Intrapersonal Communication

Intrapersonal communication is influenced in the main by a person's age, gender, socio-cultural beliefs, education, life and work experience, environmental factors and the situational context in which interpersonal communication takes place. Here too these factors are interdependent. These factors influence how we see ourselves and how we believe we are perceived by others. If intrapersonal communication is the dialogue one has in one's head, how then is this influenced by the above factors? Consider the 23year old police constable called to attend a motor vehicle accident involving a 19 year old female of Caucasian background and a 65 year old male of Greek heritage who demonstrates both a strong Greek accent and limited English language skills. Here the constable's intrapersonal communication will be influenced by: the age gap – has the constable any previous experience of communicating with older people, with people who have limited English language skills? Socio-cultural considerations – what exposure has the constable had with people of Greek heritage, are there cultural factors to consider here? Previous experience – has the constable had a positive or negative prior interaction with a similar member of society? Education – what does the constable know about communicating with people from a non-English speaking background the choice of language and its formality and simplicity? What of the environmental factors? has this incident occurred when the officer is at the end of a 12 hour shift, is there a fatigue factor, is it cold, raining, a large number of bystanders, is this the constable's first attendance at a motor vehicle accident?- is there a fear of 'getting it wrong'? The considerations are limitless, however, this situation demonstrates the connect between the officer's habitus, life experience, education, age etc with the intrapersonal communication they have prior to the interpersonal communication which will need to take place. Whilst there are elements which influence a person's intrapersonal communication, such as age, gender, cultural and educational experiences over which they have had no control, once a person recognises these influences and understands, through education, their value, they are then able to manage and include those which will support their development as competent communicators.

A discussion of intrapersonal communication is not complete without due consideration of the influence of self concept/self awareness. How do we develop a self perception? Firstly, it is important to acknowledge that self perception is an ever changing concept. How we perceived ourselves and the image we portray to others is different as we age, mature and experience the world: the image we perceive of ourselves at 15years old will be markedly altered to the one we perceive at the age of 35 or 60 years old. Our self perception is developed through the feedback we receive from others, how they see us, how they react to us and through the manner in which we choose to be seen. Self perception is developed by understanding our strengths and weaknesses, being receptive and intuitive to the responses from those with whom we interact. It is a well know adage that we never see ourselves as others see us, why? The explanation lies at the core of communication challenges, the players are humans and each one is influenced by all of those factors previously discussed therefore it is highly unlikely that any two people will have identical thoughts, feelings, views of the world and of people with whom they have contact. Our self concept develops though understanding ourselves, our self awareness, managing our self awareness, understanding our relationships with others and managing our relationship with others.

Why is understanding the perception we portray to others important to a police officer and how does this influence communication? Let us place this into context: consider what victim of a crime against the person – sexual assault, domestic violence, child abuse is going to feel comfortable talking about the more intimate details of the crime with an officer who has an aura of uncaring clinical efficiency, treating the situation as ' another job to be processed'. Now the officer has been praised in the work place for their efficiency, their attention to detail their reliability in rate of solving crimes and therefore have a self concept that they are good at their job, believe their perception by others is that they are a dependable process orientated, hardworking, officer with a focus on crime reduction. On this feedback, it would be appropriate that the officer sees themselves as efficient, effective and meeting the needs of victims i.e. speedy resolution. What they do not necessarily see is to the victim of crime, they appear officious and lacking in empathy. It does not automatically follow that because a person is efficient and hardworking that they also intuitively display an empathetic, caring nature. Here there is a disconnect between perceptions which has the potential to damage both good police work and a sustainable supportive outcome for the victim. The role of self concept is deeply embedded in the later discussion of communication strategies.

Interpersonal Communication

To understand the role of interpersonal communication in the development of communication competence it is critical to understand what factors are considered elements of interpersonal communication and their influence on the effectiveness and quality of the resultant communication interaction. As briefly mentioned, earlier in the chapter, interpersonal communication is that communication which takes place between a person and one or several other people i.e. between or inter person. Similar to intrapersonal communication, age, gender, socio-cultural, environmental, life and work experience, education and the situational context of the communication are all factors which influence the communication interaction. However, in interpersonal communication there is the additional consideration that these factors influence all of the individual parties in the communication interaction, to differing degrees and all individuals bring to the communication their own intrapersonal communication.

The common denominator is that all parties are involved in the communication process as a receiver or sender of a message simultaneously. This communication process is described in Figure 1. Here communication is seen as a continuous process and all parties influence the process through their choice of the communication channel and the verbal and non verbal communication tools for delivering and responding to a message.

How then does age influence the communication cycle? Consider the 45 year old police officer who attends a neighbourhood noise complaint at 11.30p.m. to learn at the location there is an 18th birthday celebration underway with more than 100 people in attendance who appear to be affected by alcohol or drug consumption. If there is no illegal behaviour occurring and the officer approaches the 18year old male to seek cooperation to keep the party noise down to a level which does not unduly disturb the neighbours, there are numerous potential intrapersonal dialogues which can impact on the interpersonal communication here: i.e. the 18year old may think what does this crusty oldie want to do spoiling my fun, doesn't he remember what it was like to be young! We're not doing anything wrong! The officer on the other hand, whilst attempting a reasonable approach may be thinking- these young ones think they rule the world, why don't they grow up would make my job a lot easier! He may also be mindful of the last such incident he attended where the outcome was far from desirable with several arrests. The influence of age is intrinsically linked to societal trends i.e. the 'gen y, gen x' debate the global perception that today's youth are disconnected to their elders and consequently do not show respect. It is not unusual for young police officers to be faced with elderly victims who want to talk to an older officer, mistakenly believing that all young people do not care for or respect the elderly.

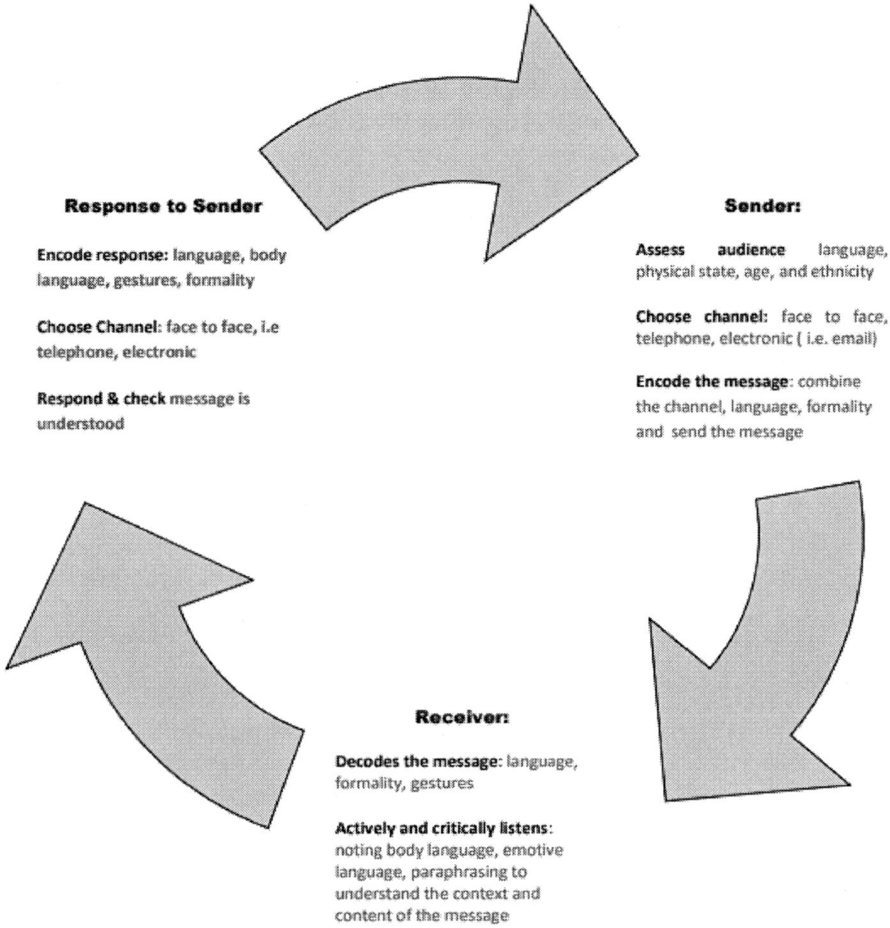

Figure 1. Continuous communication process.

Source: https://www.researchgate.net/publication/273451041_Communications_in_Policing

Intimately interwoven with the issue of age is language. The meaning of words changes through their generational use. A simple example is found in the use of the words 'cool', 'gay' 'brother' which have different meanings depending on the age group in which they are being used. To the elderly woman, brother would mean a genuine male blood relative, whilst for younger people brother means blood relative and/or friend/gang member. The pace with which the meanings change is rapid, and if in doubt the first source is an English language dictionary, for other variations, the most reliable source lies with the person who uses the word, what does it mean to them.

The influence of gender is not dissimilar to that of age and as with all of the influences. Seemingly straightforward policing incidents can be dramatically influenced by the gender of those involved in the communication interaction. In considering the following examples, include consideration of age and the potentially disparate intrapersonal thoughts the parties bring to the interaction. The distraught mother who reports a missing child, the attending officer is a young male. The mother's reaction? – the officer is too young to understand, he is not a mother, he cannot understand what it is like to lose a child? Unfortunately for the victim, in this situation if the attending officer were a female, there is no guarantee they are also a mother. What might the officer be thinking? – we have a process, which manages these situations, the woman should trust this process. Similarly, how does gender impact on a situation where a female officer attends a domestic disturbance which is revealed to be a dispute between same sex male partners? The female from a middle eastern background involved as a victim of crime, here issues of gender are interwoven with cultural beliefs, resulting in the female not wanting to talk to a male police officer about the crime. At this point, you will be able to discern a pattern building, whereby all of the influencing factors on interpersonal communication do not act independently, rather they are interdependent. Socio-cultural factors are an explicit example of this interdependence and influence socio-cultural factors permeate across all communication contexts.

The global mobilisation of ethnic groups has created a changing cultural landscape. What does this mean for policing? The policing domain is a 'melting pot' of cultures, attitudes, values, religious beliefs, language, and behavioural norms. Cultural diversity is a complex subject; here the focus is exploring the overarching themes which impact communication at the frontline of policing. For more detailed analysis and discussion of cultural diversity and policing. The ethical dimensions of western society encourage sensitivity to cultural differences in a process of creating a society in which those from diverse cultural backgrounds can coexist in a peaceful environment. Mastering communication competence in this culturally diverse domain will enhance the quality and effectiveness of policing. It is unrealistic to expect police officers to have a deep understanding of all cultures, what is important is to acknowledge the most influential generic factors which influence communication across cultures. The first of these is the nature and status of policing.

The perception and in some cases the experience people have with policing. The very presence of an officer in uniform can conjure up terrifying memories for those who in other countries have been persecuted. Here lies a conundrum, an attending officer is unlikely to know how they may be perceived by the person with whom they are interacting, again the intrapersonal communication is called into account. The challenge for the police officer is to acknowledge that an assumption that the person with whom they interact will understand the rule of law by which they are governed is false. There are numerous reasons for this, the most common of which can be a limited comprehension of the English language, mixed with the trauma of the moment in which they find they are interacting with a police officer, a genuine fear of the unknown (i.e. what have they done wrong and what will happen to them).

The second significant socio-cultural element is one often less tangible, however, equally influential, stereotyping. The difficulty here is that firstly, individuals can be unaware that their words and actions demonstrate stereotyping and secondly, these words and actions can be inherently subtle but influential to the communication interaction. The highway patrol officer who attends two parked vehicles beside the highway, the drivers appear to be of Somalian descent and the officer has attended several drug raids involving Sudanese people in the neighbourhood in previous days. This officer suspects there is illegal activity occurring based on the ethnicity of the drivers and the neighbourhood. The drivers (who have stopped because they are lost) believe the police target all Somalians and are therefore anxious with the officer's presence. Here we have two contrasting perspectives before any communicating has taken place.

The third significant socio-cultural factor to be considered is that of use of language. Whilst there is the potential for the communication to be taking place between those who do not speak the same language, there is also the manner in which language is used. The use of formal or social language. In policing this is often a fine line. If the language is too formal, the recipient may not understand, by contrast if the language is too social/informal the meaning may be misinterpreted and/or purposefully misinterpreted. (This does not include those situations which require police officers to deliver information in line with legislative requirements.) To place this into context, consider the following situation: police officers attending a late night disturbance at a licenced premise would not expect the alcohol affected patrons to respond positively to a lengthy, legally worded formal request to vacate the premises. A brief, simply worded instruction is likely to achieve the desired outcome more readily." Right folks, it is time for you to leave now"

The life and work experience of the sender and receiver in the communication cycle impacts on the successful interpretation of messages. The extent to which a person has interacted with people from diverse cultures, either socially or in the work context, the extent to which they have lived, played sport, socialised, worked with children, youths, adults, parents, the elderly and in what context all have an influence on a person's ability to communicate effectively. The broader the life and work experience which embraces diverse situations and people, the greater the opportunity to understand others and learn from the communication experience.

The police officer who has children or siblings has an increased capacity to understand the language and perception of a distraught young child lost in a major public place or involved in a motor vehicle accident. Equally, the adult member of the public who witnesses a hit and run accident who is from the health profession, and familiar with human injuries and the importance of detail, has a strengthened ability to clearly articulate what they witnessed. Embedded in a person's life and work experience are both the formal education they receive and the education which life teaches them. As this experience is unique to each individual it follows that the content and context of their education that is applied in communication is also unique and in the main unpredictable.

The final factor to be discussed which significantly impacts on interpersonal communication relates to the environmental/situational context of the communication interaction.

It is acknowledged in the policing profession, that police have limited communication with members of the public in times of celebration, realistically, police – citizen interactions are at times when the member of the public is experiencing trauma/and requires assistance or has behaved unlawfully and is or will be apprehended. The trauma may take many forms, injury, fear, distress, grief and manifest into behaviour which for the individual when in a less traumatic state would be unusual/abnormal. In a state of trauma whilst a person's senses are often heightened it does not transpose that they have clarity of thought or action. This state impedes clear interpersonal communication for police, not only are their messages not heard, the message they receive may be incomprehensible. The reflective communicator would be asking - Was the interaction successful, was the intent of the message received and understood the same intent with which it was sent?

COMMUNICATION STRATEGIES

Non Verbal Language

Developing skills which allow police to acknowledge embrace and demonstrate an understanding of the positive and negative influences on their interpersonal communication is a continuous challenge paralleled by the constant changes within the elements themselves (i.e. use of language, cultural attitudes and behaviours, situational context). There are key communication concepts which support the development of strategies for addressing barriers in police/citizen interactions namely, empathy, active listening, verbal and non verbal language, and conflict management. For police officers, these concepts are all inclusive when communicating; they are not effective in isolation. It is the application of the skills which reflect these strategies which will provide for ethical, responsible, productive communication and for the individual build communication competence.

Empathy

It is widely acknowledged that empathetic behaviour is demonstrating an understanding of how another person feels, 'walking in their shoes', and viewing the world through their eyes. A note of caution, empathy should not be confused with sympathy. Sympathy involves emotion and responding and mirroring another's emotions. Appreciatively there are times when it is difficult to separate human emotion for police officers (attending incidents of human injury and loss) being empathetic assists with this separation, allowing them to focus on the police role.

Being an empathetic communicator acknowledges the emotions of the other party, how the person is feeling. Empathy is displayed through verbal language and non verbal language (refer to later discussion), and demonstrates a commitment to the conversation and for each participant, that the other has taken their share of responsibility to support the communication interaction. An empathic communicator would choose words which demonstrate their interest "I can see you are upset this must be very difficult for you, (acknowledging how they feel) however, please help me to understand what happened here..."(places the individual in the centre of the communication).

Paralanguage

Words are not the only important component, paralanguage, the tone, pitch, volume of the voice and the speed of delivery share an equal role for the clear intent of the words to be understood. Hence in the above case, a soft tone, medium rate of delivery would suggest acknowledgement of the distress felt by the individual, and that whilst the police officer knows time may be of the essence, the individual should take their time as distress may cause them to rush and be incomprehensible. The desired outcome is that the person feels listened to and valued and is more likely to provide as much information as they are capable of at the time. In terms of policing, more information initially, fast tracks the process of investigation. Consider the alternative: "yeah, you're upset but I just need the facts" spoken in rapid fire fashion, with an abrupt matter-of-fact tone", how do you think the individual might feel? What chance of them feeling comforted and comfortable and divulging as much information as possible? Empathy relieves tension.

Words similar to those in the good example above may be used in all policing encounters; the delivery will need adjustment dependent of the situation. To the man who has just been assaulted in a violent fight and is 'fired up' an officer can use similar words, as they acknowledge the person is upset, however, they are also acknowledging the officer is there to help, but needs the persons cooperation "I can see you're upset, t want to help you, we need to have your injuries seen to then if you can tell me what happened tonight."

Active Listening and Body Language

The use of empathy does not stop at the initial contact, it must continue in the conversation to be of ultimate value. How is this achieved? Through applying the skills of active listening. What is active listening? Active listening is demonstrating through both verbal and non verbal language that you are involved and committed to the communication exchange. Non verbal communication is that which is displayed through body language and paralanguage. The table below summaries the role of our body language, the list is not exhaustive, it serves to provide an insight into how thoughts and feelings are demonstrated through non verbal language, they work interdependently so a listener should read them as a 'package' to understand the intent of the message being sent. The thoughtful communicator will choose to use their body language to ensure the message they send verbally is supported by their non verbal communication. At times it is only body language that is used to convey a message and here the importance of choosing the correct expression and knowing how to read the body language of others becomes paramount.

The policing domain is littered with such situations, often they are quick second reactions between policing partners when attending an incident or between police and members of the public, in any situation, the ability to read body language can mean the difference between serious injuries or a peaceful outcome. The officer who indicates with the gesture of his hand to his partner – you go to the left, and I'll go to the right.

The member of the public who gives a dramatic finger up gesture to the police officer indicates disrespect, I am not listening. No words are spoken in these two examples and yet the message is clear.

Parts of the body	Expression
Eyes	Rolling the eyes – disbelief, boredom Widening of the eyes – surprise, interest, or fear Screwing up of the eyes – suspicion, distaste, anger Eye contact: actively listening, confident and interested, assessing the other person/people (especially

	relevant to policing – the eyes are the window to the soul Maintaining eye contact creates inclusiveness with those in the communication interaction Strong eye contact can imply aggression especially when accompanied by other verbal or non verbal communication Maintaining eye contact can convey status, here too, this is a valuable tool for police officers Avoiding eye contact: may indicate indifference (bored) or subservience (acknowledging status) or politeness (do not wish to impose/intrude0
Mouth	Smiling – happy, pleasant thoughts, pleased Down-turned mouth – sad, grief, disappointment Grimace – fear, suspicion, dislike
Facial muscles	Relaxed – calm Tightened – pensive, distressed, angry
Hands	Clenched fists – angry, impatient, stressed Open upward palm – friendly, conciliatory, open to negotiation
Arms	Folded across the body – negative body language : I am not listening, not open to negotiation or conciliation, I am in charge Arms relaxed by the side of the body: calm, comfortable with the situation Arms out in front of the body palms opened out: wait, stop, stand back, don't come closer Arms out in front palms upwards: come closer, I am open to the conversation
Body	Slouched: disinterest, bored, not actively listening Standing up straight: listening, respected, dependable, confident
Body placement	Leaning in to the conversation: attentive , actively listening Standing aside, back from the conversation: non committed to the conversation
Head	Turned away: not interested, not actively listening Nodding: actively listening, responsive and engaged
Gestures	Universal gestures for example: outstretched arm palm upwards = STOP, Turning ones back – ignoring, uninterested, disengaged, disrespectful There are a multitude of gestures, some culturally specific , the key to understanding is to place these in context with all other cues in the communication encounter

Critical listening

Critical listening provides an avenue through which to apply active listening skills. For effective communication, and this is particularly pertinent in the realm of policing, whilst acknowledging how someone is feeling it is also paramount to hear through the emotion to what is being said. Critical listening requires the use of paraphrasing, demonstrating that the message has been heard by repeating the key points to check for understanding that the message has been received and understood correctly. This provides an opportunity for both parties to accept responsibility for the message, remember the parties are both senders and receivers at the same time. The officer who is faced with an angry person swearing and shouting that he has been robbed at a busy intersection late at night will need to hear through the emotion to find out the facts of the incident. In these circumstances, history tells us that asking the person to calm down is not always the most effective tactic unless an explanation is provided. Put yourself in the man's shoes (empathy) he needs to know what the benefit to him is if he does calm down. Check the difference between the following two officer responses: (1) "Mate, calm down, calm down, look just calm down or I will have to arrest you' in a stern, demanding voice, the volume attempting to reach over the top of the victim or (2) "Mate calm down, I can't help you until I understand what has happened, I need you to tell me so I can get the facts straight, so just calm down and you can check I've understood what you are saying".. spoken with an assertive, strong voice, not shouting, but insistent. As illustrated in the example above paralanguage combined with verbal language can have a dramatic affect on a communication interaction. The words spoken can be comprehensively altered by the paralanguage used in delivery, consider the following: "Yes officer I am okay about the mess the kids have made here, I'll get it cleaned up" said in a loud menacing, angry tone, up right stance and clenched fists. Clearly, the person is not happy, and yet the words suggest that they are okay. It is the attentive police officer who seeks these indicators that will understand the true meaning behind the message.

One of the most explicit areas of policing in which this is particularly valuable is interviewing. Irrespective of whether conversation management or cognitive interviewing is taking place, reading the body language displayed by the interviewee is essential to the progress and outcome of an interview. Similarly, the non verbal language and paralanguage chosen by the interviewing police officer is crucial to the management of the interview progress and outcome, it may ultimately determine who is in charge of the interview. The often overlooked skill of strategically using periods/moments of silence in conversation has the capacity to provide opportunity to assess the progress of the communication and the comfort zone of the participants.

Silence is considered a component in communication as valuable as all others. The situational context of the communication determines the use of silence. The officer who has the patience to allow periods of silence during conversation with a distraught, or anxious person, often reaps the rewards, silence allows communicators time to think, recall events and impressions, think about what has been said and what next to say. It is the use of silence as a control mechanism over someone's emotion that is the essence of the power of silence in communication. Silence can be uncomfortable especially when it is used purposefully as negative reinforcement, the 'silent treatment' as it has long been referred to for example. The strength of silence is misused by those who do not understand it's power, the offender for example being questioned whose motive is not to reveal information mistakenly believes that giving the officer the 'silent treatment' will in some measure assist his cause and provide him with emotional leverage over the communication interaction – who do you think has the emotional leverage here? There is a place for the use of silence as positive reinforcement. The investigating officer in communication with a young couple over the tragic drowning of their child would intersperse the communication with silence as a form of respect, relieving the anxiety of the couple, allowing them time to work through their thoughts and emotions. What would be gained by rushing such an interview?

Verbal language

Verbal language is the vocabulary/ words used in communication. If only it were that simple, whilst there is a dictionary meaning for words (denotation), as we discovered in our discussion on language previously there is also the meanings others have for the words in their world (youth vs. elderly) the connotations and/

or hidden and emotional meanings people apply to words. For policing, this can be akin to navigating a maze. The challenge is in avoiding the use of words which have may have diametrically opposed meanings depending on the context in which they are used, dependent upon the cultural group in whose presence they are used and avoiding revealing unpredictable emotional responses. The word 'understand' for example, seemingly simple in meaning, however, recall the previous example of the young woman who had reported her child missing. In an attempt to be empathetic the officer says "I understand how you feel...." It is quite likely that the woman, in an emotionally heightened state will seize on this statement, demanding how would the officer understand? Have they lost a child? Careful choice of words can avoid such situations: I can appreciate/see you must be distraught, I want to help you, please can you tell me...." In a politically correct age, there is documented best practice for politically correct language, in essence, non discriminatory and non sexist language and the combination of political correctness and assertive language provides an officer with the best possible chance of remaining in control of police/citizen interactions. It is timely at this point to briefly discuss the concept of assertiveness as it is indefinably linked to verbal and non verbal language. The nature of policing draws officers into situations which are fraught with tension and anger. Anger met with anger does not resolve issues; more likely exacerbates situations and is unproductive in the process of resolving the underlying problem. Anger is an emotion and officers need skills to manage situations without being drawn into the emotion of others. Assertiveness is a powerful tool for the officer to have in his communication kit bag. To be assertive is to maintain a bottom line, whilst using respectful verbal language, supported by appropriate non threatening body language, informing of the benefit to others of compliance (what's in it for them) allowing the other party to make a choice. The use of non emotive words assists in deescalating emotionally charged situations. The officer who maintains an approach which reflects ethical, polite, empathetic and critical listening techniques has a solid base from which to be excused for misinterpretations by others.

Conflict Management

It is in the management of conflict that the ability to address the influencing factors of interpersonal and intrapersonal communication is evidenced. Conflict in its multitude of forms is ever present in policing, from the unhappy neighbour to major public riots or tragedies and all manner of incidents requiring police response in between. The following point indicates the core guiding principles for responding to conflict which are applicable in the policing environment.

1. Assess the situation by observing the non verbal cues and critically listening for the message
2. Focus on being professional and remain objective do not react emotionally, remain assertive
3. Respond empathetically with genuine interest and concern. Use supportive statements
4. Paraphrase your understanding of the problem and ask questions to clarify the issue. Use questions to keep control of the encounter

5. Where possible ask the person to suggest the outcome

The conflict management model is transferable to all communication encounters. Each phase of the model allows for the application of active listening, verbal and non verbal language, empathy, socio-cultural understanding to the myriad of unique situational contexts in policing. This process supports demonstrating respect and professionalism whilst remaining in control of the communication encounter. At this point revisiting the case of the angry male shouting incoherently that he has been robbed at a busy city intersection late at night provides an opportunity to consider whether the application of the conflict management model draws together the key principles of interpersonal and intrapersonal communication. Place yourself in the role of the attending police officer:

- What should the officer say/do first?
  Be polite, announce the officer's presence, ask if the male is injured in an assertive, medium paced delivery
- What body language – hand gestures, facial expressions, eye movement, body stance should be used?
  Upright, confident stance, arm outstretched palm hand upward in the universally accepted stop position, establish eye contact, relaxed facial muscles
- What socio-cultural issues are there to consider?
  Potential anti-police sentiment and on behalf of the police officer- this could be the third angry, male the officer has attended to on a busy night- the intrapersonal communication has to be acknowledged and managed
- Is age an influencing factor here?
  Irrespective of age the person should be treated with due respect, if elderly they may be confused, this needs to be established through the initial contact and opening dialogue
- Are there other factors which might need to be considered? Is the male drug or alcohol affected, or suffering a mental illness?
  In initial contact, assess the situation, look for the non verbal clues: is the male upright and balanced, state of dress, clarity of speech, dilated pupils
- Is language comprehension a potential influence here?
  In initial contact, one of the verbal clues to be checked and if necessary the officer may need to choose verbal language to accommodate any limited language literacy displayed be the male
- How can the officer control the communication interaction?
  The male wants attention, to be the focus of the officer's attention. Using questions to keep the male focused on the information the officer needs. Questions will assist in calming the male and allowing the officer to hear through the emotion to the real message behind the words and behaviour being exhibited by the male.
- How can the officer maintain a state of calm and cooperation from the male?
  Be assertive, maintain a bottom line, informing and restating where

necessary that the officer needs information in order to assist. Paraphrasing the information to check for accuracy

Models and guidelines are designed to be flexible and adaptable within the bounds of the situational context of the police/citizen interaction. As evidenced in the above scenario, the officer response is innately determined by the reactions of the male and adapted to the circumstances.

Written/Electronic Communication

A discussion of communication in the policing context would not be complete without consideration of protocols for best practice for written communication. The key principles of best practice for interpersonal communication are equally applicable in the context of written communication. Intrapersonal communication influences the content and context of written communication, the decision to send a text message, or make a telephone call or meet with a person face to face is determined by the situational context and with which method of delivery the sender is more confident. Clearly, a major difference with written communication is the absence of vital supporting clues such as body language; this increases the challenge for both the sender and receiver. The choice of words becomes the dominant factor and can bring success or failure. With the many technologies now used for the transmittal of the written word and the trend to shorten messages i.e. the accepted use of 'text language' and 140 character twitter messages, both attracting the omission of potentially enlightening words, increases the likelihood of misinterpretation.

The connotations people attach to words become of increasing importance and either hinders or supports the successful transmission and receipt of messages. In the often fast paced work of policing, the 'niceties' of messages is overlooked in preference to 'getting the job done'. As indicated previously, this is fraught with hazards, it is important to take the time to write explicitly and ensure that the message is unambiguous, will not offend, the words are appropriate, acknowledge cultural sensitivity and there is less likelihood the message will be misinterpreted by the receiver.

motive words are clear indicates of the state of mind of the sender, these become vital clues. Here as with interpersonal communication, emotive words are useful in supporting a message, however, they remain clues and the receiver needs to read beyond the emotion to understand the true meaning of the message. Additional considerations in written communication are the potential lack of confidentiality, for example emails and text messages are easily forwarded to others and can remain in the public domain and the permanency of the written word, not easily erased.

Guiding principles for written communication

- Assess the audience
- Choose language and formality which suits the audience and context
- Avoid ambiguity – write clearly choose words with a low risk of misinterpretation
- Demonstrate cultural and ethical sensitivity
- Check for understanding- use paraphrasing And Remember your written word may be displayed in the public domain

Telephone Communication

The elements which influence intrapersonal and interpersonal communication are actively engaged in telephone communication, with the exception of body language. Paralanguage becomes the dominant factor, the pitch, tone, volume use of pauses are the vital clues in receiving and sending a message. Critical listening is the key to telephone communication. Listening for the meaning behind the words, combining these with the situational context of the message provides the opportunity to avoid misunderstandings. Paraphrasing is essential in this communication medium, summarising and repeating the main points to check for accuracy may be the defining action between life and death. Whilst paraphrasing is considered essential in all telephone communication it becomes increasingly important when limited command of the English language is a factor. Unfortunately, when under stress/trauma a person will instinctively lapse into their native language in the urgent desire to send a message.. There is a mistaken belief that raising the volume of the voice will result in a person having a better understanding of English. Watch for this the next time you observe communication between a native English speaker and a non English speaker As with written communication, the emotive words are a valuable guide to understanding the meaning of the message. Critically listening will allow the receiver to disentangle the core message from the emotion of the situation. Similarly, the sender should be conscious of the words they choose to avoid misunderstanding and provide precise, clear information.

The guiding principles for telephone communication are founded in guidelines for managing conflict and written communication:

- Speak clearly
- Assess the audience
- Choose language and formality which suits the audience and context
- Let the speaker's emotion be your window into their world
- Be empathetic
- Critically Listen
- Demonstrate cultural and ethical sensitivity
- Check for understanding- use paraphrasing

THE IMPORTANCE OF WRITING SKILLS IN POLICING

Law enforcement agencies of all types are part of large bureaucracies whether they are directly or indirectly linked and rely heavily on written documents, and the presentation based on them, to communicate for their individual missions. Law enforcement leaders have found poorly written documents could have negative consequences as there is a constant scrutiny on police officers and the criminal justice system. Police officer writings, whether in reports, press releases, or evaluations, are important to the perception of the organization's effectiveness. As the time between incident and media reporting closes, it is imperative police writings are clear, concise, and understood by the citizens as to avoid backlash and protest. Skillful writing enables an officer to think critically in investigations, form good arguments, and increase communication skills. Well-written reports provide a clear picture of an event and the circumstances surrounding it as well as providing an excellent reference source when testifying in court or creating intelligence briefs.

"The ability of a police officer to accurately report and record events and investigations is a cornerstone requirement of our profession. I have seen police officers lose their jobs and criminal investigations due to poor reporting practices. Poor documentation and reporting also contributes to a mistrust from the public and a lack of accountability."

Types of Writing in Policing

Law enforcement officers are required to write a variety of different reports and reviews, yet the attention paid to these reports is often neglected. Line officers will write reports on incidents, uses of force, car crashes, internal communications, and daily activity. Other types of officers, like detectives, are writing investigative reports, follow-up supplements, prosecution summaries, search warrants, operations plans, and threat assessments. Supervisory officers write employee evaluations and must ensure the subordinates report writing is checked for mistakes or inaccuracies. Police administrators will write supervisor evaluations, grants, policy and procedure, departmental directives, activity reports, press releases, and budget reports. All levels of police officers will be asked to provide memorandums, emails, and social media posts, which provide unnecessary perspectives if not written correctly.

During a law enforcement officer's career, they will write on a variety topics and issues, and although officers are not writing scholarly articles, they must be articulate, concise, and clear in their writing. Police are often asked to produce documents like notes and statements during court proceedings representing a direct reflection of how the officers thinks through problems and collects their thoughts.

Improving Writing Skills in Policing

Research has shown police training academies do not provide adequate training in writing skills and that community policing, use of force, and problem-solving training have flooded the curriculum to such an extent there is no room for writing skills training beyond the basics. Suggested models of curriculum seem to still negate the importance of writing as they do not include any training hours into the program to address it. Further research into police writing skills could help in many ways and the lack of literature on writing skills in policing shows a distinct need for research in the area so that improvement designs can be constructed.

Improving the writing skills of officers is not only needed, it is challenging. One study showed that ninety percent of mid-level professionals said effective writing was a skill of great importance in their daily tasks. Part of increasing an officer's professionalism is ensuring their reports are reflective of the manner in which they wish to be perceived.

Professional policing websites describe a few ways that police officers can improve their reports. One is to avoid writing abbreviations or police lingo when writing reports. Often times, the reader will not know what the meaning is, and it confuses them and could be attributed to the constant use of third person when first person is clearer and simpler. Other issues are grammatical and spelling errors where run on sentences and false possessives are used regularly.

The literature has shown that an officer who possesses a higher education than high school and who has good writing skills, has the likelihood to perform better than officers who do not. Scholars say this is because the college degree requirements will enhance the capabilities in the areas of problem solving, critical thinking, and communication skills which lead to a more mature and responsible officer. It is shown that becoming a well-written professional is parallel to understanding other cognitive levels. This could be interpreted as being a good writer shows a higher level of critical thinking and problem-solving skills needed in law enforcement.

It has been seen that deliberate practice of writing has led to an improvement in the performance of tasks which are related to written composition, such as report writing. Officer report writing needs the same attention where practice and experience in writing about different situations and stress levels will increase effectiveness (Reynolds, 2014). It takes two decades to develop good writing habits and a writing routine, which is generally developed in grade school, middle school, high school, and college (Kellogg, 2008). Writing effectively has been proven to be the result of the level of confidence in the person, therefore practicing will increase confidence.

Benefits of Higher Education in Law Enforcement

There has long been a call for a college education requirement for police officers, either as a prerequisite or with a structured time to attain it. The new standard in policing of higher education has changed in the last few decades as the high school diploma used to be a symbol of higher education, and now the four-year college degree has replaced it. Law enforcement leaders have consistently pushed to hire highly educated people to fill their ranks.

Higher education in law enforcement is an extremely important component of the day to day activities officers as it impacts the relationship with citizens, problem solving, and crime fighting. Due to the influx of modern policing strategies, such as community policing and problem-oriented policing, require officers to think more critically on a higher level than ever before. The perspective of a college educated officers could be because citizens feel that the responsibilities and roles of officers have changed in a way where an intellectual person who has an awareness of the social, political and historical context of what is occurring in needed. A college education instils a certain level of professionalism and maturity which is needed in all levels of law enforcement. Officers with a college education, even when not completed, had increased communications skills, decision-making skills, and writing skills.

Policy Proposal

It is obvious that well written reports are important in many professions and in law enforcement, they are the life's blood of the criminal justice system. One would think there would be a great deal of policy devoted to this in departmental policies and procedures. The research has shown this is not the case and most departments have no structured policy on the style or quality of writing within their organization. Instead, most writing styles and procedures start with field training officers who regurgitate what they are taught. Many officer writings contain numerous mechanical errors and lack illustrative descriptions or sense of scene setting along with bad technical writing issues.

The first goal presented is to improve the structural and mechanical issues in police writing. These are the grammatical, spelling, and sentence structure problems commonly seen in police officer report writing. These small, seemingly insignificant, writing problems can have grave results in the legal and law enforcement professions. Small mechanical issues can ruin a case for a myriad of reasons, most of all they reflect poorly on the credibility of the officer.

Secondly, officers must improve the clarity of their writing. When constructing a report to document an incident, it is vital to be as detailed and thorough as possible while also being concise and direct. Due to the reliance of the report in the criminal justice field, it is imperative that the officer's writing is impeccably clear and direct. The officer should approach the narration of the report as a story told in a novel.

Lastly, agencies need to establish writing procedures in regard to hiring requirements and field training standards. This is an important goal because if the standard can be set at the beginning, then the bar for writing will be raised and remedial training will be greatly reduced. This goal not only helps correct the current problem, but also looks ahead at future issues to curb them. The setting of these goals will provide a direction for agencies and officers to focus their efforts. These goals have been set to directly reflect the nature and scope of the problem at hand. The achievement of these goals will greatly improve the quality and clarity of officer writings and will be met by completing certain objectives.

Objectives

To meet each of the proposed goals, several objectives must be achieved and are proposed as a road map to what must be achieved so officers can become effective writers as well as ensuring future officers are well trained in writing skills. The first objective presented is to teach police recruits the mechanical writing skills needed in police writing such as grammatical, spelling, capitalization, and sentence structure skills. These skills are extremely important in a legal environment and if an officer is unable to spell commonly used legal words or continuously misspells than this could be used against them. Defence attorneys will challenge officers on the validity of the report and attempt to show that errors represent a level of laziness, inattention to detail, or downright falsification.

The second objective is placing a focus on the contextual issues found in police writing such as scene setting, descriptions, and proper documentation of the event. A basic check of police report writing shows that context is measured by how clear, concise, and well-organized the report is. A clear report is one that properly identifies all people involved, provides a detailed description of the environment, as well as a storyline which is easily followed. A concise report is one that uses precise language to describe the incident while providing enough detail to accurately answer all the investigatory questions. A well-organized report is formatted in a manner that one can easily extract information and understand what occurred.

The third objective addresses the agency's need to create hiring requirements ensuring the applicant is able to write on professionally so that remedial training is not necessary. A current review of local agencies hiring requirements, in the state of North Carolina, shows that the state requires a reading comprehension test (12 NCAC 09B .0203(e)) is administered early in the hiring process. The applicant is required to score at the state's tenth grade reading level. This requirement does not adequately reflect the applicant's writing ability and only shows reading comprehension levels. Law enforcement leaders should begin implement a writing skills test, or statement of purpose, providing the agency with an example of the applicant's ability to formulate sentences, use grammar, and form thoughts effectively.

The fourth and last objective is re-evaluation of the agency's field training program as it pertains to the new officer's writing skills. The officer should be evaluated on every writing presented during their duty. The standard of a higher level of writing is set during this field training phase so as to create good habits to last an entire career. This change will lead to the leader building process and create higher level law enforcement leaders.

PRINCIPLES OF REPORT WRITING

Writing an accurate, clear, readable police report is an essential part of officer responsibilities. Good narrative report writing frequently makes the difference between successful or unsuccessful prosecution of an offender. Officers should be aware of and apply the general principles of good report writing for purposes of enforcement and to protect themselves and their agency against civil litigation and related charges.

Many police officers view the police report as a necessary evil of their job that primarily fulfills the needs of administrators and prosecutors. This is a serious misconception that often undermines this essential police activity. An officer's case or incident report often makes the crucial difference between a suspect being charged or released, convicted or acquitted. Therefore, the police report may have a greater short-term impact on the local community than any other form of writing.

Through the years, jurisdictions have developed standard report formats to simplify the collection of accurate crime data. The statistical part of the forms permits officers to check the appropriate box, mark an "X" in the correct space or circle the appropriate word or phrase, thereby allowing statistical information to be captured quickly and accurately. With this information, local governments can determine the nature and extent of crime in their backyard. From a larger perspective, the standardization of statistical crime data has been instrumental in tracing the growth and complexity of criminal behaviour. Uniform Crime Reporting data as collected by local law enforcement agencies for the FBI provides the necessary means for comparing the crime problems of one city or area to another. But statistical data does little to help in the prosecution of individual cases. The real problem lies in the narrative portion of the report.

From a prosecutorial standpoint, the most common deficiency of police reports is that they lack detail, accuracy and clarity. The officer generally has the information needed but does not or cannot communicate it through the report. The officer may not include information in the report because he doesn't feel comfortable with his ability to express the facts, because he doesn't feel the case merits this level of effort or that it will be prosecuted, or simply because his time is limited. Sometimes the officer just doesn't believe the information is valuable. Whatever the reason, failing to record information in the report is a serious problem.

Reasons for Writing a Report

There are four generally accepted reasons for a police officer to write a report: for historical records, as a management tool, as an aid for testifying in court and as a guard against civil or related actions that may be brought against the officer or the agency. Historical records are critical to the department, the public and elected officials. Among other things, these records provide the ability to see how well an agency is doing compared to previous years or to other jurisdictions.

From a managerial perspective, police reports are also important to the local budget process. The information that they provide, for example, can mean the difference between hiring a construction worker or a police officer. Law enforcement professionals recognized the need for good records as long ago as 1829, when Sir Robert Peel persuaded the British Parliament to pass the Metropolitan Police Bill. Peel included two records-related tenets in his proposed reform of police services. He wrote: "The absence of crime will but prove the efficiency of police" and that "the deployment of police strength by both time and area is essential." Determining the level of crime and responding with the proper deployment of personnel is at least as important today as in the early 1800s.

The third basic reason for writing a report focuses on the narrative portion of the police report. The objective of police reports, according to the International City Management Association publication Local Government Police Management, is, "...to develop a system that yields the most complete and accurate information for police use." When written properly, the officer has the best possible tool for helping him recollect necessary details to present the case successfully in court. As a tool for use in the prosecution of criminal cases, officers must not report conclusions or opinions as if they were facts.

The fourth purpose for the police report, simply stated, is to protect the officer and the agency from false accusations. Frequently, officers fail to write about their behaviour during an incident because the action may be controversial or involve the use of force. Many officers have been led to believe that providing detailed descriptions of and reasons for their actions could raise uncomfortable questions. In fact, the opposite is true.

A detailed, factual statement explaining an officer's actions is usually the best way to avoid charges of improper or illegal conduct. The five "C's" of good police reports are: complete, clear, concise, concrete and correct. To successfully meet these five requirements, officers must use commonly accepted English that does not contain police jargon or technical terms unless absolutely necessary.

Complete

To make a complete report, an officer must understand the elements of a particular crime and be able to answer the six basic questions that police hear about so often. It is much easier to tell someone to answer the Who, What, Where, When, Why and How questions than it is to do it. There are literally dozens of questions relating to these six basic ones. These may include but are not limited to the following examples: Who was the victim? Who wrote the report? Who discovered the crime or incident? Who were witnesses? Who committed the offense? Whom did the officer interview? Who marked the evidence?

What type of offense was committed? What actions did the criminal take? What actions did the officer take? What evidence was located? What was done with the evidence? What tools or weapons were used? What further action is needed?

Where did the offense occur? Where was the evidence found? Where were the witnesses? Where is the perpetrator? Where was the suspect caught? Where was the evidence marked?

When did the incident occur? When was it discovered? When was it reported? When was the victim last seen? When did the officer arrive on the scene? When were the photographs taken?

How was the offense committed? How did the perpetrator enter the crime scene? How did he exit? How did you make the arrest? How did you get the information? How did the suspect get information to select this particular crime target?

Why was the offense committed? Why did it occur at that particular time or place? Why were witnesses afraid to talk? Why did the suspect select the tool or weapon used?

Of course these questions are not all-inclusive nor does each pertain to every event or incident. However, officers must take the time to ask such key questions as these, then try to answer them as they relate to the particular case.

Studies of reports in two police departments revealed that of the 39 evidentiary questions needed by prosecutors to present a robbery case effectively, less than 50 percent of the questions were adequately answered in one department and only about 25 percent in the other department. This research, while limited in scope, supports the views of many prosecutors that police reports often lack essential detail and completeness. It also suggests that officers in some departments make better reports than do their counterparts in other agencies.

The reason for these noticeable differences in the quality of police reports between departments is unknown. It may have a direct correlation with differences in the education, training and the level of communication between the police agency and the prosecutor's office. To prepare reports that meet the needs of the prosecutor, management from both agencies must communicate candidly and openly. If prosecutors continuously find police reports weak, the prosecutor's office must work more closely with the law enforcement agency. By working together, every officer knows the questions that must be answered based on the specific criminal offense.

Police management must see to it that all personnel are properly trained and understand the documentation needed by the agency and the prosecutor. Using a basic outline format for the narrative portion of the police report can help officers prepare a comprehensive report.

In particular, police supervisors should try to focus on the prosecutor's needs as they review each report. In too many cases, such reviews are limited to an assessment of the accuracy of dates and completeness of statistical data. The most important information of any report is found in the narrative. In this context, the reviewing officer must be willing and able to show an officer the shortcomings of the report. Using a pre-formatted narrative outline will make the review and evaluation task easier.

Clear

A police report may be complete but still lack clarity. Collecting the information needed for a good report is vital, but organizing and focusing the information is equally important. A police report contains an abundance of facts that must be coordinated and focused in order to relay useable information. However, in doing so, there is little room for an officer's opinions and conclusions. Readers must be able to draw sufficient understanding from the facts to formulate their own conclusions. Ideally, everyone who reads the same report will be guided to the same general conclusions. There are four basic strategies to accomplish this goal.

First, the officer should use direct and explicit language. The writer should not use "iffy" words and phrases nor should he omit a direct quotation from a witness and attempt to paraphrase it. Sometimes this is done in order to avoid street or gutter language commonly encountered. While this is understandable, in editing the witness's or suspect's language, the officer may significantly alter the meaning or diminish the clarity of the original message.

Second, the officer should try to avoid police jargon whenever possible. For example, do not write, "I arrested the suspect, Mr. Jones, who appeared to be a signal 24." Instead, write, "I arrested Mr. Jones, who at the time of arrest was waving his arms wildly about and shouting: "God told me to kill him, God said he was evil." The first statement contained the fact that the officer arrested Mr. Jones. However, the phrase "who appeared to be a signal 24" was the officer's opinion, not a statement of fact, and used a local police code reference for a "demented person." The description of Mr. Jones waving his arms is a factual statement and clearly shows the circumstances at the time of arrest. Mr. Jones may not be demented except in the eyes of the officer, and few police officers are trained to diagnose the mental health of a suspect.

Use short words and short sentences to express yourself. Large or technical words may sound authoritative, but they seldom add meaning to a report. Always write to express, not to impress.

Also, the active voice is more expressive than the passive voice. In the active voice, the subject acts; in the passive voice, the subject is acted upon. Notice how much stronger the sentence sounds in the active voice compared to the passive.

Examples:

> *I shot the perpetrator (active). The perpetrator was shot by me (passive).*
>
> *The mayor and council announced a cost-of-living pay raise for police (active). A cost of living pay raise for police was announced by the mayor and council (passive).*
>
> *Officer Williams tagged and bagged the evidence (active). The evidence was tagged and bagged by officer Williams (passive).*

Police writing should emphasize who does what.

The third element of clarity involves organizing thoughts before writing. While this may seem difficult initially, it is really quite simple. While most of the crimes and events reported by the police are different in some respects, they are similar in others. Therefore, the officer can structure the police report in advance if the communication between the police agency and the prosecutor is open and candid.

Most incident and crime reports can be organized chronologically. The initial paragraph may relate to preliminary information such as establishing jurisdiction and venue. Example: On Thursday, April 1, 1993, I, Officer John Jones, was dispatched to 234 74th St. S.W. on a burglary-in-progress call. The second portion of the report details anything that occurred on the way to the scene. Example: While proceeding west on Indiana Blvd. toward 74th St. this officer observed a red Ford Mustang occupied by a young white male who failed to stop at the stop sign. The next three elements of the report should describe the actors upon arrival on the scene, after the officer was on the scene and finally, the disposition or conclusion. This basic report format can be completed by the officer recording observations and events in the appropriate areas briefly and concisely.

If we edit that part of the report shown in the previous paragraph using short sentences, it will read better as follows: "As I drove west on Indiana Blvd, I saw a red Mustang run the stop sign on 74th St. The Mustang was going north on 74th St. The driver was a young white male." Since all the actions and activities were completed when the report was written, it should be easy to remember to use the past tense. The only time the present tense should be used in police reports is when victims, witnesses or perpetrators are being quoted.

The fourth strategy for good report writing involves using pronouns. Writing can be improved through the use of pronouns, provided the pronoun refers clearly and unmistakably to the noun it replaces. Compare the following statements: Confusing: "When Jenkins became partners with Smith in May, he did not know he would be such a good cop." The first "he" seems to refer to Jenkins, but who would be such a good cop? Better: "When Jenkins became Smith's partner in May, he did not know Smith would be such a good cop."

Compare the following for clarity. Confusing: "Bill held the sandwich in one hand and the microphone in the other, eating it while he talked." Common sense tells us that Bill ate the sandwich, not the microphone. But the pronoun it could refer to either. Better: "Bill held the sandwich in one hand and the microphone in the other, eating the sandwich while he talked." Similarly, which of the following is better? "Mary's partner said she couldn't arrest the suspect" or "Mary's partner told her not to arrest the suspect." In the first example, the reader cannot be sure who couldn't arrest the suspect: Mary or her partner. The second example is better because it clearly tells the reader what the writer intended.

Concise

Conciseness and clarity are directly related. A police report should only be as long as necessary to provide requisite information. The Little, Brown Handbook published by Little, Brown & Co., states: "Conciseness - brevity of expression - aids emphasis no matter what the sentence structure. Unnecessary words detract from necessary words. They clutter sentences and obscure ideas." The language in the report should be simple and direct. The efficiency of any report is found partly in the economy of words. Get the message across in the shortest and easiest way possible. Simplicity is the key. To be concise, separate each idea into its own sentence. Do not try to combine several thoughts into one long sentence. Length confuses the reader. Reading tests have demonstrated that shorter sentences are easier to read. One of the best ways to eliminate long sentences is to replace connective words such as "and" and "but" with a period. Example: "Mr. Jones told me that he had received a phone call from Elliott Jenkins, but he didn't remember the time of the call." This sentence reads better as: "Mr. Jones told me he had received a phone call from Elliott Jenkins. He didn't remember the time of the call." If the connective word needs to be retained to maintain continuity of thought, it is generally better to start the next sentence with that word.

Concrete

The language used in the police report must be specific. Officers must stick to the facts while including sufficient detail. Vaguely worded sentences may result in different readers reaching different conclusions. Sometimes the officer has no choice but to be vague in the report, but specific information should be used when it is available. Review the following examples: Abstract - "The majority of witnesses said that the suspect had blonde hair." Specific - "Four of the five witness said that the suspect had blonde hair." Abstract - "I told the victim I would call him in the near future." Specific - "I told the victim I would call him on Thursday at about 1700 hours." Abstract - "A large crowd had gathered by the time I arrived on the scene." Specific - "Approximately 50 to 60 people were present when I arrived on the scene." Avoid using cliches in reports. Cliches are defined as trite expressions or ideas. When the cliche was originated, it probably had a special significance or emphasis attached to it. But time has eroded the purpose and meaning to the extent that cliches are practically useless. They add nothing to the police report. Keep statements like these out of your reports: dead as a doornail, depths of despair, hasty retreat, birds of a feather flock together, sink or swim, the whole nine yards and similar expressions.

Correct

An officer can satisfy all other requirements of a good police report, but if it is incorrect, it is of little value. The best way to prevent incorrect reports is to proofread. Make sure each sentence makes complete sense. Does the verb match the noun or pronoun? If the noun is singular, the verb also must be singular. Is the sentence complete? Is the idea communicated clearly? Are sentences too long and confusing? Would dividing the sentence into two or more sentences make the thought flow faster and better? Look for transposed letters and numbers. Corrections must be made before the report is submitted. Double-check all days, dates and times mentioned in the report. Carefully proofreading your report should identify these and related types of common errors.

If errors are missed even after proofing, reading the report backward may help. In this way, reading is slower, and errors may be identified more easily. The report reflects an officer's level of education, degree of competence and professionalism. As such, the credibility of the officer is in many ways linked to how well his report is written.

Another potential problem area involves spelling. When spelling the names of victims, witnesses and suspects, officers often automatically use the spelling that is familiar to them. Smith could be spelled S-m-y-t-h; Culpepper could be spelled C-u-l-l-p-e-p-p-e-r, and the name one thinks is Johnson may be Johnston. When in doubt, an officer should always ask for the correct spelling. Most of us like to be called by our correct name and resent it when it is misspelled. Officers should remember that misspelling records of names and addresses may result in misdirected subpoenas and missed court dates. Another solution is to make and keep a list of words that are misspelled most often.

The 40-40-20 Rule

Looking at the report writing process in three stages helps to understand it better. The first stage is writing detailed notes into a prepared format. This is done by combining words, phrases and a few complete sentences. Placing comments into an existing format will reduce the time needed to organize thoughts into an effective report. It may be useful to separate each idea with a bullet, asterisk or other recognizable symbol. This style can even be retained in the final report if it makes the report more readable, complete and concise. After taking notes, write the first draft using the basic prestructured format. Be sure to double-space between lines in the first draft to provide room for revisions. This entire process should take about 40 percent of the total time needed to complete a good report. This approach can be examined more closely by applying it to a case example - in this instance, writing an arrest report for driving while intoxicated. Following is a sample DWI report format. The statements relate to notes made about the case.

A. Preliminary:

- Routine patrol in area of Indiana and 74th St. in Unit 714.
- April 1, 1993: 1345 hours

B. Observations:

- Red Mustang traveling North on Indiana from 74th St.
- Vehicle being driven very slowly
- Vehicle almost struck two parked cars on Indiana
- Vehicle crossed street and struck curb
- Took two blocks to get driver to stop after engaging blue lights and siren

C. Actions before Arrest:

- Car stopped at Indiana and 77th St.
- Driver a W/F
- Asked for D.L. and insurance
- Smelled strong odor of alcohol on her breath
- D.L. showed her as Mary Jones W.F. 34 Y.O.A.
- Lives at 4567 Tupolo Dr.
- Did 3 field sobriety tests:

1. Straight line 15 ft. (lost balance, almost fell)
2. Stand on one foot with eyes shut (could not do)
3. Lean back and touch nose with forefinger (touched high on forehead with left, low on forehead with right)

D. Actions After Arrest:

- read implied consent
- She informed me she had been drinking since early morning

- Tried to give me $50 to let her go.

E. Conclusion:

- Left Unit 625 with Mustang to impound
- Took Ms. Jones to station and gave Certified Intoximeter test.
- Completed booking report
- Allowed Jones to make phone call

REFERENCES

1. https://www.linkedin.com/pulse/importance-writing-skills-policing-m-brad-stewart/
2. https://www.theiacp.org/sites/default/files/2018-08/434%20Principles%20of%20Report%20Writing.pdf
3. https://onlinedegrees.sandiego.edu/police-communication-important-today/
4. Beisler, F., Scheeres, H., & Pinner, D. (1987). Communication barriers. In Communication skills (pp. 7-15). Melbourne: Pitman Publishing.
5. Billings-Harris, L. ( ). The diversity advantage: a guide to making diversity work.
6. Buchholz, S., & Roth, T. (1987). Creating the high-performance team. New York: John Wiley & Sons.
7. DeVito, J.A. (2009). Human Communication: The basic Course. (11th ed.). United States of America: Pearson.4.
8. Cielens, M. & Aquino, M. (1999).The business of communicating. (4th ed.). Roseville, NSW: Irwin/McGraw-Hill.
9. Cushner, K. 2005. Communicating across international and domestic cultures. Crime & Justice International, vol.21, no.88, pp.11-15.

8 POLICE POWERS: SEARCH AND ARREST

INTRODUCTION

The powers of the police to stop and search, particularly in public, has been the subject of particular scrutiny in recent years. The excessive and arbitrary use of such powers was held to have been a major contributory factor to the underlying resentment, notably between younger people and the police, which led to the inner city riots in 1981. The law and procedures governing stops and searches by the police who have not, at that stage, made an arrest.

Police powers related to arrest and search are fundamental aspects of law enforcement, granting officers the authority to maintain public order and investigate crimes. The power of arrest allows police to detain individuals suspected of committing a crime, ensuring they appear before the court and preventing further offenses. This power must be exercised with reasonable grounds, balancing the need for security with individual rights. In conjunction with arrest powers, search powers enable officers to locate and seize evidence pertinent to criminal investigations. These searches can be conducted with or without a warrant, depending on the situation's urgency and legal requirements. Warrantless searches are permissible under specific circumstances, such as during an arrest or when evidence is in plain view. However, to protect citizens' privacy, these powers are regulated by laws and judicial oversight to prevent abuse. Together, the powers of arrest and search are critical tools for law enforcement, but their application must always adhere to legal standards and respect civil liberties.

One of the most popularized conceptions of an arrest is the scenario whereby a police officer takes a suspect by the arm who is then led to a waiting police car having first been cautioned. In the American style, one would expect the suspect to be 'read his rights' whilst being handcuffed. These arrests usually occur in the street or other public places, or even in private property, but this is not the only situation under which a person may be arrested. A person may already be at a police station voluntarily, in order to 'assist the police with their enquiries', but could later be arrested.

POWERS OF THE POLICE

The powers of the police in England and Wales are defined largely by statute law, with the main sources of power being the Police and Criminal Evidence Act 1984 and the Police Act 1996. This article covers the powers of police officers of territorial police forces only, but a police officer in one of the UK's special police forces (most commonly a member of the British Transport Police) can utilize extended jurisdiction powers outside of their normal jurisdiction in certain defined situations as set out in statute. In law, police powers are given to constables (both full-time and volunteer special constables). All police officers in England and Wales are "constables" in law whatever their rank. Certain police powers are also available to a limited extent to police community support officers and other non-warranted positions such as police civilian investigators or designated detention officers employed by some police forces even though they are not constables.

There are several general powers constables have that normal members of the public do not, including:

- the power to detain people in certain circumstances
- the power to stop and search people/vehicles in certain circumstances
- various powers of entry in certain circumstances
- the power to seize and retain property in certain circumstances
- the power to arrest people with or without warrant for any offence and in various other circumstances. (A significantly wider power than that provided to members of the public, often described as "citizen's arrest")
- the power to direct the behavior of persons and vehicles on highways and in other public places
- the power to demand name/address and certain documents of anyone driving a motor vehicle on a public road

The powers have various limits and generally require a clear reason for their exercise to be made known to a person subject of to one of the above powers, unless impractical due to the persons behavior or unusual circumstances.

Once a person has been arrested his/her vehicle or residence can be searched without the need for a warrant to be obtained for the purpose of obtaining evidence connected to the offence causing the arrest, as long as the offence or suspected offence was indictable. This power is provided by Section 18(1) or 18(5) and/or 32(2) of PACE 1984 depending on the circumstances. If a person is arrested in a premises or were in a premises immediately before arrest, Section 32(2) states a Constable has the power "to enter and search any premises in which he was when arrested or immediately before he was arrested for evidence relating to the offence". Constables and PCSOs also have the power under this section to search an individual for items that may assist or facilitate an escape from custody (i.e. an arrest or detention).

Source of Powers

The basic powers of the police derive from the Police Act 1996, which covers attestation (section 29), jurisdiction (section 30) and a number of other matters. Day to day, common law features greatly in relation to use of force (self defence &

defence of others) and a number of other areas. The Police and Criminal Evidence Act 1984 is a key piece of legislation in relation to policing which was amended by the Serious Organized Crime and Police Act 2005, significantly, in relation to powers of arrest. Another notable piece of legislation is the Police Reform Act 2002. This act extended limited policing powers to those within the police family who are not warranted constables, such as PCSOs and others.

Exclusive Powers

The Policing and Crime Act 2017 identified a set of powers exclusive to constables that could not be conferred on police staff such as Police Community Support Officers. Section 28(4)(a) states a PCSO will be able to be designated with "any power or duty of a constable. These excluded powers would be:

- Any power or duty of a constable to make an arrest under s24 PACE 1984
- Any power or duty of a constable to stop and search an individual or a vehicle or other thing
- The power of a constable, under section 36(4) of the Police and Criminal Evidence Act 1984, to perform the functions of a custody officer at a designated police station if a custody officer is not readily available to perform them
- Any power that is exercisable only by a constable of a particular rank
- Any power of a constable under
  - the Terrorism Act 2000;
  - the Terrorism Act 2006;
  - the Counter-Terrorism Act 2008;
  - the Terrorism Prevention and Investigation Measures Act 2011;
  - the Counter-Terrorism and Security Act 2015
- Any power of a constable under the Official Secrets Act 1911 to 1989
- The power of a constable to make an application on behalf of the Commissioner of Police of the Metropolis under section 6 of the Regulation of Investigatory Powers Act 2000

Search without Warrant

Premises

A Constable may enter and search any premises occupied or controlled by a person who is under arrest for an indictable offence, if they have reasonable grounds for believing that there is on the premises evidence (other than items subject to legal privilege) that relates to that offence, or to some other indictable offence which is connected with or similar to that offence. This power, under section 18(1) of PACE, requires the authority of a police officer of at least the rank of Inspector and is normally conducted whilst a person is in police custody at a police station. Under PACE section 18(5), such a search of premises may be conducted prior to the arrested person being detained in police custody and prior to an authority by an Inspector if the presence of the person at a place (other than a police station) is necessary for the effective investigation of the offence. However an Inspector must be informed following such a search. This power is used much less than 18(1). Under section 32 of PACE, a constable has the power, if a person has been arrested for an indictable offence, to enter and search any premises in which he was when arrested or immediately before s/he was arrested for evidence relating to the offence.

People or Vehicles

Search without Arrest

The Police and Criminal Evidence Act 1984 (PACE) was enacted to correct problems with the implementation of the powers used by the police. The "sus" law allowed police to stop, search, and subsequently arrest a "suspected person" without warrant, reason or evidence. Due to the unfair implementation of this law within the black community, there were riots in some parts of the country in majority black areas in the early 1980s and "sus" was repealed in 1981. The vast majority of search powers now require "reasonable suspicion" of an offence to be present, although this has not prevented stop-and-search from being used disproportionately against black people, who are over nine times more likely to be searched than white people, Asian people nearly three times more likely to be searched and BAME members in general four times more likely. This disparity can also be seen when looking at arrests, as a black person is over three times as likely to be arrested and the whole BAME group nearly twice as likely. Constables cannot carry out "consensual" searches of a person unless a power to search exists.

Before searching anyone or anything (except an unattended vehicle), a constable in plain clothes must identify himself as a constable and show his warrant card or similar, and a constable (in uniform or otherwise) must state:

- the constable's rank/grade, collar/warrant number, surname and the name of the police station to which he is attached,
- the legal power being used to conduct the search,
- that the detained person is detained for the purpose of a search,
- the object being searched for (if applicable),
- the grounds for the search, and
- that a copy of the search form will be available on demand for three months.

Before searching an unattended vehicle, a constable must leave a notice (inside the vehicle unless it is not reasonably practicable to do so without damaging the vehicle) stating:

- that the vehicle has been searched,
- the name of the police station to which the constable is attached,
- that an application for compensation for any damage caused by the search may be made to that police station, and
- that a copy of the search record will be available on demand (if one was made).

The above provisions do not apply to searches under section 6 of PACE or section 27(2) of the Aviation Security Act 1982, which both relate to vehicles leaving goods handling areas where searches are routine. A search without arrest is unlawful if it appears to the constable, after first detaining the person or vehicle, that the search is not required or it is impracticable. A person or vehicle may be detained for the purposes of a search for as long as is reasonably required to permit a search to be carried out either at the place where the person or vehicle was first detained or nearby. Whilst in public, a constable cannot require a person to remove any of his clothing other than an outer coat, jacket or gloves (except in the case of a search under sections 43, 43A or 47A of the Terrorism Act 2000, which additionally permits the removal of footwear and headgear.

Search after Arrest

A Constable may search a person who has been arrested (unless the arrest was at a police station) if the Constable has reasonable grounds for believing that the arrested person may present a danger to himself or others. A Constable may also (unless the arrest was at a police station) search an arrested person for anything which he might use to assist him to escape from lawful custody, or which might be evidence relating to an offence. This power is given to both Constables and PCSOs by Section 32 of the Police and Criminal Evidence act 1984. A Constable may search a person arrested under section 41 of the Terrorism Act 2000 to discover whether he has in his possession anything which may constitute evidence that he is a terrorist.

Searches in Detention

The Custody Officer must record everything which an arrested person has with him at the police station and may search a person to the extent that he considers it necessary to do so, but may not conduct an intimate search for these purposes. The Custody Officer may seize anything, but may only seize clothes or personal effects if the Custody Officer:

- believes that the person from whom they are seized may use them:
- to cause physical injury to himself or any other person,
- to damage property,
- to interfere with evidence,
- to assist him to escape, or
- has reasonable grounds for believing that they may be evidence relating to an offence.

An Inspector also has a limited power to order a search of an arrested person in order to facilitate establishing the identity of a person, particularly by discovering tattoos or other marks. Where such a search requires more than the removal of the arrested person's outer clothing, the provisions of Code to the Police and Criminal Evidence Act 1984 relating to strip searches apply. An intimate search is a search of the bodily orifices (other than the mouth). It should be conducted by a suitably qualified person unless this is impracticable and done in the presence of two other people. An intimate search requires the authorization of an inspector and may only be made in one of the following circumstances:

Condition	**Consent**	**Place**
The inspector reasonably believes • that the detainee has concealed on him anything he could use and might use in police detention or custody of the court to cause physical injury to himself or others; and • that the article in question cannot be found unless the detainee is intimately searched.	Consent is not necessary for the search to take place and reasonable force may be used to conduct the search.	Police station, hospital, surgery or other medical premises.

The inspector reasonably believes • that the detainee may have a Class A drug concealed on him; • that the detainee was in possession of the drug before his arrest with intention to illegally supply or export it; and • that it cannot be found unless the detainee is intimately searched.	Consent for the search is necessary. If the detainee refuses to give consent, proper inferences may be drawn but force may not be used.	Hospital, surgery or other medical premises.

REASONABLE GROUNDS FOR SUSPECTING

The term 'reasonable grounds for suspecting' is mentioned in PACE under a number of provisions and not just s 1, but this statute does not define its meaning. Therefore, we have to examine a variety of sources in order to ascertain both its definition and how it should be applied. To begin with, the question of reasonable suspicion is tested objectively, meaning: facts and circumstances which would lead an impartial third party to form the belief or suspicion in question.' One of the main complaints from particularly young people in the areas affected by the inner city riots of 1981, especially those from the ethnic community, was that the police had arbitrarily or randomly exercised their stop and search powers simply by virtue of the fact that those persons were on the street. In some cases, the police were alleged to have made statements that they merely had a feeling that those suspects were generally 'up to no good'. The latter constitutes a purely subjective approach to suspicion, which is forbidden under PACE and the Codes of Practice.

Guidance as to what constitutes the objective test of suspicion is given in Code A which state:

- Reasonable grounds for suspicion depend on the circumstances in each case. There must be an objective basis for that suspicion based on facts, information, and/or intelligence which are relevant to the likelihood of finding an article of a certain kind or, in the case of searches under section 43 of the Terrorism Act 2000, to the likelihood that the person is a terrorist. Reasonable suspicion can never be supported on the basis of personal factors alone without reliable supporting intelligence or information or some specific behavior by the person concerned. For example, a person's race, age, appearance, or the fact that the person is known to have a previous conviction, cannot be used alone or in combination with each other as the reason for searching that person. Reasonable suspicion cannot be based on generalizations or stereotypical images of certain groups or categories of people as more likely to be involved in criminal activity.
- Reasonable suspicion can sometimes exist without specific information or intelligence and on the basis of some level of generalization stemming from the behavior of a person. For example, if an officer encounters someone on the street at night who is obviously trying to hide something, the officer may (depending on the other surrounding circumstances) base such suspicion on the fact that this kind of behavior is often linked to stolen or prohibited articles being carried. Similarly, for the purposes of section 43 of the Terrorism Act 2000, suspicion that a person is a terrorist may arise from the person's behavior at or near a location which has been

identified as a potential target for terrorists.

- However, reasonable suspicion should normally be linked to accurate and current intelligence or information, such as information describing an article being carried, a suspected offender, or a person who has been seen carrying a type of article known to have been stolen recently from premises in the area. Searches based on accurate and current intelligence or information are more likely to be effective. Targeting searches in a particular area at specified crime problems increases their effectiveness and minimizes inconvenience to law-abiding members of the public. It also helps in justifying the use of searches both to those who are searched and to the general public. This does not however prevent stop and search powers being exercised in other locations where such powers may be exercised and reasonable suspicion exists.
- Searches are more likely to be effective, legitimate, and secure public confidence when reasonable suspicion is based on a range of factors. The overall use of these powers is more likely to be effective when up to date and accurate intelligence or information is communicated to officers and they are well-informed about local crime patterns.
- Where there is reliable information or intelligence that members of a group or gang habitually carry knives unlawfully or weapons or controlled drugs, and wear a distinctive item of clothing or other means of identification to indicate their membership of the group or gang, that distinctive item of clothing or other means of identification may provide reasonable grounds to stop and search a person.
- A police officer may have reasonable grounds to suspect that a person is in innocent possession of a stolen or prohibited article or other item for which he or she is empowered to search. In that case the officer may stop and search the person even though there would be no power of arrest.
- Under section 43(1) of the Terrorism Act 2000 a constable may stop and search a person whom the officer reasonably suspects to be a terrorist to discover whether the person is in possession of anything which may constitute evidence that the person is a terrorist. These searches may only be carried out by an officer of the same sex as the person searched.
- An officer who has reasonable grounds for suspicion may detain the person concerned in order to carry out a search. Before carrying out a search the officer may ask questions about the person's behavior or presence in circumstances which gave rise to the suspicion. As a result of questioning the detained person, the reasonable grounds for suspicion necessary to detain that person may be confirmed or, because of a satisfactory explanation, be eliminated. Questioning may also reveal reasonable grounds to suspect the possession of a different kind of unlawful article from that originally suspected. Reasonable grounds for suspicion, however, cannot be provided retrospectively by such questioning during a person's detention or by refusal to answer any questions put.
- If, as a result of questioning before a search, or other circumstances which come to the attention of the officer, there ceases to be reasonable grounds

for suspecting that an article is being carried of a kind for which there is a power to stop and search, no search may take place. In the absence of any other lawful power to detain, the person is free to leave at will and must be so informed.

- There is no power to stop or detain a person in order to find grounds for a search. Police officers have many encounters with members of the public which do not involve detaining people against their will. If reasonable grounds for suspicion emerge during such an encounter, the officer may search the person even though no grounds existed when the encounter began. In an officer is detaining someone for the purpose of a search, he or she should inform the person as soon as detention begins.

The issue of reasonable suspicion has been subject to judicial interpretation in a number of cases, which include the following. In Black v DPP (1995), the police entered premises belonging to the defendant's brother in accordance with a search warrant under the Misuse of Drugs Act 1971. While the search was in progress, the defendant arrived, carrying a bag and was suspected by the police of attending the premises in order to buy or sell drugs. The police wished to search the defendant and asked him to enter the premises for this purpose, but he became aggressive, threw the bag down and then attempted to leave the premises. He was charged and later convicted of obstruction under s 23(4)(a) of the 1971 Act. The Divisional Court held that a person merely arriving at the address of a known drug dealer did not amount to conduct which constituted reasonable grounds for suspecting that person of possessing a controlled drug and that the defendant's behavior after he was detained could not retrospectively provide such grounds. The defendant's conviction was quashed.

In Samuels v Commissioner of Police for the Metropolis (1999), S sued the police for damages under what may generally be termed unlawful detention. Earlier, he had been acquitted of the charge of assault on police. S was stopped by a police officer whilst walking home and was asked where he was going. S did not venture any significant information and stated that he had the right to go where he wanted. He then continued his journey but, when he was nearly home, the police officer stated that he wished to search S, because he suspected him of being in possession of a prohibited article. The officer later gave evidence that he thought S may have been carrying a screwdriver and his manner of walking was suspicious. It was ruled by the trial judge that the stop and search of S was based on reasonable grounds. The Court of Appeal, however, had to consider whether that suspicion was reasonable. In allowing the appeal, the court held that if the police officer did not have the prerequisite reasonable suspicion before he approached S, then the conduct of S immediately afterwards could not transform an unreasonable suspicion into one which was reasonable.

It is important to note that a police officer does not have the power to stop a person against their will in order to establish any grounds for suspicion; neither may a person's refusal to answer questions constitute reasonable suspicion. In Rice v Connolly (1966), it was held that citizens are under no general legal duty to answer questions put to them by the police. However, such refusal may reinforce a police officer's existing suspicion, but this may not singularly justify stopping and detaining a person. The essence of reasonable suspicion, within the context of

PACE, is that there must be a tangible and positive condition present to justify the use of police powers of stop and search under s 1.

Under other legislation, namely s 60 of the Criminal Justice and Public Order Act 1994 (as amended) and s 44 of the Terrorism Act 2000, a number of stop and search powers have been conferred upon the police which do not require reasonable suspicion as a prerequisite for these powers to be exercised.

Another important term used frequently in PACE is 'reasonable grounds for believing'. What is the difference between reasonable grounds to believe and reasonable grounds to suspect? First, a much higher criteria is set when the exercise of certain police powers require reasonable belief, rather than suspicion. This is because many of the powers requiring reasonable belief generally impose a greater restriction on the liberty of those against whom they are being used.

Secondly, it has been propounded that many of the powers under PACE that require reasonable belief are often exercised following decisions made as a result of consultation and reflection, whereas many powers requiring reasonable suspicion are often made in street situations, requiring quick, if not instant, decisions.

SERIOUS VIOLENCE REDUCTION ORDERS

The Conservative party's 2019 manifesto committed to tackle knife crime by targeting known knife carriers and making it easier for the police to stop and search those previously convicted of knife crime offences. The Police, Crime, Sentencing and Courts Act 2022 ("PCSC Act") introduced SVROs. These are a new court order that can be issued to people for using, or having on them, a knife or offensive weapon when they committed an offence.

The legislation requires that SVROs be piloted before national roll-out and the Secretary of State must lay a report before Parliament of the outcome of the pilot. In May 2022, the Government confirmed it would be piloting SVROs in Merseyside, Thames Valley, Sussex and West Midlands police forces before a decision is made on roll-out across England and Wales.

Serious Violence Reduction Orders Work

The prosecution must apply to the court for an SVRO to be applied to an individual upon their conviction. The court can issue an SVRO if it is satisfied that "on the balance of probabilities" either of the following two conditions has been met:

- the individual used a knife or offensive weapon during the commission of an offence, or had a knife or offensive weapon on them when they committed an offence (regardless of whether it was used); or
- the individual knew or "ought to have known" that another person who used a knife or offensive weapon in the commission of the offence was going to do so, or that another person who committed the offence had a knife or offensive weapon with them at the time.

To issue an SVRO to someone, the court must "think it is necessary" to protect the public, protect a specific individual or to prevent further offending involving an offensive weapon/bladed article.

SVROs can only be issued to individuals aged 18 or over. SVROs can be applied for a minimum of six months to a maximum of two years. The Crown

Prosecution Service and the chief officer of the relevant police can apply to the courts for an SVRO to be varied, renewed, or discharged.

The police have the power to stop and search anyone with an SVRO "for the purpose of ascertaining whether the person has a bladed article or offensive weapon with them".

Breach of an SVRO, including intentionally obstructing the police in exercising their stop and search power, is a criminal offence punishable by a sentence of up to two years' imprisonment, an unlimited fine, or both.

The Secretary of State will be given legislative powers to specify additional requirements or prohibitions that can imposed on an individual by a SVRO, but only once the Government has completed its pilot.

Serious Violence Reduction Orders Compare to Existing Stop and Search Powers

Once an individual has received an SVRO, officers will not have to meet any legal test to search them for an offensive weapon. There is no other modern-day search power that allows the police to stop and search an individual without having either reasonable grounds or authorization from a senior officer to do so. Whilst section 60 searches can be used by officers to search people without suspicion, it must be authorized by senior police officers, there are pre-conditions that must be met, and restrictions around its use as described above.

It is also the only search power that encourages officers to stop and search individuals on the basis of a previous conviction. Until SVROs it was unlawful – and still is for other search powers - to search someone solely because they have a relevant offending history. This is to prevent prejudice against people with previous convictions.

New Proposed Stop and Search Powers: Protests

The Public Order Bill was introduced to the House of Commons on 11 May 2022. The aim of the Bill is to provide the police with greater powers to respond to protesters that cause serious disruption by affixing themselves to objects, buildings or land (known as "locking-on"); obstructing major transport works; interfering with national infrastructure; or building / occupying tunnels.

The Bill includes proposals to extend stop and search powers to enable the police to search people in relation to protest in two ways:

- ***Searches on suspicion***: Clause 9 of the Bill would amend section 1 of PACE to allow officers to stop and search a person or vehicle if they have "reasonable grounds" for suspecting that they will find an article that is intended to be used in, or has been made for, relevant "protest-related offences".
- ***Suspicion-less searches***: Clause 10 would introduce a power that would operate in a similar way to section 60 search powers. Senior police officers (above the rank of inspector) would be able to authorize uniformed officers within a specified locality and time period to conduct stop and searches for objects that have been used in/connected with "protest-related offences" or may be intended for use in a protest-related offence. Following authorization, police officers would be able to conduct searches

on individuals whether or not they have any grounds for suspecting that person of having such an object on them.

The proposals were met with concern from commentators and have received a significant level of opposition. The Government's intention to introduce further powers for police to search people without reasonable grounds has been particularly controversial in light of existing concerns surrounding section 60 and potential infringements on people's human rights.

Prior to the Public Order Bill's introduction into Parliament, HMICFRS assessed the Government's proposals for expanding the powers the police have to respond to protests. HMICFRS found broad support amongst the National Police Chiefs Council (NPCC) - the coordinating body for UK police forces - and many senior police officers for protest stop and search powers who viewed it as a positive preventative and deterrent measure. HMICFRS offered its own support for the search powers but recognized that the powers were "controversial" and caveated its support, stating that the measures "must be subject to strong and effective safeguards."

MAKING A LAWFUL STOP AND SEARCH

Officers must meet certain legal standards whilst conducting any stop and search. Failure to meet these standards will result in the unlawful use of their stop and search powers. Other standards represent guidance that officers should follow as good practice but failure to meet these does not affect the lawfulness of a stop and search encounter.

General Principles

Officers must complete their search as soon as possible, taking no longer than is reasonable and without being excessively thorough. For example if an officer is searching for something large like a bat or crowbar, they cannot spend a long time searching a person's pockets. Officers must treat people with dignity and respect during a stop and search encounter. They are required to consider a person's vulnerabilities before conducting a search and exercise their search powers accordingly. They should make every effort to be polite even when those they are searching appear confrontational.

Communication

Officers must give those they have stopped to search certain information. They must tell them their name (except where officers reasonably believe that giving their name might put them in danger), their police station, the object they are trying to find and the legal basis of the search (including the reason for a section 60 search being authorized). Officers must inform those they are searching of their rights to have a copy of the search record. Plain clothes officers must take reasonable steps to show their warrant card to those they are searching.

Removing Clothing

Officers can require people to remove their outer coat or jacket, gloves, headwear or shoes in public. Officers may require people to remove more clothing when they have reasonable grounds but this must be done out of public view. Searches must also be carried out near to where the person was stopped. This means that officers must not take people to a place unreasonably far away to conduct more thorough searches. Any search involving the removal of more clothing than an outer coat, jacket, gloves, headwear or shoes must be conducted by an officer of the same sex as those they are searching. Searches which expose intimate parts of the body must be conducted at a nearby police station or other appropriate location out of view but this cannot be a police vehicle. Officers should consult their supervisor before taking a person they have stopped to a police station for an intimate search.

Use of Force

Officers must seek the cooperation of those they are searching but they may use reasonable force as a "last resort". This means that they can handcuff people to conduct a search in some circumstances. However, they should not routinely handcuff those they search. Automatically handcuffing someone without seeking their compliance with a search would be a breach of PACE Code A.

In a spotlight report published by HMICFRS in 2021 on stop and search and the use of force, the Inspectorate found "anecdotal evidence that the use of handcuffs during stop and search encounters is becoming routine in some forces." Following the Inspectorate's findings, in April 2022, the IOPC published its learning report on stop and search which also stated the routine use of handcuffs pre-arrest was a common theme amongst its investigations of stop and search and that in some cases it may have caused situations with those the police are searching to escalate.

Experimental statistics published for 2020/21, indicates that overall Black people were approximately 5.7 times more likely to have force used on them by the police than White people (across all tactics) and eight times more likely to be 'compliant handcuffed' than White people.

USE OF STOP AND SEARCH

To ensure lawful and effective use of search powers, officers are legally required to record stop and search encounters and forces must monitor those records. To further improve trust in policing, forces are also expected to engage their local communities in oversight and scrutiny of their search powers. However, record keeping and data collection on stop and search has traditionally been inconsistent and attracted criticism in the past for its gaps. In response to this, the Home Office has taken recent steps to improve the availability of data on stop and search however police watchdogs have raised concern that forces are themselves not doing enough to analyses the use of their search powers.

Monitoring Stop and Search

There are certain requirements for recording and monitoring stop and search encounters that legally police must follow and additional guidance on monitoring that should be followed as good practice.

Concerns with Forces Monitoring

HMICFRS has been repeatedly critical of how forces monitor their own records and argues that forces could do more to further improve and maintain standards. In 2020, HMICFRS published a spotlight report that provided an overview of the inspections carried out across 19 police forces and reported on the use of their powers. On stop and search, the inspectorate reported:

- five of the 19 forces were not monitoring a "wide enough range of data" to allow them to "fully understand" how their officers were using stop and search;
- six had "insufficient external scrutiny arrangements"; and
- "Only ten forces reviewed body-worn video footage of stop and search encounters as part of either their internal or external scrutiny".

Best Practice

All police forces in England and Wales have subscribed to Home Office's BUSS guidance on monitoring stop and search. This guidance requires officers to include information on the outcome of searches that do not result in an arrest in their written records of searches (ie if they issued an out-of-court disposal or when no further action was taken). Under BUSS, officers should also inform people they have stopped and searched of their right to complain.

Community Scrutiny

Police forces must make arrangements for their stop and search records to be scrutinized by community representatives but exactly how they do this is up to them.

Most police forces operate monitoring panels consisting of local leaders and community volunteers. These panels scrutinize the operational use of stop and search and communicate local experiences to officers.

In March 2019 the Home Office announced they were asking the College of Policing to create new guidelines on stop and search community engagement. In August 2019 the College of Policing published draft revisions to its APP guidance on stop and search. New guidance was published in July 2020.

The revised APP provides more advice on how forces should operate their local scrutiny panels and monitor body-worn video of stop and search encounters. Forces are expected to "have regard" to this new guidance but it does not form part of their legal requirements.

Through BUSS forces also operate "ride along" schemes which allow members of the public to join officers so they can see stop and searches in action and provide feedback based on their observations. Forces also pledge to explain how they are using stop and searches when the number of complaints from the community reaches a local threshold.

Number of Searches

Police officers conducted around 700,000 stop and searches in 2020/21. The number of annual searches fell year on year between 2009/10 (the year the current data series began) and 2017/18. However, the use of stop and search has begun to rise again, with the number of searches more than doubling since 2017/18. Police leaders say they have increased their use of stop and search as part of their response to rising levels of violent crime, including violent crime connected to illegal drug dealing.

120 Both the previous and current Conservative governments have supported an increased use of stop and search as part of their policy on violent crime which involves increased police enforcement alongside investing in early intervention projects to support at risk youth.

Reason for Searching

Whilst police leaders say stop and search is being targeted to those that they suspect are carrying knives and weapons this is not reflected in the data. Around 69% of all reasonable grounds searches in 2020/21 were conducted to find controlled drugs. HMICFRS says the high prevalence of drug possession searches indicates that enforcement "efforts are not being effectively focused on force priorities".

The high proportion of searches conducted to find drugs is frequently criticized by those that campaign against the use of stop and search. Stop Watch has argued that it demonstrates that stop and search is used to "over-police vulnerable communities for low level drug possession". HMICFRS says the high proportion of drug searches contributes to "ethnic disproportionality" in stop and search rates "despite evidence that there is no correlation between ethnicity and rates of drug use".

Stop and Search Use by Police Force

There is little correlation between the type of area a force polices (urban/ rural) and the number of searches it conducts. Most forces conducted between three and six searches for every 1,000 people who live in their police force area. However, there are two notable outliers, the MPS and Merseyside Police, both of which police very urban areas. The MPS and Merseyside conducted 31 and 24 searches for every 1,000 people who live in their police force areas respectively.

Impact of Stop and Search

Stop and search is a contentious police power. It can be one of the most intrusive interactions that members of the public have with the police and there is ongoing debate over the way this power is exercised and the potentially harmful impact it can have. Poorly targeted and conducted stop and search is widely accepted to damage police community relations and there is growing recognition of the potentially traumatic impact it can have on individuals. Those opposed to stop and search argue that its history of poor use and long-standing ethnic disparities in search rates demonstrate that it is a fundamentally flawed police power. However, those in policing claim it is a legitimate policing tactic and an important tool in combating violence and drugs. They argue that when stop and search is targeted and conducted in line with the law and guidance, police can confiscate dangerous and prohibited items without undermining public trust in the police. Evidence regarding the impact of stop and search on crime is mixed. There is little evidence to suggest that stop and search provides an effective deterrent to offending. The use of stop and search appears to cause only marginal positive effects on levels of some crime types. Stop and search may be more effective at detection than deterrence, but most searches result in officers finding nothing and have no linked criminal justice outcome.

The Impact of Stop and Search on Black and Minority Ethnic Communities

People from Black, Asian, and Minority Ethnic backgrounds are consistently more likely to be stopped and searched than White people. The disparity is most stark for Black people. Recent statistics show that:

- Black people are searched at a rate of 53 per 1,000;

- Asian people at a rate of 18 per 1,000; and
- White people at a rate of 7.5 per 1,000.

Overall, in 2020/21, Black, Asian and minority ethnic people were 3.5 times more likely to be stopped and searched than White people. Black people were seven times more likely to be stopped and searched than White people.

Policing leaders recognize they must monitor their use of stop and search in order to better understand the causes and consequences of ethnic disparities in search rates. However, poor monitoring of ethnicity has been a consistent cause of concern raised by the Inspectorate. In February 2021, HMICFRS concluded that disparity in search rates by ethnicity is likely being underreported after finding that, on average, 17% of police stop and search records were missing ethnicity information (the proportion of search records missing ethnicity information ranged between forces from 2% to 34%).

HMICFRS went on to say that no force "fully understands the impact of the use of [stop and search] powers". The Inspectorate concluded that too many forces do not analyze and monitor stop and search sufficiently or take action on the disparities they identify. Therefore, they state, "no force can satisfactorily explain why" ethnic disproportionality persists in search records.

The IOPC echoed the Inspectorate's findings and also pushed for forces to do more to understand the disproportionate impact of policing tactics on certain communities and groups. They noted this is particularly important for Black people who have faced the most stark disparities. The IOPC says:

- Forces should be conducting equality impact assessments and community impact assessments to understand and mitigate risks of discrimination and stereotyping associated with a policing response.

Moving Vehicles

Under s 2(9)(b), only a police officer in uniform may stop a moving vehicle. With regard to motor vehicles, this, inter alia, has a practical application, since a plain clothes officer would be indistinguishable from any other citizen and drivers of such conveyances would be unlikely to stop. Section 2(9)(b), however, does not prevent a vehicle being searched by a non-uniformed police officer once it has already stopped or is parked unattended. There is a general power for uniformed police officers to stop motor vehicles under s 163 of the Road Traffic Act 1988 and, once a vehicle has been stopped, the powers of s 1 of PACE can then be applied. It should be noted that if reasonable suspicion is focused on something which the vehicle may be carrying, the power to search should be confined to the vehicle and anything in or on it. This should not extend to anyone in the vehicle, unless they are reasonably suspected of carrying stolen or prohibited articles themselves. This being the case, the same search procedures mentioned above will apply as they do to persons who are not in vehicles. Whether or not just the vehicle is searched, the person in charge of the vehicle (usually the driver) should also be given the same information as persons who are about to be searched namely, the officer's name and station, the grounds and object of the search and the availability of a record of the search if applied for within a year, or an on the spot record (subject to the exceptions mentioned below). Apart from the overall requirement under Code A that any search should be conducted with reasonable expedition (para 3.3), it was held in Lodwick v Saunders (1985) that a police officer is entitled to detain a vehicle for a reasonable time in order to carry out the necessary procedures, so as to make an arrest if the vehicle is suspected of being stolen.

OVERVIEW OF POLICE POWERS OF ARREST

As well as recognizing the need to reform police powers of stop and search the Philips Royal Commission were also aware of a similar need to rationalize police powers of arrest which, likewise, consisted of a patchwork of statutory and common law provisions:

- There is a lack of clarity and an uneasy and confused mixture of common law and statutory powers of arrest, the latter having grown piecemeal and without any consistent rationale.

The Government accepted this point in principle, but did not accept all of the Commission's proposals as to how this problem could be remedied. In the end, the enactment of the Police and Criminal Evidence Act 1984 (PACE), among a number of other things, rationalized and preserved many statutory police powers of arrest that existed prior to its enactment. All such powers work through PACE, especially in terms of its procedures. These statutes include the Prison Act 1952, the Bail Act 1976, the Criminal Law Act 1977, the Public Order Act 1936, the Children and Young Persons Act 1969 and the Mental Health Act 1983. These were preserved basically because of the need to take certain vulnerable persons into police custody or to apprehend persons unlawfully at large. A substantial number of statutes conferring arrest powers on the police have been enacted since PACE. These include the Sporting Events (Control of Alcohol, etc) Act 1985, the Public Order Act 1986, the Criminal Justice and Public Order Act 1994, the Terrorism Act 2000, the Criminal Justice and Police Act 2001 and the Police Reform Act 2002 to name but a few.

Circumstances under Which a Person Can Be Arrested

A person can be arrested under several circumstances. The police are a machinery of the State vested with powers to arrest persons who have violated or committed offences under law. Section 41 CrPC provides for arrest of a person without warrant from a Magistrate under several circumstances when any person actually concerned or reasonably suspected to be concerned in a cognizable offence; any person who, in the presence of such an officer, has committed or has been accused of committing a non-cognizable offence and refuses to give his true name or address; any person concerned or reasonably suspected to be concerned in any act committed at any place outside India, any person belong to one or more of the categories of persons specified in Section 109 or 110 of CPC and so on. The police are also empowered to arrest person(s) under several other circumstances. They can arrest for securing attendance of an accused at trial; to prevent from commission of any offence; to remove obstruction to the police; and for retaking a person who has escaped from custody.

How Arrest is Made

Section 46 (1) provides for as to how arrest is to be made. According to the section whether the arrest to be made is with warrant or without warrant, it is necessary that in making such arrest, the police officer or other person making the arrest actually touches or confines the body of the person to be arrested unless there be a submission to custody by word or action. However, an oral declaration of arrest without actual contact or submission to custody will not amount to arrest.

The Code of Criminal Procedure has vested the police with the following powers for effecting an arrest:

(1) ***Use of force by the Police while making Arrest***: The police may use necessary force to arrest a person if the person to be arrested resists the arrest or attempts to evade the arrest under Section 46(2) of CrPC. However, the power to use necessary force for making an arrest shall not extend to causing the death of a person who is not accused of an offence punishable with death or with imprisonment for life under Section 46(3) of CrPC. The person arrested is not to be subjected to more restraint than is necessary to prevent his escape as set out in Section 49 of CrPC.

(2) ***The police should not handcuff Accuse in normal circumstances***: The investigating police are restrained from handcuffing the arrested persons without the prior permission from the concerned Magistrate. Time and again the Supreme Court has emphasized the need for exercising caution while handcuffing a person arrested. The Apex Court is not happy about indiscriminate handcuffing of arrested persons by the police, in spite of the courts warnings. Thus, the Supreme Court has ordered in Citizens for Democracy v State of Assam, (1995)3 SCC 743: 1995 SCC (Cri.) 600, that: "In all the cases where a person arrested by the police is produced before the Magistrate and judicial or non-judicial remand is given by the Magistrate, the person concerned shall not be handcuffed unless special orders in this respect are obtained from the Magistrate at the time of the grant of the remand. When the police arrest a person in execution of a warrant of arrest obtained from a Magistrate the person so arrested shall not be handcuffed unless the police have also obtained orders from the Magistrate for the handcuffing of the person to be so arrested. Where a person is arrested by the police without warrant the police officer concerned may, if he is satisfied, on the basis of the guidelines given by us that it is necessary to handcuff such a person, he may do so till the time he is taken to the police station and thereafter his production before the Magistrate. Further use of fetters thereafter can only be under the orders of the Magistrate as already indicated by us."

(3) ***The Police power to search a place***: Under Section 47 of CrPC the police are empowered to effect search a place and an occupier of a house is under a legal duty to afford to the police, and to any person acting under a warrant of arrest, all the facilities to search the house for the purpose of making arrests. If such facilities are denied or obstructions are put in the search, the police shall have power to use force for getting entry into the house for search and also for the purpose of liberating himself in case he is detained in the house. These powers are subject to reasonable restrictions if the part of the house to be searched is in occupation of any pardanashin woman. In such instances either she should be called out of the house or the search is to done in the presence of a woman or a woman police.

(4) ***The police power to pursue Offenders any place in India***: under Section 48 of CrPC a police officer may, for the purpose of arresting without warrant any person whom he is authorized to arrest, pursue such a person into any place in India. This provision facilitates the police to conduct and complete investigation of a case in hand promptly and effectively. In case the arrest is to be made by the investigating police under a warrant, Section 77 of CrPC makes it clear that the warrant may be executed at any place in India. However, when a warrant of arrest is to be executed outside the local jurisdiction of the court issuing it, a special procedure as prescribed in Sections 78-81 of CrPC will have to be followed.

(5) ***The police power to obtain assistance***: A police officer can reasonably ask any person to assist him in the taking of or preventing the escape of any other person whom he (the officer) is authorized to arrest under Section 37 of CrPC. The person asked to assist is under a legal obligation to give assistance and any intentional failure on his part is punishable under Section 187 IPC.

(6) ***Power to require Subordinate Officer to arrest***: An officer- in- charge of a police station, or any police officer holding investigation of CrPC, can require any subordinate officer to arrest without a warrant (other than in his presence) any person who may lawfully be arrested without a warrant, and shall deliver to the officer so required an order in writing, specifying the person to be arrested and the offence or other cause for which the arrest is to be made under Section 55 of CrPC.

(7) ***Power to re-arrest escapee***: Section 60 of CrPC provides for if a person in lawful custody escapes or is rescued, the person from whose custody he escaped or was rescued may immediately pursue and arrest him in any place in India. The person making such re-arrest shall have the same powers and duties as mentioned above in respect of using force for arrest, and of search of place etc.

After-Arrest Procedures

(1) ***Search of arrested person***: Whenever an arrested person cannot legally be admitted to bail, or is unable to furnish bail, the police officer making the arrest (or to whom the arrested person is made over after arrest by a private person) may search such a person, and place in safe custody all articles, other than necessary wearing apparel, found upon him. A receipt showing the articles so seized shall be given to such a person. The police's failure to take out a recovery memo is an irregularity and was however held not vitiating the trial. Where the arrested person is a woman the search shall be made by another woman with strict regard to her decency as provided under Section 51 of CrPC.

(2) ***Seizure of offensive weapons***: The police officer or other person making any arrest may take any offensive weapons from the person arrested which he has in his person, and shall deliver all weapons so taken to the court or officer before which or whom the arrested person is to be produced under Section 52 of CrPC.

(3) ***Medical examination of accused***: If the offence with which the arrested person is charged is of such a nature and is alleged to have been committed under such circumstances that the evidence as to the commission of the offence would be afforded by the medical examination of such an arrested person, then, at the instance of a police officer not below the rank of a subinspector, such examination could be made by a registered medical practitioner in order to ascertain the facts that might afford such evidence. For the purposes of such medical examination such force as is reasonably necessary could also be used. If the person to be so examined is a woman the examination shall be made by, or under the supervision of, a registered lady medical practitioner as provided under Section 53 of CrPC. Such medical examination has been held to be not violation of Article 20(3) of the Constitution as it would not amount to compelling the arrested person "to be a witness" against himself. The examination is not restrictively confined to what is visible on the body itself. It may include testing of blood, sputum, semen, urine, etc. depending upon the nature of the case. If the process of examination is reasonable, then the discomfort, pain or hurt caused to the examinee in such examination is justified under Section 53 CrPC.

By giving an elaborate explanation as to the meaning of 'examination' and 'registered medical practitioner', the Code of Criminal Procedure (Amendment) Act 2005 has incorporated sections 53-A and 54(2) and laid down the procedures for the conduct of medical examination.

Section 53-A CrPC makes special provisions for rape cases. It is enacted that in a rape case the accused could be sent for medical examination by a registered medical practitioner working in a hospital run by the Government or local authority and in their absence within a radius of 16 kilometers, any other registered medical practitioner acting at the request of a police officer not below the rank of sub-inspector. For the purpose of such examination such force as is necessary can also be used.

The registered medical practitioner has to prepare the report with supporting reasons for his conclusions on each aspect, detailing the names and address of the accused and the person taking the accused to the medical practitioner, age of the accused, marks of injury on the person of the accused, the description of material taken from the accused person for DNA profiling and other material particulars. The exact time of the commencement and completion of examination will also be noted in the report and a copy of the report will be sent to the police officer and the magistrate. In case of the examination taking place at the instance of the accused under subsection (1) a copy will be given to him also under Section 54 CrPC. Accused persons who are on bail can also be subjected for medical examination.

Section 311-A CrPC authorizes the Magistrate to direct any person including an accused to give specimen signatures or handwriting for the purpose of investigation or other proceedings. But this order shall not be made if he was at any time arrested in connections with such investigation.

(4) ***Reports of arrest to be sent to District Magistrate***: Every police officer-in- charge of a police station is required to report to the District Magistrate

the cases of all persons arrested without warrant, within the limits of his station under Section 58 CrPC.

(5) ***Person arrested not to be discharged except on Bond or Bail***: A person who has been arrested by a police officer shall not be discharged except on his own bond or on bail or under the special order of a Magistrate under Section 59 CrPC.

Rights of Arrested Person

The Code of Criminal Procedure, the Indian Constitution, various judgments of the Supreme Court and other International Human Rights Covenants and Conventions have laid down several standard procedures as to the rights of arrested person. These rights are enforceable at different phases of arrest of a person and violation of which would invite serious disciplinary and penal action against the delinquent police officer.

(1) ***Right to be informed of the grounds for arrest***: In every case of arrest with or without a warrant the person arresting shall communicate to the arrested person, without delay, the grounds for his arrest under Section 50 CrPC. This is a precious right of the arrested person and has been recognized by the Constitution under Article 22(1). Timely information of the grounds of arrest serves the arrested person in many ways. It gives him an opportunity to remove any mistake, misapprehension or misunderstanding, if any, in the mind of the arresting authority. It also enables him to apply for bail, or for a writ of habeas corpus, or to make other expeditious arrangements for his defence.

Under Section 50-A CrPC it obligatory on the part of the police officer not only to inform the friend or relative of the arrested person about his arrest etc., but also to make an entry in a register maintained by the police. The Magistrate is also under an obligation to satisfy himself about the compliance of the law by the police in this regard.

(2) ***Right to be informed of right to Bail***: Every police officer arresting, without a warrant, any person other than a person accused of a non-bailable offence, is required to inform the person arrested that he is entitled to be released on bail and that he may arrange for sureties on his behalf under Section 50(2) CrPC. Only when he fails to arrange sureties he need not be released on bail.

(3) ***Right to be produced before a Magistrate without delay***: In case of every arrest, whether the arrest has been made with or without a warrant, the person arresting is required, without unnecessary delay and subject to the provisions regarding bail, to produce the arrested person before the Magistrate or officer-in-charge of a police station having jurisdiction in the case under Sections 56 and 76 of CrPC.

(4) ***Right to consult a Legal Practitioner***: Both the Constitution and the provisions of the CrPC respectively recognize the right of every arrested person to consult a legal practitioner of his choice under Article 22(1) and Section 303 of CrPC. The right begins from the moment of arrest. The consultation with the lawyer may be in the presence of the police officer but not within his hearing.

(5) ***Right of an arrested Indigent Person to free legal aid and to be informed about it***: In Khatri v. State of Bihar, (1981) 1 SCC 627, the Supreme Court has held that the State is under a constitutional mandate (implicit in Article 21) to provide free legal aid to an indigent accused person, and that this constitutional obligation to provide legal aid does not arise only when the trial commences but also when the accused is for the first time produced before the Magistrate as also when he is remanded from time to time. However, this constitutional right of an indigent accused to get free legal aid may prove to be illusory unless he is promptly and duly informed about it by the court when he is produced before it. The Supreme Court has therefore cast a duty on all Magistrates and courts to inform the indigent accused about his right to get free legal aid.

(6) ***Right to be examined by a Medical practitioner***: If any arrested person alleges, at the time when he is produced before a Magistrate or at any time during the period of his detention in custody, that the examination of his body will afford evidence which will disprove the commission by him of any offence or which will establish the commission by any other person of any offence against his body, then the Magistrate, on the request of the arrested person, is required to direct the examination of his body by a registered medical practitioner. However, the Magistrate need not give such a direction if he considers that the request for medical examination has been made by the arrested person for the purpose of vexation or delay or for defeating the ends of justice under Section 54 CrPC. According to the direction of Supreme Court, the arrested accused person must be informed by the Magistrate about his right to be medically examined in terms of Section 54 CrPC.

The following guidelines for the police who are in to investigation and policing:

- The police personnel carrying out the arrest and handling the interrogation of the arrestee should bear accurate, visible and clear identification and name tags with their designations. The particulars of all such police personnel who handle interrogation of the arrestee must be recorded in a register.
- That the police officer carrying out the arrest of the arrestee shall prepare a memo of arrest at the time of arrest and such memo shall be attested by at least one witness, who may either be a member of the family of the arrestee or a respectable person of the locality from where the arrest is made. It shall also be countersigned by the arrestee and shall contain the time and date of arrest.
- The time, place of arrest and venue of custody of an arrestee must be notified by the police where the next friend or relative of the arrestee lives outside the district or town through the Legal Aid Organization in the district and the police station of the area concerned telegraphically within a period of 8 to 12 hours after the arrest.
- The arrestee should be subjected to medical examination by a trained doctor every 48 hours during his detention in custody by a doctor on the panel of approved doctors appointed by the Director, Health Services

of the State or Union Territory concerned. The Director, Health Services should prepare such a panel for all tehsils and districts as well.

- Copies of all the documents including the memo of arrest referred to above should be sent to the Illaqa Magistrate for his record.
- The arrestee may be permitted to meet his lawyer during interrogation, though not throughout interrogation.
- A Police control room should be provided at all districts and State Head Quarters, where information regarding the arrest and the place of custody of the arrestee shall be communicated by the officer causing the arrest, within 12 hours of effecting the arrest and at the Police Control Room it should be displayed on a conspicuous Notice board.

Failure to comply with the requirements herein above mentioned shall, apart from rendering the official concerned liable for departmental action, also render him liable to be punished for contempt of court and the proceedings for contempt of court may be instituted in any High Court of the county having territorial jurisdiction over the matter.

Consequences of Non-Compliance with the Provisions Relating to Arrest

Non-compliance of the provisions of arrest will result in several serious consequences on violators. A trial will not be void simply because the provisions relating to arrest have not been fully complied with. Though the illegality or irregularity in making an arrest would not vitiate the trial of the arrested person, it would be quite material if such a person is prosecuted on a charge of resistance to or escape from lawful custody. If the arrest is illegal, the person who is being so arrested can exercise the right of private defence in accordance with, and subject to, the provisions contained in Sections 96 to 106 of the IPC. If the public servant having authority to make arrests knowingly exercises that authority in contravention of law and effects an illegal arrest, he can be prosecuted for an offence under Section 220 of the IPC. Apart from this special provision, any person who illegally arrests another is punishable under Section 342 of the IPC for wrongful confinement. If the arrest is illegal, it is a sort of false imprisonment, and the arrested person in entitled to claim damages from the person who made such an arrest.

Misuse of Power of Arrest

Notwithstanding the safeguards contained in the Code of Criminal Procedure and the Constitution referred to above, the fact remains that the power of arrest is wrongly and illegally exercised in a large number of cases all over the country. Very often this power is utilized to extort monies and other valuable property or at the instance of an enemy of the person arrested. Even in case of civil disputes, this power is being resorted to on the basis of a false allegation against a party to a civil dispute at the instance of his opponent. The vast discretion given by the CrPC to arrest a person even in the case of a bailable offence (not only where the bailable offence is cognizable but also where it is non-cognizable) and the further power to make preventive arrests (e.g. under section 151 of the CrPC and the several city police enactments), clothe the police with extraordinary power which can easily be abused. Neither there is any in-house mechanism in the police department to check such misuse or abuse nor does the complaint of such misuse or abuse to higher police officers bear fruit except in some exceptional cases.

Balancing of Societal Interests and Protection of Rights of the Accused

We are not unaware that crime rate is going up in our country for various reasons which need not be recounted here. Terrorism, drugs and organized crime have become so acute that special measures have become necessary to fight them not only at the national level but also at the international level. We also take note of the fact that quite a number of policemen risk their lives in discharge of their duties and that they are specially targeted by the criminal and terrorist gangs.

We recognize that in certain situations e.g., like the one obtaining in Kashmir today, a literal compliance with several legal and constitutional safeguards may not be practicable but we must also take note of and provide for the generality of the situation all over the country and not be deflected by certain specific, temporary situations. We must also take note of the fact that very often it is the poor who suffer most at the hands of Police. Their poverty itself makes them suspects. This was said, though from a different angle, by George Bernard Shaw. He said "poverty is crime". But nowadays, even middle classes and other well-to-do people, who do not have access to political power-wielders, also are becoming targets of Police excesses. We recognize that ensuring a balance between societal interest in peace and protection of the rights of the accused is a difficult one but it has to be done. We also recognize the fundamental significance of the Human Rights, which are implicit in Part III of our Constitution and of the necessity to preserve, protect and promote the Rule of Law which constitutes the bedrock of our constitutional system.

DETENTION OF THE PERSON ARRESTED

There are two Sections-57 and 167- CrPC provide for detention of accused person. The legislative intention of incorporating these two sections is to expect investigation undertaken by the police is promptly and effectively completed in the first instance within 24 hours under Section 57, if not, under Section 167 within 15 days from the date when the person arrested was first produced before the Magistrate.

Detention of Accused under Section 57 CrPC

In case of every arrest, the police officer making arrest is required to produce the arrested person without unnecessary delay before the Magistrate; and it has been categorically provided that such a delay in no case shall exceed 24 hours exclusive of the time necessary for the journey from the place of arrest to the Magistrate's court under Section 57 and proviso to Section 76 CrPC. If it is not complied with, the detention shall be unlawful. When the arrested person is produced before the Magistrate it is his duty either to release him on bail or to remand him. Such remand would continue till the trail is over. Illegal detention may entail award of compensation by the court. The tendency of police officers authorized to arrest, to note the time of arrest in such a manner that the accused's production before the Magistrate would well within 24 hours of the arrest. This perverse act of the police officers came to be criticized by Apex court and many High Courts in many instances. The Courts ruled that the arrest commences with the restraint placed on the liberty of the accused and not with the time of arrest recorded by the police officer. The right has also been incorporated in the Constitution as one of the fundamental rights under Article 22(2). This right has been created with a view (i) to prevent arrest and detention for the purpose of extracting confessions, or as a means of compelling people to give information; (ii) to prevent police stations being used as though they were prisoners- a purpose for which they are unsuitable; and (iii) to afford an early recourse to a judicial officer independent of the police on all questions of bail or discharge. This healthy provision contained in Section 57 enables Magistrate to keep a check over the police investigation and it is necessary that the Magistrate should try to enforce this requirement and where it is found disobeyed, he should punish such erring police indiscriminately without being soft towards them.

Detention of Accused under Section 167

Under the Section 57 CrPC police officer is empowered to detain in custody a person arrested without warrant for a period not exceeding 24 hours under all the circumstances of the case. If the investigation could not be completed within that period, the police should forward the accused to the nearest Magistrate under sub-section (1) of Section 167. The Magistrate can then authorize his detention in such custody as he thinks for a term not exceeding fifteen days. When an arrested accused is produced before the Magistrate he may release him on bail, or he may order his detention in police custody. If he does neither, the Magistrate would take the accused to judicial custody.

Where a person is not arrested by the police, but surrenders himself before the court, remand order under Section 167 cannot be passed, as he is not in police custody when the police apply for remand. However, if he is taken to judicial custody on such surrender, the police officer who is investigating the case against that accused can approach the Magistrate with an application to issue body warrant to prison authorities to produce the accused before the court, hear him and then pass suitable orders to hand over him to the police officer for investigation.

SEARCH AND SEIZURE AT THE SCENE OF CRIME

As soon as the investigating police officer arrives at the scene of crime, he should, as a golden rule, never alter the position of the scene of crime, pick up, even touch any object before it has been minutely described in an official note, and a photograph taken of it. He should contact the man who reached the scene first and make enquires. He should ensure that the scene of crime is not interfered with. He should not allow any unauthorized person to meddle in the inspection of the scene. He should avoid crowding at the spot and all thoughtless interference, as they always result in the destruction of clues. He should never leave the inspection of the scene to his subordinates especially those who are untrained. He should never take anything to be trivial but make his inspection thorough and minute; and search methodically, patiently and in a definite order. He should summon some local and independent witnesses to assist him to draw panchanama as required under Section 100 of CrPC. The investigating police officer effecting the search should take down accurate and detailed notes, supported by accurate sketches drawn to scale, showing the whole lay-out and the exact places where the articles, etc., were found. An article is in a certain room or on a particular table. Its exact position must be noted and, if necessary, an enlarged sketch of that portion of the scene must be drawn by a qualified draftsman. In all important cases photograph and video graph should be taken of the scene and of the objects on which any useful clues are found. Sketches are useful in criminal investigation and prosecution as they reduce the length of case diaries and make a much more exact impression on the mind than written reports. They make lucid explanation of an intricate case fairly easy. They introduce method into investigation and help judges, magistrates, and others to an accurate understanding of case. They also enrich the powers of observation of investigating police officer. The sketches should be prepared to scale indicating the compass point and mentioning the distance correctly. Invariably he should use a ruler, scale and compass for measurements at the scene of crime. He should use the expressions such as 'on the right' and 'on the left;' North, South, East and West for directions and for distance measurement 'inch', 'feet', 'meter' etc.

Search and Seizure at Different Places under Sections 165 and 166 Read with Section 100 CRPC

Section 165 CrPC is enacted as an exception to this general law of searches because it is recognized that in certain exceptional emergencies it is necessary to empower responsible police officers to carryout searches without first applying to the courts for authority. The legislature has, however, attempted to restrict and limit the powers of the police under the section and provided the concerned citizens with safeguards in order to prevent the abuse of the powers. As set out in Section 165 CrPC an officer-in-charge of a police station or an investigating officer, having reasonable grounds for believing that anything necessary for the purpose of investigation of any offence which he is authorized to investigate may be found in any place within the limits of the police station of which he is in charge or to which he is attached and that such thing cannot in his opinion be otherwise obtained without undue delay, may search the place. Before making the search, the investigating police officer must record his grounds of his belief; specify therein the thing for which the search is made. This is known as "record of reasons." If the investigating police officer is unable to conduct the search in person, he may require any officer subordinate to him to make the search, after recording in writing his reasons for so doing. The subordinate police officer so deputed should be given order in writing specifying the place where and the thing for which the search is to be made. Copies of records made above should be sent to the nearest Magistrate empowered to take cognizance of the offence.

When a search has to be conducted in the jurisdiction of another station, whether in the same or a different district, an officer- in- charge of a police station making an investigation may require under sub-section (1) of Section 166 CrPC, the officer-in- charge of the former station to make a search or cause search to be made. But, where there is reason to believe that the delay occasioned by such a procedure might result in evidence being concealed or destroyed, the investigating police officer may, under sub-section (3) of the Section 166 of CrPC, make the search himself or cause the search to be made, in which case, he shall forthwith send a notice of the search together with a copy of the list prepared under Section 100 CrPC to the officer- in charge of the police station, within the limits of which the place searched is situated and to the nearest Magistrate empowered to take cognizance of the offence.

Procedures to be followed during Search and Seizure U/S 100 of CRPC

The investigating police officer while conducting search has to bear in mind the following procedures and follow them accordingly. Any deviations or violations of the procedures laid down under the Section 100 of CrPC will adversely affect the prosecution case and vitiate the trial as well. The procedures in simplified form are as follows:

- The free ingress and reasonable facilities are to be made under both for search under a warrant as well as for a search without a warrant.
- The police officer or other conducting the search is empowered to enter the place and in order to effect an entrance into such a place can break open an outer or inner door or window of any house or place if after notification of his authority and purpose, and demand of admittance duly made, he could not otherwise obtain admittance. Section 47(2) provides a safeguard in favor of a pardanashin woman and the same would apply in case of a search also. Further, it has been held that if in the exercise of the power or the performance of the official duty, improper or unlawful obstruction or resistance is encountered, there must be the right to use reasonable means to remove the obstruction or overcome the resistance. This accords with common sense and does not seem contrary to any principle of law.
- In order to obviate the chance of any person stealthily taking away on his person any article or thing for which the search of a place is to be made, sub-section (3) of Section 100 provides for the search of such a person. The provision is necessary to prevent the object of the search getting frustrated. If the person to be searched is a woman, then, in order to protect her modesty it has been provided that the search shall be made by another woman with strict regard to decency.
- The search is to be made in the presence of at least two independent and respectable inhabitants of the locality in which the place to be searched is situated. However, if no such inhabitant of the said locality is available or willing to be a witness to the search, the search can be made in the presence of persons of other locality. What is more important to be emphasized is the respectability of the witness rather than his locality or independence. The object of the provision is to guard against possible chicanery and unfair dealings on the part of the persons authorized to search and ensure that anything incriminating which may be said to have been found in the premises searched was really found there and was not introduced by the members of the search-party. The presence of witnesses at a search is always desirable and their absence will weaken and may sometimes destroy the admissibility of the evidence as to the finding of the articles.

  Sub-section (4) of Section 100 also lays down that the officer or other person making the search is to call the above-said persons [panch witnesses] to attend and witness the search and they make for this purpose issue a written order to them. If a person so ordered to be a witness neglects or refuses without reasonable cause to attend and witness a search, then according to sub-section (8) of Section 100 he shall be deemed to have committed an offence under Section 187 IPC.

- As far as possible a search has to be conducted in daylight. If information is received after dusk necessitating the immediate search of a house and if it is apprehended that delay till daybreak might result in evidence being concealed or destroyed, the house should be sealed and guarded and if that is not possible, search should be conducted during the night itself.
- Before entering the premises to be searched, the exterior of the place shall be inspected to see whether facilities for introducing property from outside exist.
- Before commencing search the investigating and the panch witnesses should ensure that mutual search of each other is done.
- Search and seizure must be systematic and thorough.
- Women should be allowed to withdraw while effecting search and seizure.
- Indiscriminate search and damage to property should be avoided.
- The occupant of the place of search, or his nominee, shall in every case be permitted to attend during the search. Denial of such permission may cause suspicion as to the reliability of the discoveries made out. However, where the securing of the presence of the occupier or his nominee might cause such delay as to frustrate the purpose of the search, it may be permissible to dispense with his presence.
- List of all things seized in the course of the search and of the places in which they are respectively found shall be prepared by the police officer or other person making the search and shall be signed by the panch witnesses. The signature of the accused on the search is not required under law.
- A search list shall be prepared in quadruplicate, all the copies being signed by the police officer making the search and the witnesses to the search. One copy will be handed over to the owner or occupant of the house, the second copy should be sent to the Magistrate and the third copy should be sent with the case diary to the superior officer to whom case diaries are sent. The fourth copy will form the station record.

Disposal of the Seized Property

The police are not empowered to dispose of the property seized without the order of the competent court. Under sub-section (2) of Section 102 CrPC the police are empowered to hand over the custody of the property seized which cloud not be retained in their custody for want of accommodation to any person on execution of a bond with a direction to produce before the court as and when required. So also the where the property seized under sub-section (1) is subject to speedy and natural decay and if the entitled to the possession of such property is unknown or absent and the value of such property is less than five hundred rupees, it may forthwith be sold by auction under the orders of the Superintendent of Police. In all other cases and circumstances court is empowered to dispose of the property seized as per the provisions of Sections 457 and 458 CrPC.

REFERENCES

1. Levenson, H, Fairweather, F and Cape, E, Police Powers: A Practitioner's Guide (3rd edn, London: Legal Action Group, 1996).

INDEX